BIG BILL

BIG

H.A. BRANHAM

FOREWORD BY
RICHARD PETTY

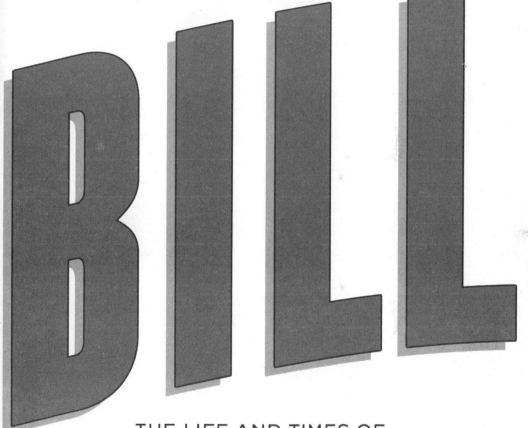

THE LIFE AND TIMES OF
NASCAR FOUNDER
BILL FRANCE SR.

Copyright © 2015 by the National Association of Stock Car Auto Racing, Inc

Fenn/McClelland & Stewart is an imprint of McClelland & Stewart, a division of Random
House of Canada Limited, a Penguin Random House Company

Fenn/McClelland & Stewart and colophon are registered trademarks of McClelland &
Stewart, a division of Random House of Canada Limited,
a Penguin Random House Company

Library and Archives Canada Cataloguing in Publication is available upon request

ISBN: 978-0-7710-1767-4
ebook ISBN: 978-0-7710-1768-1

Published simultaneously in the United States of America by Fenn/McClelland & Stewart,
a division of Random House of Canada Limited, a Penguin Random House Company

Library of Congress Control Number is available upon request

Designed by Five Seventeen
Typeset in Charter ITC by Erin Cooper
Printed and bound in the USA

Photos from France Family collection

Fenn/McClelland & Stewart,
a division of Random House of Canada Limited,
a Penguin Random House Company
www.penguinrandomhouse.ca

1   2   3   4   5   19   18   17   16   15

Penguin
Random
House

*William Henry Getty France was a leader, a dreamer,
a visionary, a man of extraordinary will and purpose.
But more than anything else, first and foremost he was
a husband and a father. And so this book is dedicated to his
wife, Anne Bledsoe France – the beloved "Annie B." –
and their two sons, William (Bill Jr.) Clifton France and
James (Jim) Carl France.*

CONTENTS

By Richard Petty

Bill France Sr.?

Well, let's just say he "ran the show."

It was "his show" and I think everybody that raced in NASCAR for him knew it was "his show." That meant that when he said "this is the way it's going to be," you knew there wouldn't be any arguing about it and that there wouldn't be any second thoughts.

I never really had any problem with that myself, but he and my daddy, Lee Petty, they sure crossed swords a few times.

But you know what? In the long run, when you look back, everybody knows that things had to be that way to keep NASCAR operating smoothly.

Being NASCAR was a new business and all, it needed a strong dictatorship, per se. And again, in retrospect, that was a good thing. No matter what the rules were or what went down in a particular circumstance, Bill Sr. was always looking at things from the perspective of what was best for racing in the future, not from a "you or me" perspective. Let me tell you, he was one forward-thinking, future-thinking individual.

He had to be that way, you know? He had to be thinking about the future when he and a bunch of guys started NASCAR. Then he goes out 10 years later and builds Daytona International Speedway and has the first Daytona 500. Everything he and his family had was 100 per cent into NASCAR. If Daytona had fallen flat he would've been out of business, but Bill Sr. didn't mind gambling on something he really believed in – and he most certainly believed in that speedway and in NASCAR.

Bill France Sr., Bill France Jr., and now Brian France – all the right guys at the right time. Bill Sr. got NASCAR started and put a real strong base under everything. Bill Jr. grew up with his dad and so he understood that part of the business, the importance of having that strong foundation.

Bill Jr. took over as NASCAR president from his father in 1972, and by then NASCAR had really grown. But Bill Jr. wasn't really a completely new generation in terms of his approach; maybe we should call him "one-half to two-thirds" of a new generation, because he saw things that Bill Sr. didn't do and acted accordingly; and he also saw things Bill Sr. did do and kept them intact. But Bill Jr. took the sport from Step 1 to Step 2, for sure.

Then Brian France came along, the third-generation leader of NASCAR, and he really did symbolize a completely new generation in terms of approach. When he came in he brought a whole new generation of thought compared to Bill Jr., who came in with a "half generation" of new thought. You hear me?

But make no mistake, it all started with Bill Sr., and one thing he was really smart about was PR. The best example was that very first Daytona 500 in 1959. We had a famous finish between my daddy and Johnny Beauchamp. Well, they finished side by side and Bill Sr. knew my daddy had won. But he said to himself, "Looky here, this thing is close enough that we can argue about it for two or three days," and that's what happened, until Bill Sr. announced on Wednesday that Lee Petty had won. If he had made that announcement right after the race, that would've been it and come Monday the interest in the first Daytona 500 would've been over with. But instead we had to wait and wait, and by the time Wednesday rolled around the whole country was waiting to see what was going to happen. The new Daytona International Speedway race track all of a sudden was humungous in the public eye.

Talladega Superspeedway turned out to be a good PR deal too, when the drivers boycotted the first-ever race there in 1969 because of safety concerns and Bill Sr. put together a field and ran the race anyway. That was the best thing ever for Talladega because before that nobody had ever heard of Talladega, Alabama. You had everybody looking at a map just trying to find out where Talladega was. So, we had all that fallout about the boycott lasting really strong for a couple of weeks. It put Talladega on the map.

Looking back, you can see Bill Sr. really put his mark on NASCAR initially and by doing that, he had complete control of what he thought was going to be the best thing for NASCAR.

Like in 1949, the very first Strictly Stock race (the forerunner of today's NASCAR Sprint Cup Series) at Charlotte, he disqualified the winner because of illegal parts! And then, in 1950, he took a bunch of points away from my daddy and a couple others because they ran in some non-NASCAR races on a week off. It might've cost a couple of them the championship.

Bill Sr. wanted to show people that he had the upper hand, right quick. But I remember that whenever he and my daddy would have a disagreement, my daddy would tell me, "It's his ball, his ball game, and it's being played on his ball field. If you don't want to play, you can go home." My daddy understood that, and since he was trying to make a living from NASCAR racing, he had to make it work.

I think Bill Sr. would be proud of NASCAR today, proud of the fact his son took it one step further than he did, and proud that his grandson has taken it another step further. Now, he wouldn't have done it the same way, but he would've sat back, and told you:

"Yeah, I had something to do with all of this."

INTRODUCTION

So many people have so many stories about Bill France Sr., who in these pages will be referred to mostly as "Big Bill" or simply, "Senior." The stories are absolute gold, the ultimate gateways to NASCAR's past. Especially telling is the manner in which some of these stories are told. Bill France Sr. died in 1992, but for those who knew him he seems to live, still.

For those of us who now work at NASCAR but never had a chance to work for Bill Sr., there is this inevitable, undeniable truth: we know we missed out on something special, notwithstanding the overwhelming force of nature that was his son, Bill France Jr., who thankfully was with us until the spring of 2007.

You know you missed out when talking to the people who did not.

People like Betty Faulk, Bill Sr.'s secretary for many years, who in her 90s still gets schoolgirl wide-eyed when recounting the old days.

Or Juanita "Lightnin'" Epton, who started the 2014 season still working in the Daytona International Speedway ticket office at the age of 93, whose tone is almost reverent when the subject is Bill Sr. or his steadfast wife of 60 years, Anne Bledsoe France.

Listen to Betty Jane France, Bill Jr.'s widow, talk about her father-in-law and you'll know that the good times rolled basically non-stop. Betty Jane was there when Senior was building a sport, building a speedway, the whole deal – and having a grand time doing so.

Senior's boys? Bill Jr. could recite his father's accomplishments in a heartbeat. Same for Jim France who, when asked how he wants his father to be remembered, says simply, "I want people to know how smart he was."

So many people, with so many Bill Sr. stories . . .

I have only one, unfortunately. But I consider it a personal keeper.

Actually, it's surreal to recycle the tale now, having told it so many times over the years with inevitable embellishment, of course.

A quick set-up:

The International Motor Sports Association (IMSA), the premier sports car sanctioning body in North America, now undergoing a rebirth under the leadership of Jim France, for years sanctioned the stellar Camel GT Series. In 1969, IMSA was founded by Bill Sr. and the husband-wife team of John and Peggy Bishop, and for a number of years the season started and ended at Daytona International Speedway – the Rolex 24 At Daytona in January and a three-hour October event.

The Daytona finale was held for the final time on October 26, 1986 – and that's the date of my Big Bill story.

A three-hour race on a Sunday afternoon was a good assignment for the auto racing journalists covering that finale. I was one of those. Post-race, with stories filed and darkness enveloping the speedway, the evening was still quite young, which meant the party would ensue momentarily. Such were the times.

And what better place to begin the party than with a "pre-game" cocktail courtesy of the speedway's hospitality suites? I was sent off in that direction by members of the speedway staff who were packing up for the night, with the mandate of returning with several drinks. No problem. I dashed out of the press box . . . down the corridor . . . into the suite . . . and quickly slid in behind the fully-stocked bar in a completely empty suite.

Nice.

And then, I was no longer alone. A door opened and in walked an elderly gentleman, slowly, surely heading my way. His eyes met mine and suddenly I was face-to-face with none other than Big Bill himself. There we were, the founder of NASCAR and a long-haired writer of casual dress with an inclination to socialize for free. I had my media credential around my neck; immediately I resigned myself that he would be asking for it, as he kicked me the hell out of his suite and banned me from the speedway for life.

Bracing for the worst, instead I got this from William Henry Getty France: He asked me to make him a drink. I have no memory of what I mixed, only that it was done quickly and properly – and politely. I handed him the glass, he thanked me, took a sip, and left the suite. My exhale was, well, loud and long.

Back to the press box, where my encounter evoked a moment of terror and then, laughter, loud and long. Bill France Sr. thought I worked for him.

"He must have seen your credential and just not looked at it that closely," said a staff member. "You are *soooo* lucky."

So there you have it. Bill Sr. and me, just two guys looking for a post-race pop.

That's my Senior story and I'll stick to it. It's all I have.

"Yeah, but I'd say that's a pretty good one," Jim France says.

"Hell, you were his bartender."

– H.A. Branham

CHAPTER I

Validation of the Vision

When plans for a NASCAR Hall of Fame were announced in February 2005, speculation immediately began about the induction process, specifically regarding how large the first class of inductees would be – and who would be chosen.

When it was announced in January 2009 that each class would consist of five people, the speculation evolved into prediction.

Everyone had an opinion.

There were shoo-ins, no doubt, for the inaugural induction on May 23, 2010, set for downtown Charlotte, North Carolina. Four of them, according to just about anyone who knew anything about NASCAR and was willing to discuss the potentially controversial subject matter.

Those four:
Richard Petty.
Dale Earnhardt.
Junior Johnson.
And . . . Bill France Sr.
After that, well . . .

There was the expected considerable momentum among fans and media for David Pearson, the popular three-time NASCAR Sprint Cup Series champion whose 105 wins ranked second all-time behind Petty's 200.

Cale Yarborough and Darrell Waltrip, also three-time champs, seemed reasonable possibilities, as did two-time titlist Ned Jarrett, legendary owner/driver and World War II hero Bud Moore, Bobby Allison, too.

And . . . Bill France Jr.

A wide gulf of public opinion separated the two Bills going into the voting process, which transpired on October 14, 2009, in Charlotte. After hours of deliberation by a voting panel representing constituencies from throughout the NASCAR industry – including the media – ballots were tabulated by the renowned accounting firm of Ernst & Young. That firm was on hand not because of the numbers involved but rather to demonstrate the legitimacy of the voting process.

Ernst & Young was not needed to ensure Bill Sr.'s inclusion. He was a lock. Bill Jr. was a longshot. That represented no attack on Bill Jr.'s credentials, but rather the result of a growing feeling that the France family shouldn't get two of the first five slots. And after all, the argument went, Bill Jr. would be a lock in 2011.

Debate was intense during the voting panel sessions. Support for Bill Jr. grew as the debate continued. When votes were cast, he was in.

The rest of the "first five": Petty, Earnhardt, Johnson – and Bill Sr.

The vote for Bill Sr. wasn't unanimous but awfully close to it, a result that at once can be seen as legitimizing and ludicrous. Should there really have even been a vote regarding NASCAR's founder? Couldn't that simply have been an automatic situation? If it had been determined to start the process by making Bill Sr. the first inductee and moving on to actual give-and-take on the other nominees, few would've argued. Of course, a process was in place. Rules had to be followed. And after all, during his years of running NASCAR, Bill France Sr. was all about process, about rules, about order.

Ramsey Poston, former managing director of communications for NASCAR, moderated that first voting panel session, which was akin to herding cats, albeit after a slow, almost sleepy start.

That first year was full of anticipation and anxiousness, with panel members jammed into a room at the Charlotte Convention Center adjacent to the Hall of Fame.

"It was a special day; we all knew it was going to be special," Poston said. "We had a little breakfast reception that morning before the voting session and I remember looking around and seeing Richard Petty, Junior Johnson, Bud Moore, Cotton Owens – and then, there was NASCAR president Mike Helton coming in and mingling with everybody. It was something, and it hit me that it was probably the first time, possibly ever, all of these individuals had been in one room together. That was pretty neat.

"No one was really sure how it would go and when we first started the session, everyone was sort of shy and quiet; no one seemed to really want to say much. But then, the broadcasters – as I recall, FOX's Mike Joy – stood up first and that got everyone going.

"With Bill France Jr., eventually it came down to a debate between him and David Pearson.

"But as far as Bill France Sr. goes, that wasn't really a discussion as much as it was a coronation."

"Coronation, yes . . . that describes it perfectly," said voting panel member and legendary motorsports journalist Tom Higgins. "It was a given that Big Bill and Richard Petty were going into the hall the first year. I don't remember one negative comment about Bill Sr. being inducted. It was unanimous praise all around and if the vote wasn't unanimous, well, that's insanity."

The 150,000-square-foot NASCAR Hall of Fame, part of the Hall of Fame Complex in uptown Charlotte, was long overdue, especially when compared to the long-standing halls in other major sports – baseball in Cooperstown, New York; basketball in Springfield, Massachusetts; pro football in Canton, Ohio. Those facilities are meccas for ardent fans of each sport.

NASCAR fans, by contrast, had always been presented with a smorgasbord of halls, all admirable in their own right but none approaching the NASCAR-centric credibility that could rival other sports. The International Motorsports Hall of Fame at Talladega has an illustrious inductee roll but it also honors individuals from all forms of racing. Various media-driven versions – the

Southeastern-based National Motorsports Press Association, the Eastern Motorsports Press Association, the California-based American Auto Racing Writers and Broadcasters Association – all have traditions of their own and fervent memberships that take their halls quite seriously.

Still, something more was needed to further nudge NASCAR into the realm of big-time sports that Bill France Sr. had envisioned so many years before.

"NASCAR's overriding goal is to have a world class Hall of Fame," said NASCAR chairman/CEO Brian France, Bill Sr.'s grandson, when the hall concept was announced in February 2005. "We want it to be a special place that brings NASCAR's history to life. Our hope is for longtime fans to have the opportunity to relive NASCAR's greatest moments and for new fans to learn about them."

Bill Sr. would've loved the NASCAR Hall of Fame.

Just as he would have loved the decision to make him the very first inductee at the very first induction ceremony.

"It wasn't an accident that he was the first one," said NASCAR Hall of Fame Executive Director Winston Kelley. "It was very intentional – as it should've been."

For the first several years of the NASCAR Hall of Fame induction ceremonies, the inductee acceptance speeches were preceded by inductors' speeches, designed to both honor and introduce the inductees. Some were fellow NASCAR notables. Some were family or friends. In the case of posthumous inductions, the inductors' role was enhanced greatly. In the case of Bill France Sr.'s posthumous induction, a very special inductor was required, to say the least.

It was originally thought that Jim France would induct his father. As NASCAR's vice chairman and the chairman of the International Speedway Corporation (ISC), he has had his own remarkable career in motorsports while somehow flying under the general public's radar. Jim is an intensely private individual and also, those close to him say, an emotional man, which led to him reconsidering the task of standing up before a television audience and talking about his father for an extended period of time. He opted to deliver a briefer acceptance speech, which, upon further review, made more sense anyway.

Jim France turned to an old friend, John Cassidy, for help with the longer remarks. "Jimmy called me and said he wanted me to make the speech," Cassidy said. "I told him I would be honored. Jimmy dearly loved his father . . ."

Cassidy immediately went to work, as he has been doing for more than 50 years when it comes to the France family. Cassidy, then a robust 80 years old, is one of the last living direct links to Bill France Sr. and stands as one of the most interesting characters in the man's colorful life.

Cassidy has long had NASCAR and its sister company, International Speedway Corporation (also founded by Bill Sr.) as clients, serving as a main adviser to Bill Sr. – and later, Bill Jr. – on legal matters such as antitrust, securities, competition rules, membership rights in voluntary organizations, and contracts. Cassidy was a founding partner in the Washington, D.C., law firm of Miller, Cassidy, Larroca & Lewin, LLP, which was merged into Baker Botts, LLP in January 2001. Cassidy founded his firm in 1965 after serving as a trial attorney in the criminal and tax divisions of the United States Department of Justice and as special assistant to the Attorney General of the United States, Robert F. Kennedy.

Bill Sr. had sought Cassidy's help for the first time in 1961, when Kennedy was aggressively battling organized crime, working on prosecuting members of the Teamsters and, particularly, Jimmy Hoffa. The Teamsters had targeted NASCAR, and Bill France Sr. was on alert, absolutely convinced that unionization would cause the downfall of his sport.

"Senior had come up to D.C. to see Bobby about his Hoffa problem," Cassidy recounted. "I was sitting in my office and the phone rang. It was Bobby. He said, 'I've got a fella in my office who says his name is Bill France. He has something to do with something called NASCAR and all I know is that NASCAR has something to do with motorsports. Jimmy Hoffa is trying to move in and take it over and we can't let that happen because this France guy . . . he's one of us. So I'm sending him down to your office and I want you to help him and NASCAR.'

"And with that, the door opens and Senior, wearing one of those funny little hats he liked to wear, just fills the doorway. He looks at me and says, 'Are you John Cassidy?' I told him I was. He says, 'Well, you and I are about to take a long ride together.' We then embarked on what became a long journey."

And so they did, a ride that lasted until the day Bill France Sr. took his last breath.

Cassidy, still practicing law these days with Baker Botts (Baker, as in former U.S. Secretary of State and former White House Chief of Staff James Baker), took the job of inducting Bill France Sr. very seriously.

He worked on the speech for more than a month, going so far as enlisting his partner Baker as an editor. Baker had his own special affinity for Bill France Sr.; during George H.W. Bush's 1988 presidential campaign, Bill Sr. had come out in support of Bush, who went on to defeat Michael Dukakis and named Baker his secretary of state. Senior's support led to others backing Bush and ultimately, to a third-consecutive Republican term in the White House.

"Baker never forgot that," Cassidy said.

Baker edited Cassidy's speech but, more importantly, supplied a vital tip on how to handle the inevitable emotions that would wash over him while on the stage.

"Baker asked me, 'You were very close to Senior, weren't you?' I told him that I was, especially after he came up to my father's funeral in 1967. That was very touching. Bill Sr. thereafter treated me like a son over the years. He was a father figure to me after my father died – which I will never forget.

"Baker then said, 'I'm a little concerned about the speech. And it's not so much the speech itself. You can give a speech. But what are you going to do if you become emotional?' I said I would tough it out the best I could. That wasn't good enough for Baker. He said, 'I'm going to give you a trick.'

"He told me, 'Whenever you give a speech with an emotional component, there are two types of people in the audience – those who hope you'll break down and cry and those who are rooting for you and hope you don't. You have to do something to get your mind off that concept. The trick: When you stand at the lectern, hold on real tight with both hands and raise one foot off the ground. Stand on one foot and you will not get emotional.'

"That's what I did and it worked. It tricks the brain, gets your mind off the moment."

Once his initial speech draft was turned into NASCAR, the work continued, with Cassidy primarily collaborating with the late Jim Hunter, then NASCAR's vice president of communications. Soon, however, a dilemma developed for organizers of the induction ceremony, scheduled to be broadcast on television. With each new draft, Cassidy's speech got longer, considerably exceeding the time allotment established in the show's script. A debate within NASCAR was squelched quickly by Hunter, with the induction only several days away.

"Goddamn it . . . the speech is fine the way it is!" Hunter told staff members. "Leave it the fuck alone. After all, this is Bill France Sr. we're talking about! I don't want to hear any more about this. Understand?"

It was understood.

As it turned out, all was fine. Cassidy self-edited on the fly, replacing a sizable portion of the prepared text with off-the-cuff storytelling. The end product was an eloquent portrayal of a man whose dreams and vision were being validated in the best way possible.

Cassidy mixed historical tidbits with personal tales and reminiscences of Bill Sr.'s life – and added his own perspective throughout, such as:

"People frequently say Bill Sr. was a 'visionary.' I don't dispute that, but I prefer to call him a 'dreamer who was also a man of action' . . . someone who turned dreams into reality. Not only did Bill follow his dreams . . . he expected the rest of us to do likewise."

Or this:

"Bill Sr. never forgot the humble beginnings from which both he and NASCAR sprung, and . . . while he walked with ease in the corridors of power in Washington and elsewhere . . . he walked with equal grace through the infields and garages during NASCAR events.

"A walk with Bill Sr. through an infield was truly a walk among good friends . . . most of them greeting him as 'Bill.'"

And finally, this:

"Bill's dreams of growth for NASCAR were only exceeded by his desire that stock car racing become a recognized and respected professional sport in America. If he were here today he would be the first to acknowledge NASCAR has exceeded his dreams."

Jim France then accepted the honor of induction, along with the first-ever commemorative NASCAR Hall of Fame ring, for his late father – but came on to the stage with a special surprise in store.

"On behalf of everyone in our family, thank you, John, for that introduction and great tribute to my father," he began. "Let me begin by saying that our family is very proud to be involved in this memorable afternoon for the induction of my father and my brother Bill. We would like to thank the Hall of Fame voting panel for including them in this inaugural class with Junior, Richard, and Dale, truly the iconic heroes of NASCAR."

Jim France talked for only perhaps a minute more before sharing his surprise.

"In closing, I would like to offer the donation of this ring back to the NASCAR Hall of Fame for display wherever they would choose. Thank you."

And with that, the coronation was complete.

CHAPTER 2

An Early Racing Sensibility

n the mid-2000s, when NASCAR started truly expanding beyond its Southeastern roots, repercussions surfaced among core fans – and do to this day from time to time. Such desires by the organization were viewed as some sort of heresy by many who considered NASCAR almost a Southern possession. Part and parcel of this viewpoint was the assumption that NASCAR's founding family members were Southern as well. As the years passed following NASCAR's 1947 founding, it had largely been forgotten by the core fan base that Bill France Sr. was a native of Washington, D.C., growing up just a short distance from the White House – and growing up with an inherent big-city and international sensibility. While Bill Sr.

meshed well with whatever rural clientele he dealt with, he remained a big-city urbanite at heart and moved easily within those circles throughout his life.

Something else that grew to be largely forgotten – or actually, maybe never truly acknowledged in the first place – is that Bill Sr. grew up in a region of the United States that possesses a rich racing history.

But more on that later.

Born September 26, 1909, to William Henry France and Emma Graham France, the boy immediately was given a name that personified "bigness" – William Henry Getty France. So technically, he was not a "Junior." The addition of "Senior" to his name would come along years later when he also had a son named Bill. The addition of "Getty" had a purpose. The renowned Getty family possessed a fortune built in the oil business. Being given their name as part of his own would serve as a personal, constant reminder to Bill France of the possibilities for success the world presented.

Growing up taller than almost all of his schoolmates, "Big Bill" became an inevitable nickname at an early age. It stuck, and with almost each passing year it seemed to be more and more an appropriate fit.

"Big Bill" seems appropriate indeed when viewed within the context of his ancestry on his mother's side. His *eighth* great-grandfather lived life large, to say the least. That was James Graham, the Fifth Earl and First Marquis of Montrose, known in Scottish history as the "Great Montrose."

Graham was a 1600's Scottish nobleman and soldier who fought for King Charles I in as the English Civil War developed from 1644–46 and again in 1650. He was renowned for spectacular victories, taking foes by surprise via superior battle tactics. He also was renowned for being beheaded by military dictator Oliver Cromwell's troops in 1650. Not only was great-grandfather Graham beheaded, his body was cut into four parts and sent to the four major towns of Scotland. Ten years later when the monarchy was restored following Cromwell's death, King Charles II took the throne. James Graham's body parts were actually collected and he was buried with great ceremony at St. Giles Cathedral in Edinburgh. That burial area is known as the Montrose Isle, where the Dukes of Montrose are interred.

Bill Sr.'s mother had emigrated from Ireland along with her parents and her aunt, Susan Shaw, while his father had farmed in Virginia before moving to Washington, where he worked as a clerk at Park Savings Bank. Banking was the family business. Bill Sr.'s uncle Ed Graham had been a runner for the Central National Bank of Washington and worked his way up to vice president of the National Bank of Washington. Emma Graham was a cashier at Riggs Bank. And as a youngster, Bill Sr. worked after school as a runner for Commercial National, riding his bike from bank to bank.

All of this flies in the face of his approach to business later in life. While Bill Sr. became renowned for many things, frugality did not make the list.*

Bill Sr. the banker, then, was not meant to be. And how could it have been? As his former chief lieutenant at NASCAR, Jim Foster, writes in his uncompleted manuscript on Bill Sr.'s life:

---

* More than one family member will tell you still that were it not for his longtime wife, Anne, NASCAR might not have survived financially.

"Bill France was a dreamer from birth. And his dreams weren't about reading, writing and arithmetic, nor did he dream about white-collar jobs and earning a lot of money. His mind was on fast cars and motorcycles, and like most young kids, [he was] anxious to become 16 when he could drive cars like the ones he saw on R Street near the Capitol in D.C. where he and his friends played daily."

And play they did, including some magical childhood days in nearby Rock Creek Park.

Much of the park's magic remains intact today, juxtaposed against the city with which it coexists. Rock Creek Park's main section consists of 1,754 acres in what is known as the Rock Creek Valley in D.C. It is, in many ways, the district's version of New York City's Central Park, affording residents an oasis of sorts amid the ultimate asphalt jungle. The park boasts a variety of recreational facilities and is tremendously popular among walkers, runners, and cyclists. Years ago it was also a favorite swimming hole, despite the unpredictability of the creek's currents, depending on where people chose to swim.

Bill Sr. and his older brother, James, loved Rock Creek, a place in the park made for childhood memories. All that changed on June 25, 1920. The two young boys – Bill was 10, James 13 – were wading when, according to a *Washington Post* account, James apparently stepped over a deep embankment into the creek's deeper waters. The Post reported that none of the friends with James that day could swim well enough to save him. Today, neither swimming nor wading is allowed in Rock Creek. "That was a tremendously traumatic event for Senior," John Cassidy says, an opinion not based solely on conjecture.

"I used to have a law office years ago in D.C. that overlooked a small portion of Rock Creek. One day back in the late 1970s, Senior came to see me and he walked over to a corner of my office and looked out the window, and down at the creek. He asked me, 'What is that water down there?' When I told him he suddenly got very quiet.

"Senior said, 'That creek has a real meaning for me, John.' And when he turned back around from the window, his eyes were misted over. This really struck me, because I never saw Senior cry and he seldom became emotional. But this was different. I saw a side of him that day I had never seen before – or after.

"For the rest of the time I had that office, whenever he came to see me, the first he did was walk to the corner and look down at Rock Creek without saying anything.

"He just wanted to take a look, you know?"

Bill Sr., always silent when spending his few minutes gazing out of Cassidy's office window, carried the memory of losing his brother likewise silently.

"He never talked to me about it at all," said his longtime secretary Betty Faulk. "He may have talked to other people about it, but not to me."

Added his former assistant Judy Jones: "Why would he? He was gone. Nothing he could do."

Bill Sr., growing up without his older brother, immersed himself in his love for anything that involved wheels. Two or four, it did not matter, as long as maximum speed was involved. This compulsion started modestly.

The Frances moved to a home on 13th; Bill Sr.'s aunt Esther Speidel lived next door to the Frances with her husband, Fred, who happened to own an Indian motorcycle. Fred Speidel – an early hero! Bill Sr. came to admire Fred and become fascinated with the motorcycle, dreaming of the day he would be old enough to ride it himself. The kid had good taste; Indian Motorcycle Company is an American classic, the country's first motorcycle company. Founded in 1901, the company's bikes evolved from winning races to helping American soldiers win both world wars. Even after the Frances moved to another area of D.C. to live with Bill Sr.'s grandmother Emma Graham, he stayed in touch with Fred and, de facto, with Fred's Indian.

Bill Sr. went on to attend Gage Primary School and Columbia Junior High in the district. Inevitably he was tabbed by classmates and coaches as a potential basketball star as he started nearing his eventual six-foot-five adult height when he entered the seventh grade at Central High School. Bill Sr. apparently had some semblance of game; he had played on a church league team called the Calvary Reds.

Neither basketball nor books, however, was to his liking. Hard work and dreams of racing were more his style. He stuck it out at Central long enough to complete seventh grade. Not long after he started eighth grade, he dropped out.

As a teenager, he looked for jobs, and many ended up having something to do with the automobile, in large part because of his dream of racing in the Indianapolis 500. So he pumped gas back in the days when service stations – filling stations, as they were called – did that for customers, at no charge. He changed tires, too. And he advanced his skill set, eventually working for a Washington service station chain as a battery and electrical system repairman . . . running a front-end machine for a Ford dealer . . . working as a front-end specialist for a Buick dealership.

It was during this period that his Uncle Fred started letting him take the Indian out for a spin. Jim Foster wrote that "Bill Sr. and his pals got to know the District of Columbia police on a first-name basis, with many warnings for speeding and violating noise ordinances, but Bill Sr. seldom got a ticket because the police in D.C. knew him and liked him. Everyone he met was charmed by his 'aw shucks' attitude, his friendly smile, and his show of maturity beyond his years."

Thus, early on, Bill Sr. was developing a personality that would carry him through his life, fast times and slow, good times and bad. What many friends and family would later describe as an "aura" surrounding his every move might well be traceable to a gangly teenager talking his way out of speeding tickets. Humble beginnings for a giant of American motorsports, granted, but one can almost envision the scene transpiring on a muggy D.C. summer night, Bill Sr. pleading his case while making friends in the process.

Further Foster insight: "Although Bill was honest, sincere, and personable, many of the older family members referred to him as a 'black sheep' as they were concerned about his free-wheeling lifestyle, especially his lust for speed."

Bill Sr. quit school. The reasons were simple. He had grown tired of studying, unless the studying had something to do with automobiles – that was his focus. He would go watch races after school, or skip school just to be around race cars at tracks around Washington. So, actually, he was still studying, only it was the racing styles of great drivers like Peter DePaolo and Ralph DePalma.

DePalma was of special interest to Bill Sr. Winner of the Indianapolis 500 in 1915, DePalma went to Daytona Beach, Florida, in February 1919 and drove a Packard to a world speed record of 149.875 miles per hour over a mile of oceanfront sand. Years later one of the grandstands at the Daytona International Speedway that Bill Sr. would build was named in DePalma's honor.

When Bill Sr. reached the age of 16, he got the grudging okay from his father to occasionally drive the family's Model T Ford. Unbeknownst was that the Model T was being raced at a board track in nearby Laurel, Maryland. This is another bit of Bill Sr.'s past that had a tie to his future.

The 1.125-mile wood Laurel Speedway had turns banked at an incredible 48 degrees; years later, Daytona's 31 degrees of banking must have seemed routine to Bill Sr.

Laurel was unique, outlandish – and not wholly a good idea.

It was right up a teenage Bill France's alley.

Check out this Laurel assessment from the *Washington Post*:

"A wide board track, wrapping 80 acres of ground as a ribbon might encircle an ostrich egg, with a huge grandstand overlooking it all, is ready today to vibrate under the great motor gruel, the inaugural race at the Washington-Baltimore automobile speedway.

"Never level and in places almost up and down, it is [an arena for] speed-crazed drivers, out on a Roman holiday to entertain the populace and in so doing to lower the world's speed records."

Fred Speidel's son, Bill, was seven years old at the time. Bill Sr. was able to get Fred's car keys by saying he was taking the kid for a ride. Which was true, more or less. Often, they rode to Laurel Speedway.

At Laurel, the people operating the track let him drive the Model T around the apron, but the temptation of going up into the racing groove on the banking was too much for Bill Sr.. He could get up there but the Model T wouldn't stick. Finally, his father noticed the Ford's tires were wearing out way too quickly and drove down to the Ford dealer to complain. Bill Sr. accompanied his father but then had to keep silent, listening to what must've been a strange conversation about the unusually balding tires.

"There's the old story that's been told a lot, about Bill France Sr. and the Laurel track," racing historian Larry Jendras said. "The story goes that all the laps he was able to take around Laurel proved to be an inspiration for him years later when he built Daytona International Speedway and how he wanted to shape the high banks there."

Laurel Speedway's brief existence – it was active for merely two years before being abandoned and torn down – belied its impact on American motorsports. Its inaugural race, on July 11, 1925, was won by Pete DePaolo with 60,000 spectators on hand. DePaolo had won the Indianapolis 500 just six weeks earlier. The report on the event was a front-page story – front page of the main section, not a sports-specific area – in the next day's *Washington Post*. DePaolo was one of many top-notch wheelmen of the era who raced there. It was a perfect place for an impressionable teenager already excited about motorsports to be nudged over the edge into a full-blown, heart-and-soul commitment. That's what happened to Bill France Sr.

But the lure of Laurel was accompanied by other influences.

Bill Sr.'s uncle Jim Graham decided he and Fred Speidel needed a place to satisfy their need for speed. Graham bought a 100-acre farm near Olney, Maryland. Here was plenty of room to ride motorcycles away from the potential problems to be encountered on big-city streets.

In addition to the main house the property had a structure that had been used in the 1800s as slave quarters. Bill Sr. decided to turn it into his first garage, where he would build his first race car.

He and a friend named Hugh Ostemeyer built a rudimentary wooden chassis and covered it with canvas. It was an unusual project and very inexpensive, but perhaps not as strange as one might think. Factory-produced cars in those days were rudimentary in their own way. France dropped a Model T engine into his home-made chassis and installed a seat belt – something few drivers of the era used.

Bill Sr. raced his prized ride at Pikesville, Maryland, on a five-eighths-mile dirt track. Later known as Milford Mill Speedway, the facility personified the immense popularity of auto racing in the D.C.-Baltimore area in the early part of the 20th century, into which Bill France tapped.

"Anywhere you got close to Pennsylvania [you had racing]," Jendras said. "Pennsylvania had so many fairgrounds and if you had fairgrounds you had race tracks. Racing was popular [in the area]. And for years we had a NASCAR track, in Beltsville, Maryland."

Beltsville Speedway, a half-mile asphalt oval, represented a continuation of the race fervor that affected Bill Sr. during his younger days. The track, originally known as Baltimore-Washington Speedway, hosted 10 races in what is now known as the NASCAR Sprint Cup Series, from 1965–70. The list of winners is a mixture of current and almost-certain future members of the NASCAR Hall of Fame: Ned Jarrett (1965), Tiny Lund (1966), Bobby Allison (1966), Jim Paschal (1967), Richard Petty (1967 and '69), David Pearson (1968), and Bobby Isaac (1968,

'69, '70). Beltsville, near the Baltimore-Washington Parkway, closed in 1978 after a number of years of battling noise ordinances imposed by Prince George's County.

In 1985, the area's last speedway closed, but that obscures a long history of auto racing in a region that most people relate to as a horse-racing hotbed, due to Pimlico and its status as host track for the second leg of the Triple Crown, the Preakness. Likewise obscured is the influence the region's racing had on Bill Sr., who clearly was a racer in his heart and soul long before he came to Daytona Beach.

Jendras, perhaps the definitive historian when it comes to auto racing in the Baltimore-D.C. area, writes that "with the popularity of auto racing growing across the nation during recent years, newer fans may not realize the long history the sport has in [the area]. Competition between two or more autos can be traced in Baltimore back to November 1900. The event took place at The Gentleman's Driving Park located across from the famous Pimlico Race Course horse track. . . . Auto racing in the 1920s and '30s often used the ready-made tracks at county fairs or horse-racing facilities. Baltimore was no different, as cars took to Prospect Park, which was located on Eastern Avenue between Baltimore and Essex. . . . The first speedway built especially for cars was Pikesville Speedway, later known as Milford Mill Speedway. Located on Milford Mill Road between Reisterstown Road and Liberty Road, Pikesville Speedway was in operation from 1930–35. One of the most familiar faces in all of auto racing, Bill France, founder of NASCAR, drove some races there during his early career as a driver."

Indeed he did, and while the homemade machine wasn't a winning car, who cared? Bill Sr. was honing skills at 90 mph in the straights, his resolve to become a "major league" driver becoming more entrenched into his very being. Indianapolis remained the primary goal.

That resolve was juxtaposed by the desire of his basketball coach in D.C., who urged him to return to high school. Bill Sr. had grown to six-foot-five but it didn't matter. He was interested in only one sport.

"I just liked to go fast," he told Jim Foster. "I don't think I was unusual. I knew I wanted to be a race driver. Go out and ask every kid who likes to drive fast if he'd like to be a race driver and he'll say yes."

Bill Sr.'s racing and car construction were sidelined briefly when he was injured in one of his many falls off his motorcycle. He suffered a knee injury and walked on crutches for a while. There were no serious after-effects immediately but later in life he would pay a price. He had repeated battles with gout, and when he was stricken, his knee often would swell and cause him considerable pain. Ultimately, he would have a kneecap removed, leaving him with a noticeable limp.

Injuries did nothing to dissuade the young France from his racing dreams. But around the age of 20, in 1929, he began to realize that he would have to work a good deal more to keep those dreams alive, in addition to maintaining an increasingly active social life. Bill Sr. had become interested in women and the interest was reciprocal in many cases.

Early in 1931, at the age of 21, Bill Sr.'s life would be changed forever when his mother asked him to drive her to the hospital to visit a relative. The Speidels had divorced in 1930 and Bill's Aunt Esther was left with their son, Billy, and his two brothers. Billy had Bright's Disease and was a patient at the hospital. Bill Sr. was happy to drive his mother that night. It got him out of the house and behind the steering wheel of a car.

They had not been at the hospital long before a nurse entered the room. There was something about her that piqued Bill Sr.'s interest. She was not only pretty, but her soft voice and mannerisms kept his attention.

She left the room briefly but returned to check on young Billy. This time she introduced herself as Anne Bledsoe and Bill Sr. engaged her in conversation. She had just completed nursing school and was living in Washington.

For the next few days Bill Sr. forgot about his passion for going fast and thought only about this intriguing woman he had met. He called her for a date and was slightly surprised when she said yes. He borrowed the family car and picked Anne up at the hospital after she got off work. Money was scarce so a movie was out of the question. Bill Sr. drove her out to the farm to show her his motorcycle and race cars.

For the first time in his life he was actually infatuated with something other than a car or motorcycle. He knew he wanted to know more about her and see her again. Soon they found common ground beyond mutual infatuation.

Anne Bledsoe was born in Nathan's Creek, North Carolina, on October 27, 1904 (nearly five years before Bill Sr.). Anne's father, Marcus, was an eighth-generation Bledsoe. He was a descendent of George Bledsoe (1635–1705), who emigrated from England to North Cumberland, Virginia, in 1652. He and his wife, Virginia Cox Bledsoe, had six children.

After only three months of dating, Bill Sr. proposed. Her immediate response reflected her overall cautious, conservative approach to life – 180 degrees in opposition to her husband-to-be, who never saw a risk he didn't want to take.

"She said, 'Now Bill, are you sure about this?'" Bill Sr. recalled. He was sure.

So was Bill Sr.'s family, believing the new bride would be able to "settle down" his racing wanderlust.

They were married on June 23, 1931. Anne moved in with Bill Sr. and while she continued to work as a nurse, France continued to spend his days underneath cars, repairing brakes and transmissions in the summer and changing frozen batteries and installing chains in the winter months. Obviously he would have preferred to work on race cars and drive them.

In September 1932 the couple learned that a baby was on the way. Immediately, Bill Sr. turned serious regarding work and, most importantly, money. On April 4, 1933, William Clifton France was born. Officially there was no Junior attached to his name, just as his father technically wasn't a Senior. The Junior-Senior thing simply became a necessity over time.

Bill Sr. worked hard to support his family, as his wife had quit her nursing job. He found a little row house on Park Road for $25 a week, and moved his new family in.

Bill Sr. was working hard, focusing on married life and fatherhood – but that didn't stop him from visiting nearby race tracks. And he spent a considerable amount of his free time tuning up his newest race car, a Riley that he drove at four of the area's tracks.

One lesson he learned as a young racer would serve him well when he became a promoter in the late 1930s. Breaking news: Race promoters in the early part of the 20th century oftentimes could not be trusted! If they were not directly influencing the outcome during the actual races to help favored drivers or over-looking post-race violations to benefit drivers who were personal friends, they were inventing myriad plots to avoid paying competitors the prize money they were due.

Bill Sr. told what he swore was a true story, of entering a race at Pikesville where the winner's purse was advertised as $500. He raced hard to finish third – and was handed a $10 bill.

"I asked the promoter, 'I only get $10 dollars for third? How much did the winner get?' He said, 'Fifty dollars; I just made the announcement about $500 for the public, to help boost interest for the race.'"

Such post-race experiences – and others that were similar – stuck with Bill Sr. It would prod him to make life better for drivers in the years ahead.

In the late summer of 1934 – Bill Jr. was 16 months old – Bill Sr. had had enough of working on frozen cars during the winter and making very little money in return. He told Anne he wanted to move the family to Florida, maybe as far south as Miami, where it would be a warmer atmosphere for his work and for young Billy to grow up. Anne's conservative nature again was evident. Spending money was always a mental roadblock with her. She asked her husband point-blank how the excursion to Florida would be financed.

"Now Bill, where are we going to get the money?"

His reply: "I'll find it."

Bill Sr.'s Uncle Ed loaned him $300 for the move. Meanwhile, his Uncle Jim, steadfastly in the "black sheep" camp when it came to his nephew, told Ed, "You'll never see that money again."

The $300 was spent judiciously. Bill Sr. took care of a few out-standing small debts. He purchased some wheels, tires, and other parts to build a small wooden house trailer for the several-day trip.

In October 1934, with cold weather closing in on D.C., he left town with $25 in cash after depositing $75 in a D.C. bank. He packed the crude trailer with tools and other belongings, hitched it to his Hupmobile – a beloved make of car that fell victim to the Depression era – and headed south to Florida with Anne by his side and Billy in her arms. They would stop to eat and to rest but spent only one night in the trailer.

Bill France Sr. was anxious to get to Florida.

CHAPTER 3

Coming to Daytona

Best to set the record straight right from the start, regarding the reason Bill France and his wife and child took up residency in Daytona Beach in the fall of 1934.

This means debunking the well-worn story that the Frances stayed because they were stranded, with their Hupmobile having broken down as they cruised along A1A en route to, perhaps, South Florida.

This isn't the first time for such a dismissal, nor will it be the last, so perhaps the best course of action is to go for the strongest dismissal possible given the passage of time. Makes sense.

Because, dismissals notwithstanding, the story simply will not die.

"My dad was a mechanic and he would've fixed the car if it needed to be fixed," says Bill Sr.'s youngest son, Jim France. "He came here the same reason a lot of people did in the 1930s. He was mainly looking for work."

Bill Sr. told an interviewer virtually the same thing in 1983, saying, "The car didn't break down. We stopped in Daytona Beach because it was the place we wanted to live."

Not nearly as sexy, that reality, as the serendipity drenched yarn spun into an urban legend. (Or is it rural legend, given NASCAR's original fan base?) Jim France credits the late *Daytona Beach News-Journal* sportswriter/editor Benny Kahn with creating the tale and then propagating it until his death in 1975.

"It made for a better story," Jim France admits.

Longtime *News-Journal* motorsports editor Godwin Kelly, who worked for Kahn and has become the modern-day incarnation of his old boss, says "this was sort of like one of those old Native American legends. It just kept getting passed down, you know: 'Hupmobile broke down . . . he ended up here in Daytona.'"

Of course, work was not the only reason Bill France rolled into Daytona. He had racing on his mind, which was nothing new. Along with his wife and child, NASCAR's future founder brought an inherent auto racing sensibility to the Sunshine State.

That sensibility received an immediate high-octane boost from Daytona's racing history, which was rich long before Bill France came to town.

The drive from D.C. had reached mid-afternoon on the third day on the road when Bill Sr. and Anne began seeing palm trees, a certain sign they were getting close to Florida. Bill Sr. was excited. He tried his damnedest to excite his wife, he told Jim Foster. "We're going to be in Daytona Beach before dark," he announced just north of the Georgia-Florida border. "That means we can take a drive on the beach . . . maybe even a swim."

While France had dreamed of driving a race car at Indianapolis, he had also spent a lot of time reading books and articles on the history of the automobile, and what little there was printed on racing at the time.

"Annie, we're going to see the 'Birthplace of Speed,'" he proclaimed as he gave the Hupmobile a little more gas.

"Now Bill," Annie cautioned. "We don't need a speeding ticket."

As they crossed the state line into Florida, France's thoughts were racing, recalling the history of speed on the sands of Ormond Beach and Daytona Beach, adjoining Florida cities that had, at the turn of century, become the automotive playground for the millionaires of the time.

While making the decision to leave the snow and ice in Washington, Bill Sr. had targeted Florida as a potential destination because he had always heard of the state's beauty and warmth. His initial thought was to settle in Miami – a large, growing city with plenty of automobiles in need of repair.

But eventually – and perhaps inevitably – he started thinking about Daytona Beach.

He did not share this with his wife.

In the mid-1930s the city of Daytona Beach owed its very existence, in large part, to automobile racing. Daytona Beach, along with Ormond Beach just to the north, had come to be known as the Birthplace of Speed in the early 1900s. Technically, the nerve center was in Ormond proper, an area that today is marked by a strip mall anchored by an Outback Steakhouse. But there was a time when the future intersection of Grenada Boulevard and A1A was abuzz with automobiles from around the world each winter, as machines and men combined forces to chase the world land speed record on the hard-packed sands of the Atlantic shoreline.

It was a formative period for American auto racing; the annual quest for speed was labeled the Winter Speed Carnival. In many ways it was the original Speedweeks, Daytona International Speedway's long-running season-opening NASCAR fortnight that culminates with the Daytona 500.

The community that Big Bill France brought his dreams to had once been an internationally known haven of dreamers – and doers. The alumni of the grand period between 1903–35 included people such as Henry Ford, Louis Chevrolet, and Ransom Olds chasing the speed marks. Standard Oil magnate John D. Rockefeller had an Ormond Beach home just a short walk from the shoreline; the home still stands today as an attraction and event center, called "The Casements." And when the racing was done, what better place for the drivers and their adoring fans to gather than the Hotel Ormond, a grand palace owned by visionary developer Henry Flagler, who complemented his construction of a railroad system along Florida's East Coast – he eventually reached Key West in 1912 – with a series of palatial-for-the-times hotels. Flagler's railroad made Ormond and Daytona reachable; his hotel made the area livable for turn-of-the-century high rollers. The Hotel Ormond, which opened on New Year's Day 1888, 15 years before the speed-record runs began, was built by John Anderson and J.D. Price and sold to Flagler the next year, whereupon the magnate expanded guest capacity to 600.*

The Hotel Ormond became one in a series of hotels that were positioned near the Florida East Coast Railway. Others were the Ponce De Leon in St. Augustine; the Royal Poinciana and the Breakers in Palm Beach; and the Royal Palm in Miami. In November 1980 the Hotel Ormond was added to the U.S. National register of Historic Places; sadly, it was torn down 12 years later and replaced by a condominium complex.

It is not a stretch to connect some historical dots between Flagler and France, two dreamers whose ambitions seemed at times preposterous.

A railroad all the way to Key West in the early 1900s?

A 2.5-mile race track in Daytona Beach 50 years later?

Six of one, half a dozen of the other.

In many ways, Henry Flagler supplied a template for ambition up and down Florida's East Coast.

Most certainly, his work in Ormond and Daytona was a template.

Flagler biographer Sidney Martin wrote this in 1949: "Although Floridians differ as to their opinion of Flagler, none can deny that he was the greatest developer the state ever had . . . from Jacksonville to Key West was injected with new life. Flagler gave Florida a future."

---

* Bill France Sr.'s final home was in Ormond Beach on John Anderson Road, which runs north-south and begins by intersecting State Road 40, adjacent to where the Hotel Ormond once stood.

Professor Seth Bramson, perhaps the premier living Flagler historian, ups the ante, calling Flagler "the single greatest name in Florida history" in his book *The Greatest Railroad Story Ever Told: Henry Flagler & the Florida East Coast Railway's Key West Extension.*

"The East Coast of Florida is his monument, it's as simple as that," Bramson says. "There's no question that Florida without Henry Flagler would today be a completely different place. The development might have come but it would've come much more slowly or differently. That was just a marvelous, marvelous period of time. All the wonderful history of the [racing] industry and business in Daytona Beach that would eventually become NASCAR, even that can be related to Flagler.

"The Ormond Hotel, for many, many years, it was *the* place, the center of social activity starting south of St. Augustine, the center of social activity really going all the way down to Brevard County. And, I would tend to believe the folks that were engaged in the early years of racing had their meetings, did their planning and probably stayed at the Ormond. This connection (between Flagler and auto racing) is so valid it's hard to believe."

Added Martin, regarding the synergy between Flagler's railroad, Hotel Ormond, and the beach races: "Automobile racing fans crowded the Ormond Beach hotel to enjoy the sport which soon made Ormond and Daytona beaches famous."

Daytona's sand eventually lost out to the Bonneville Salt Flats in Utah after 1935, as the speed records inevitably soared and technology followed. Which left a hole in the city's psyche. The Birthplace of Speed was in need.

"When the speed-record chasers stopped coming to town, it left a void," Bill France Jr. said in 2005. "Over the first 40 years or so of the 20th century, the Daytona Beach area had become synonymous with speed. So it was only natural that some community activists would try to keep that going. One of those activists was my father."

Flagler's influence had played an integral role in facilitating auto racing's birth in the Daytona Beach area.

Bill Sr.'s influence would bring the sport back to prominence – and then some, albeit with a series of stutter-steps along the way.

Bill Sr. had stopped in St. Augustine to refuel and decided he didn't want to wait until he arrived in Daytona Beach to see the ocean. He took the ocean highway (U.S. A1A), which was a slower route but definitely picturesque. When he got to Ormond Beach, he made a sharp left – on to the world-famous (at least among racing enthusiasts) hard-packed sands that stretched 23 miles to Ponce Inlet. He was jubilant and continued his selling job to his wife.

On they rolled into Daytona Beach. Just ahead was the city's landmark Main Street pier. Bill Sr. stopped the car short of the pier. He, Anne, and toddler Bill Jr. got out and went wading in the ocean. Over the course of an hour or so, Bill Sr. was trying to figure out how to tell his wife that he had quickly made up his mind on where they would build their future.

Nearly 50 years later, Bill Sr. described the moment, which was a watershed not only for the small family but also for the future of auto racing in North America, to Jim Foster:

"I just blurted it out: Anne! This is it. We're not going any farther. She asked if I was sure. . . . The first time I saw Daytona Beach I thought it was the prettiest place I'd ever seen. I'll never forget how beautiful that beach was the first time I saw it. It was a perfect fall day."

Not only was he sure, but he had already made arrangements before leaving Washington to stay with a relative just south of Daytona in Coronado Beach, near New Smyrna Beach. Anne, ever the pragmatist, wanted to know what would come next. Her husband assured her a job and a home would come easily.

And why shouldn't he have been confident? Finding work in Washington had never been hard despite a worsening economy. He had a reputation for being polite as well as being a skilled mechanic – two ways to combat the Depression. Granted, he wasn't sure how he would be accepted in Florida, although he knew a Buick dealer he had worked for in Washington would give him a good recommendation. And his confidence had soared when he noticed a Buick dealership on the Daytona Beach mainland after leaving the beach that first day.

This attitude was telling, and indicative of the style that carried Bill Sr. throughout his life. He had a personality as big as his six-foot-five stature, a fact that was noticeable as a youngster but undeniable when he reached his adult years.

Years later, his longtime secretary Betty Faulk still marvels at the memory of his presence.

"Senior would walk into a room and people would just do what he wanted," Faulk said. "I once saw the Kennedys up close and they had that same kind of charisma. It just emanated from them. Senior was that way."

And that's the sort of charisma he carried with him into the show room at Lloyd Buick in Daytona Beach. He quickly hit it off with the owner of the dealership, Sax Lloyd. A good recommendation from the D.C. dealership led to some immediate part-time work, primarily on brakes.

Serendipity was operative, as it seemingly would be throughout the life of Bill Sr.

Lloyd was a lot like him, extremely personable and down to earth. Lloyd was a pillar of the community, served on city, county, and state boards, and was involved in many charitable organizations. Through the years, Bill Sr. would find Lloyd's friendship instrumental in his quest for success.

The France family's first home at 322 Wisconsin Place, a modest two-room duplex renting for $15 a month, was only two blocks from Lloyd Buick. The Frances actually rented it before Lloyd offered some work for Bill Sr., who saw that as nothing more than a minor technicality.

Roots had been put down, albeit rather quickly.

But quickness was appropriate.

After all, the Frances had decided to make the Birthplace of Speed their new home.

Sig Haugdahl felt the community's pain when the racing went westward after 1935. Haugdahl had seen the sands come alive with speed; in fact, he was a former record holder, giving him far more emotional equity than most citizens who wanted the racing to return. It is important to remember that it was mid-Depression across the country, with the South hit especially hard by the tough times. Chances are most of the citizenry in Daytona Beach and Ormond Beach who wanted to keep the races running were motivated by an economic sensibility. Haugdahl's interest went beyond that, which should not be surprising. The man was a racer. In 1922, he had achieved a speed of 180 mph at Daytona – and was the International Motor

Contest Association dirt-track champion six consecutive years between 1927 and 1932.

Haugdahl, who ran a local garage, came up with a concept that was at once novel and outlandish: racing modified cars on a circuit that utilized both the Atlantic shoreline – low tide, of course – AND the bumpy pavement of State Road A1A, the now-legendary oceanfront road that runs the length of Florida's East Coast and eventually, following the lead of Flagler's railroad, reaches Key West.

This beach-road course approach was not a perfect setting but it was the best setting possible at the time. All these years later, the combo layouts have a secure place in NASCAR lore. Making history, though, was not the goal in 1936; it was more about extending history at the time.

Bill Sr., enthralled to begin with about the Daytona-Ormond racing history, witnessed first-hand the final year of speed runs on the beach in the winter of 1935. That fired him up further about where he lived and what the place meant to auto racing on a global scale. His enthusiasm was still largely based on being a competitor, though. The idea of promoting races may have been lurking in his mind but it was by no means foremost. Bill Sr. entered Haugdahl's race, finishing a solid fifth in the 250-mile event and at some point became a de facto partner of Haugdahl. Not the greatest move, as the city of Daytona Beach lost more than $20,000, a huge setback considering the times.

Entering that 1936 event affected France in two distinct ways: he came away more or less convinced that he could win stock car races on a regular basis, but he also became convinced that, if pressed into service, he could be successful as a promoter.

According to Foster, "He decided he would drive in every race possible, and he also wrote down all of the mistakes he had watched occur in the promotion of that 1936 race."

After the financial failure of 1936, the city of Daytona Beach decided to get out of the racing business, the romance with history notwithstanding. The Elks Club promoted the race in 1937 and also lost money, so no race was scheduled for 1938. Eventually the chamber of commerce visited with Bill Sr., who had emerged as a vocal racing proponent since coming to the area in 1934, and asked him to help find a promoter. Already Bill Sr. was becoming a local "face" in terms of racing and also in terms of notoriety overall, even though he had relatively limited means. This development was an early example of what would become a hallmark of Big Bill France's professional life: his personality and all-out zeal for something he believed in was infectious. The idea of promoting a race indeed excited Bill Sr.; by now Daytona Beach was *his* city. And, in line with his overall optimistic approach to life, he was certain he would succeed where Haugdahl and the Elks had failed. When asked if he knew of a potential promoter, Bill Sr. told city officials he was just the perfect man for the job.

The brief period at Lloyd Buick was followed by France opening his own garage and service station on the corner of Main Street and Halifax Avenue in Daytona Beach, just a short walk from the Atlantic shoreline. He and Anne moved out of the confines of the duplex on Wisconsin and into a roomier rental home on Braddock Avenue, only a block from the garage.

The garage came to be a meeting place for area racers. Bill Sr. proudly called his business the "racing headquarters" for the locals to come and work on their cars or simply to hang around and talk racing.

Bill Sr. had begun competing in the Carolinas, driving a 1937 Ford owned by Daytona Beach restaurant owner Charlie Reese with mixed results. It was a reality that would define his driving career and slowly, inexorably, steer him toward the path of managing the events rather than entering himself. Still, there were moments when Bill Sr. looked more than capable in a stock car, doing well against many drivers in the Southeast who had sharpened their skills as moonshine runners, carrying loads of illegal liquor to earn good money – and outrunning police cars in the process. Many of these part-time outlaws – called "trippers" – would remain part of his life for a number of years and a number of races down the road.

These were the years of the birth of stock car racing, which was no less than a cultural phenomenon. And no less than two-time NASCAR national champion Tim Flock, a former tripper himself, would look back after his racing days were through and declare that the birth had taken place in and around Dawsonville, Georgia, a city known to modern-day fans as the hometown of another NASCAR champion, Bill Elliott.

The noted veteran motorsports journalist Jonathan Ingram, writing for RacinToday.com, explored the cultural aspect of a growing sport:

"There are some grains of truth to Flock's story about the origins of stock car racing as an organized sport . . . [racing] reached an epidemic scale during the Great Depression, which increased demand for low-cost entertainment and bootleg whiskey. The attraction to racing stock cars found several strongholds in three distinct territories in the East in the late 1930s . . . Langhorne in Pennsylvania . . . the shores of Daytona . . . [and] Lakewood in Atlanta. Each [featured] a major venue hosting races of one hundred miles or more in length. All were close to concentrations of Americans of Scottish-Irish, German or English descent – and they were located in territories known for (bootleg whisky).

"When stock car racing arrived in the 1930s, issues surrounding individual honor so prized by the Scottish-Irish pervaded the circumstances of the races. Amidst the bellowing cars, individual rank and territory were often in dispute . . . the sport quickly came to represent the sort of defiance . . . that also helped drive the bootlegging trade."

Amid this cultural metamorphosis being played out in high drama fueled by horsepower and hard times, the hot ticket-sellers were bootleggers – men like Atlanta's Raymond Parks, the car owner who had talented drivers like Flock and Red Byron in cars prepared by legendary mechanic Red Vogt. These guys were not easy to beat on the track, much less to govern off the track. Bill France Sr., in fact, joined them in competition for a while, sometimes driving one of Parks' cars, which carried him to a handful of impressive wins and a host of solid finishes that enabled him to build a name among fans and the racing community.

Concurrent, he was building his name as an organizer and promoter. Writes Jim Foster: "Bill told Reese about the possibility of promoting a race in Daytona. He explained it was a good opportunity, but he didn't have any money. Reese, knowing Bill's honesty and hard work, agreed to supply the cash if Bill would do the work in 1938. A partnership formed. And it was the beginning of a promotional career for Bill. There had been racing on the beach for twenty years and the speed trials had made the city famous. But none was financially successful.

"That first race France and Reese sold five thousand tickets at fifty cents each and made a profit of $250 each. Bill figured if they were going to work that hard, they should make more money. He raised the admission price to one dollar in 1939 and again sold five thousand tickets, realizing a profit of $2,000 after donating 10 per cent to charity. Bill and his partner split the $2,000.

"Bill told this story many times over the years, calling it one of the best lessons he ever learned. His philosophy was, you have to take chances and learn by your mistakes."

The initial year of the France-Reese partnership is notable for another reason: it offered a glimpse into the future and Bill Sr.'s commitment to fairness as a promoter. Circumstances truly conspired to place him and Reese in an unenviable position when the 1938 race winner Smokey Purser disdained the traditional Victory Lane celebration to instead haul ass to . . . somewhere.

No detective work was needed to discern what was going on, and sure enough Purser soon was located at a nearby garage. He and some buddies were working to yank out illegal high-performance cylinder heads and get the car back to stock configuration.

Obviously Purser would have to be disqualified, giving the victory to none other than . . . runner-up Bill France!

Fair enough, but that created the immediate dilemma about the first-place prize money. Bill Sr. and Reese pow-wowed quickly and determined that the winner's purse would be awarded to the third-place driver, Lloyd Moody.

Former Charlotte Motor Speedway president H.A. "Humpy" Wheeler views the "perfect man for the job" description of Bill Sr.

for Daytona Beach promotion on a much larger scale. Wheeler thinks Bill Sr. was a perfect match for the inherent, overall ethnicity of stock car racing's original competitive base.

"In those days we needed a strong-willed person running the show," Wheeler said. "The Scotch-Irish are a hard-headed people and we needed somebody to lay down the law when it was necessary."

And who better to lay down the law than a direct descendant of a Scottish warrior? Big Bill France, remember, had the blood of the Great Montrose running through his veins. Kicking ass and taking names came naturally.

In 1939, Bill Sr. accelerated both his driving and promoting ambitions. The two beach-road races in Daytona – he finished fourth in the second one, in July – were supplemented by a stint as chief judge for races at the nearby Deland Fairgrounds, reflecting an increasing presence and reputation as a racing authority in the region where he lived.

Bill Sr. would promote races on the beach and at various tracks in North Carolina from 1938 to 1941, but the Japanese attack on Pearl Harbor on December 7, 1941, temporarily stalled his burgeoning auto racing dreams.

For much of the first half of the ensuing decade, those dreams would be stuck, idling.

The second half? Overdrive.

CHAPTER 4

The 1940s:

The Beach, the War — and NASCAR

ill France Sr.'s popularity as a driver *and* a promoter increased exponentially in 1940 and '41. Much of that had to do with his efforts outside Florida, as he became involved in promotion of events in North Carolina and Georgia, often competing in those events as well.

Concurrently, he worked non-stop to recruit drivers for his races back home in Daytona Beach. But it was during this two-year period immediately preceding the United States' involvement in World War II that Bill Sr. peaked as a driver.

The 1940 season had two competitive highlights – a break-through victory on the Daytona Beach-road course in February and an "unofficial" national championship crown. In addition to Daytona, Bill Sr. had victories at Salisbury, North Carolina, Spartanburg, South Carolina (twice) and Greensboro, North Carolina.

On July 7, 1940, Bill Sr. finally won outright on the beach-road layout, his only previous win there coming when he and Reese had disqualified Smokey Purser in 1938. Unlike that day, this time Bill Sr. got to keep the winner's purse of $600 after averaging 75 miles per hour on the 3.2-mile course with approximately 12,000 spectators on hand. It completed three consecutive wins, following a May victory at Salisbury and a July 4 triumph in Spartanburg.

The *Daytona Beach News-Journal* by this time had openly embraced him as a transplanted hometown hero, repeatedly running his photo – albeit the same smiling, portrait-type shot with a white lattice fence in the background – alongside race stories. His Daytona win led the *News-Journal* sports pages on July 8, adjacent to a piece on Boston Red Sox first baseman Jimmy Foxx being named to play in the All-Star Game for the eighth consecutive time. A footnote to the Foxx story: it mentioned that another member of the Red Sox, an outfielder named Ted Williams, had been chosen to play in the game for the very first time.

After the second Spartanburg victory, the paper reported that "France's win yesterday [November 17, 1940] probably was the greatest of his career. The 30-year-old driver has rocketed to the top in stock car racing within the last year . . ."

The same report, though, illustrated Bill Sr.'s fence-straddling between driving and promoting which, when it came right down to it, was savvy business. "In a telephone conversation with the *News-Journal* last night," the story continued, "France said he had lined up the finest field in Volusia's racing history to run at the Fairgrounds. He will return home tomorrow afternoon and immediately begin laying plans for the December 1 race in Deland."

This was double-dipping at its zenith.

Before the year was over Bill Sr. and Anne had purchased a modest home on Goodall Avenue, not far from the service station and garage. It became both an office and a place of entertainment immediately and would remain so for years to come.

Without a doubt, 1940 had been a great year for Bill and Anne France. He had accumulated five victories on the track, by far his most successful season. Meanwhile, success as a promoter in the Carolinas and in Florida had earned him additional respect in both the racing and business communities where the races were held. They had also settled into their new home, with their son Billy soon entering pre-school.

Bill Sr.'s mother had passed away and his father, William Henry France, had left Washington and moved in with Bill and Anne. He would remain in Daytona Beach, driving taxi cabs and finding other odd jobs, until his death on March 27, 1949.

The Daytona Beach-road course hosted four races in 1941, starting with the "Bundles for Britain" wartime fundraiser on March 3, won by Roy Hall. Then, on March 30 the second annual Lockhart Memorial was run, with Smokey Purser winning.

The Lockhart Memorial was another nod by Bill Sr. to the area's speed-record history, but also to the allure of the Indianapolis 500 and his one-time dream to be part of the grand spectacle.

Frank Lockhart, the winner of the 500 in 1926, became one of the casualties of the speed runs on April 25, 1928. Lockhart, driving a prototype called the Stutz Black Hawk Special streamliner, cut a tire and went careening across the sand. He was thrown from the car and killed instantly. At that point, the speed runs were in their 25th year and with each passing year the inherent treacherous nature of rocketing down the beach was looking less like heroism and more like foolishness.

The Lockhart Memorial drew some 12,000 spectators and Bill Sr. responded to the atmosphere by capturing the pole position. Smokey Purser passed Roy Hall on the final lap to win the race.

The July 27, 1941, race at the Daytona road course had atmosphere, largely because of the exploits of Bill Sr., but he had plenty of help when it came to attracting ticket buyers. The field that gathered that weekend was trumpeted as the strongest ever for a stock car event. Hyperbole or not, it may well have been just that.

Bill Sr. still managed to lead often in a group of drivers that included newcomer Fonty Flock from Atlanta, part of the colorful Flock family that would in future years become so vital to NASCAR's early popularity. Roy Hall ended up taking the checkered flag.

Four weeks later, urged on by the belief that America's involvement in the war was imminent, Bill Sr. promoted what would be the last race in Daytona Beach until 1946, on August 24. The fact that the winner would be Lloyd Seay – pronounced See – who led all 50 laps in the process, has taken on increased historical significance with each passing year.

After the Daytona victory, Seay – who had finished fourth at Daytona in July – traveled to High Point, North Carolina, and won there on August 31. From there it was a quick southwest trip to

Lakewood Speedway just south of Atlanta for the next day's Labor Day race. He got there late and missed qualifying, forcing him to start last. By Lap 35 he had assumed the lead and went on to take the victory – his third over a mercurial eight-day period.

After winning the Lakewood race, Seay drove straight to his brother Jim's home in Burlsboro, Georgia, where he stayed that night. The next morning, Seay's cousin Woodrow Anderson came to the house, raising hell about a bill for sugar that Lloyd had charged to an account under Anderson's name. Before heading south to Daytona, Seay had purchased the sugar for the stills he, his brother, and Anderson operated together. It was a straightforward business operation, albeit illegal: Woodrow and Jim made the moonshine and Lloyd delivered it unerringly at breakneck speeds through the Georgia countryside.

Accounts of what happened that morning are numerous and varied. But the bottom line is that the trio ended up at Anderson's father's house to settle matters and an argument ensued. Anderson pulled out a .32-caliber pistol and shot Jim Seay in the neck, then unloaded a round in Lloyd Seay's chest, killing him. Anderson was sentenced to life in prison but served only 10 years, a travesty by any reasonable measure.

Considering Seay was only 21 years old at the time of his death, and with NASCAR's creation coming in the not-too-distant future, the long-held consensus is that he would have been one of NASCAR's first champions, if not its dominant driver for years – he had lived.

A cousin of Roy Hall and car owner Raymond Parks – moonshiners all – Seay was described by Bill Sr. as the best pure race driver he had ever seen. Ed Hinton, the veteran writer with ESPN.com who, with the passing of Chris Economaki in 2013 inherited the unofficial "dean of motorsports journalism" title, describes Seay as an almost-certain future superstar.

"Oh yes, Seay would've been Fireball Roberts before Fireball Roberts," Hinton says with conviction. "Red Byron, Fonty Flock – all those guys were well and good but Lloyd Seay was just an incredible, charismatic personality. A friend of Seay's one time told me that Lloyd had claimed he could climb a pine tree with a '39 Ford. That pretty much summarizes Lloyd Seay right there.

"Bill France Sr. knew how good he was. I remember the first time I interviewed Big Bill back in 1974. I asked him who was the greatest driver he had ever seen. He said, 'a fellow from up around Atlanta, Georgia. Lloyd See-ay.' And he told me all about how Seay would drive on the beach, through the North Turn, with both left-side wheels completely off the ground."

On December 7, 1941, the second era of racing in Daytona Beach was cut short by the advent of World War II.

Bill Sr., at the age of 32 ineligible for the draft, went to work building "subchasers" at the Daytona Boat Works – a major employer of Volusia County residents during the war years.

Subchasers were, well, just that – nimble craft meant to chase down or at least hamper submarines. They were built and launched in a rush when the United States entered the war – with good reason. German U-boats, even before the nation's formal declaration of war, had been roaming the Atlantic Ocean, perilously close to the U.S. shoreline.

The late Ted Treadwell Jr., who served on a subchaser and authored two books on the craft, wrote that "in the summer of

1942 U-boats sank more ships and took more lives than were lost at Pearl Harbor. . . . The Germans were so bold that they landed counteragents on beaches in Maine and Florida. Most American citizens were unaware of the seriousness of our situation, but the Navy knew, and the U-boat menace became our Navy's No. 1 priority even at the cost of delaying our response to the Japanese aggression in the Pacific. . . . The U.S. Navy had been virtually destroyed at Pearl Harbor. On the entire East Coast we had only one bona fide antisubmarine vessel. Something had to be done quickly to stop the U-boats. The big shipyards were backed up with contracts for building carriers, cruisers and destroyers and steel was allocated for these as well as tanks, guns and many other military devices."

Enter the subchasers into the wartime mix. They could be built of wood in small boatyards – and could be completed quickly, in as little as two to four months. The Navy contracted approximately 50 boatyards, including Daytona Boat Works.

Early in the war, subchasers and aircraft patrols were the sole defense against the U-boat threat, and while the subchasers' actual threat to the subs was limited, there was a serious nuisance factor that helped keep the coast secure. Subchasers could detect U-boats with sonar and then attack with depth charges. This would force a submarine to stay submerged, unable to attack in return.

The work being done at the Daytona Boat Works was part of an intense community response to the war and possible threats to the coastal communities in Flagler and Volusia counties. Within a week of the Japanese attack on Pearl Harbor, Volusia residents organized a local Civil Defense chapter and, during the war, residents regularly manned the Ormond Watch Tower in Ormond by the Seas, just north of Ormond Beach, to watch for possible U-boat advances toward the shoreline.

Online records show that between 1942 and '44 a total of seventeen subchasers were built at Daytona Boat Works. Four went to Russia. Records also show that two were bombed and sunk off the coast of Italy and one was destroyed by Typhoon Louise in October 1945.

On February 15, 1943, the community was invited to the christening of U.S. Submarine Chaser 1305 and the presentation of the "Army-Navy 'E' Award for Excellence in War Production" to the Daytona Boat Works. Handling the honors for the christening: Anne Bledsoe France.

On October 24, 1944, Bill Sr. and "Annie B." welcomed their second son into the world – James Carl France, named after the uncle he would never know. Bill Sr. now had a full house down on Goodall Street and looked forward to the end of the war and resuming his racing business, to feed his growing boys – and his dreams.

Post-war, in late 1945, he went about rebuilding his racing operation and expanding his scope in the process. The first order of business: stage an event. The Daytona Beach-road course needed a tune-up after several years of inactivity, mainly the grandstands, which were falling apart due to the harsh seaside weather. That sent Bill Sr. on a hunt that led him to Southern State Fairgrounds in Charlotte, North Carolina. It also led him to a fateful meeting with Wilton Garrison, the sports editor of the *Charlotte Observer*. Bill Sr. sought publicity and he had a promotional line ready for Garrison, wanting to term the event a "national championship."

Stories of what transpired that day have been told and retold, some depicting a contentious exchange between Sr. and Garrison, others describing a cordial public relations debate. Jim Hunter had his own version; he called it a public relations "lesson" for Bill Sr. And being a former longtime sportswriter, Hunter loved to tell the story about how a "sports editor helped give Bill France Sr. the idea for starting NASCAR."

Hunter's gleeful, almost giddy take is corroborated more or less by others' recollections:

"Garrison told Senior that you couldn't have a national championship with just one race. He told him that he needed an actual season, something like a league, with point standings and year-end prize money, to be a legitimate professional sport like, for instance, baseball. He also told him he needed rules and structure if he wanted people to take the whole thing seriously."

The meeting was important – and certainly has supplied a tidbit of colorful NASCAR lore – but chances are it wasn't nearly as monumental as some might think. Bill Sr. already was all about rules and structure when it came to running individual events. It probably wasn't much of a stretch for him to start thinking about how to apply those concepts across a broader racing spectrum.

But at the same, it would also be off-base to assume that Bill Sr. wouldn't take Garrison's suggestions to heart. The air of autocracy that has come to dominate his legend aside, Bill Sr. was a smart man who knew how to collaborate – and then incorporate input he'd received into a finished product. And if that sometimes meant making the input your own, so be it.

"I knew I had a lot to learn about putting on races," Bill Sr. said in the 1980s, looking back at his post-war efforts.

Bob Flock won the Southern States race, taking advantage of a last-lap wreck by Roy Hall on the half-mile red clay track. The packed crowd left pleased, as did Bill France, who would remember the event well. From 1954–61 the track would host races in NASCAR's premier series, which at the time was nothing more than a gleam in Bill Sr.'s eye.

With the darkness of World War II lifted, the spring of 1946 was one of rebirth for stock car racing. Things moved quickly in Daytona Beach; Bill Sr. went to work repairing the weather-gutted grandstands along the beach-road course, preparing for an April 14 return to racing in the Birthplace of Speed.

The return was spectacular but, much like the show put on back in the late-summer of 1941, there was a historical value that obviously would not be known until years down the road.

You want a storyline?

Try this one: *Disabled World War II veteran comes back from war and wins at Daytona.*

Meet Red Byron.

With a left leg damaged by Japanese artillery but an unshakable will, Byron was able to find a way to overcome that daunting challenge with the encouragement of car owner Raymond Parks and the inventiveness of mechanic extraordinaire Red Vogt, an Atlanta resident who actually grew up near Bill Sr. in Washington. Vogt, who many think will one day be inducted into the NASCAR Hall of Fame, devised an alternative clutch pedal set-up. There were what came to be called "fatigue pins" welded to the pedal, allowing Byron to periodically rest his left heel between the pins. In addition, his shoe was attached to a leg brace that ran up to his left hip.

Crude, but effective. And when matched with Byron's considerable skill and incredible resolve – not to mention an intelligence
that seemed to distinguish him from many of his rivals – the end
result was a championship-caliber entry who won over fans and
media via the inevitable sentimental value.

Red Byron won that Daytona race, beating his cousin Roy Hall
and of course Bill France Sr., among others. On the heels of a win
at a February race near Orlando, also promoted by Bill Sr., Byron
had established himself immediately as a post-war stock car star.

It was only the beginning for Red Byron.

Bill Sr., meanwhile, was hard at work establishing his own star
in the form of an organization he had envisioned for years, long
before Garrison's prompting. In the second half of the 1946 season
he ended a tenuous business partnership with the New Jersey–based
sanctioning body, the American Automobile Association (AAA),
and announced the formation of his own "deal" – the National
Championship Stock Car Circuit (NCSCC). This announcement is
notable after all these years more because of two related developments that followed: Bill Sr. announced his retirement from competition at the end of the season; and the superb racer Roy Hall proved
to be a less-than-competent criminal. Hall was sentenced to six years
in prison for his part in a bank robbery that reportedly had a $40,000
payoff. A temporary payoff, granted, but a payoff nonetheless.

The Hall story doesn't end there. His burgeoning legend was
substantial before his incarceration, and it is probably safe to say
the legend was heightened with the shooting death of his cousin
Lloyd Seay. The late pop-folk singer Jim Croce (of "Bad, Bad Leroy
Brown" fame) penned a tune in the 1970s memorializing Hall,
titled "Rapid Roy, The Stock Car Boy."

Here's the takeaway: Whatever romanticism is attached to both Seay and Hall in terms of their stock car potential was not overblown. These fine Southern gentlemen weren't really gentlemen at all but rather ass-kicking, part-time criminals of the first degree. Granted, they were outlaws, but whether people liked it or not – starting with Bill France Sr. – stock car racing was an outlaw sport, tied into undeniable cultural undertones of everyday folks who didn't always follow the universally charted course of the American Dream.

The history they made, the legacies they left, are every bit as intoxicating as the liquor they hauled.

"Where the fastest that run . . . run the fastest."

That was the ambitious promotional slogan Bill Sr. applied to the National Championship Stock Car Circuit. In 1947, he had to feel as if he was on the precipice of, well, something. The NCSCC wasn't "it," but it was at least a reasonable facsimile of what Bill Sr. knew, in his heart and soul, he was after. That was the reality facing Big Bill as he prepared for the season-opening event on January 26 in Daytona Beach, which was won by Byron despite an increasing indifference to his success. Remember the storyline? Surprisingly it may have worked against Byron for a while; once one got past the emotional aspect of his war injury, he evoked little further emotion from fans. Bespectacled and soft-spoken, he was a stark contrast to larger-than-life characters such as Roy Hall, the Flocks, or even six-foot-five Bill France Sr. He was Jimmie Johnson 60 years beforehand – a good guy, admirable guy, but by no means controversial.

The 1947 NCSCC season proved to be the set-up, the opening act as it were, to a climactic 1948 inaugural NASCAR season. In '47 there were nearly 40 events, with Fonty Flock ending up as the season's champion, having won seven of the 24 races he entered. Flock got a champion's prize of $1,000 – and a four-foot-high trophy.

Under Bill Sr.'s leadership, the NCSCC was bringing increased notoriety and credibility to stock car racing. The 1947 season had been a confidence-booster for Bill Sr. and everyone who harbored aspirations for the sport. During the season Bill Sr. had spoken a number of times about initiating an annual winter meeting in Daytona Beach. He was formulating ideas that would fulfill aspirations – starting with his own.

An in-depth look at NASCAR's historic organizational meeting – from December 14–17, 1947, at the Streamline Hotel in Daytona Beach – begs the question: Who *wasn't* there?

This is at once one of the most monumental – and strangest – pieces of NASCAR history. First, some Streamline tidbits: Located at 140 South Atlantic Avenue – State Road A1A – across the street from the ocean, the place, which defines "funky," opened in 1940 and remains the oldest-standing hotel in Daytona Beach. Two firsts for the Streamline: According to a plaque outside the hotel, it was the first building in Daytona to be fireproof and was also the city's first bomb shelter.

The Streamline gathering has taken on almost mythical proportions and unless you keep your research tight, you can come up with mythical findings. First off, the number of attendees. Bill Sr. had invited important people in stock car racing from throughout the country and the reported number who showed up was approximately 40. The iconic photo of the meeting shows 24 people seated or standing around a table that is covered with papers, ashtrays filled with cigarette butts, coffee cups, and cocktail glasses. Bill Sr. is at the head of the table, of course.

A closer look at just who came to the Streamline illustrates Bill Sr.'s powers of persuasion, which were part and parcel to developing the eventual autocracy so necessary for NASCAR to survive.

His personality got them to Daytona Beach.

His sheer will got them to agree with his vision.

The group included people from various regions of the country, reflecting Bill Sr.'s recognition of the importance of national appeal for stock car racing to become a major sport that interested not only core fans of racing but also casual sports fans. This was not a Southeastern-only group that made its way to Florida. Consider:

- From New England (Providence, Rhode Island), car owner Freddie Horton.
- From the Midwest, representing roadster sanctioning bodies, Jack Peters and Ed Bruce came to not only discuss stock cars but also a potential new roadster division Bill Sr. was considering.
- Bob Richards, a former racer turned businessman from Atlanta, who had prime connections in an important market that was the home of many future "core fans."
- From Spartanburg, South Carolina, Bill Sr.'s old pal and promotional partner Alvin Hawkins. Hawkins would

become a legendary figure as the longtime promoter at a legendary track – Bowman Gray Stadium in Winston-Salem, North Carolina.

- Bill Tuthill, a businessman and first-rate promoter from New Rochelle, New York, ran the Streamline Hotel meetings for Bill Sr. and when the gathering was complete, was named NASCAR's first executive secretary.

Here's a further rundown of the Streamline attendees, from the 2010 biography of Bill France Jr., *The Man Who Made NASCAR:*

"There were drivers – Bob and Fonty Flock of Atlanta, who would become two stars of NASCAR's first decade; Sam Packard of Jamestown, Rhode Island; Joe Ross of Boston; Chick DiNatale from Trenton, New Jersey; the 1946 national stock car champion Ed Samples of Atlanta, who Bill Sr. named to head up NASCAR's technical committee; the immensely popular local, Marshall Teague, who worked at Big Bill's gas station as a teenager and came away from the Streamline meetings with the title of NASCAR's first treasurer; and the Atlanta driver-owners who would win NASCAR's first championships, driver Red Byron and car owner Raymond Parks. . . . There were mechanics – Jimmy Cox of Mount Airy, North Carolina, and the superb Red Vogt out of Atlanta.

"There were more promoters – none more important than Joe Littlejohn of Spartanburg, South Carolina, who raced against Bill Sr. before World War II. His reputation and influence throughout the Southeast was formidable. . . . There were people from the Daytona Beach Chamber of Commerce – Lucky

Sauer and Jimmy Roberts. Here was an early nod by Bill Sr. to the importance of politicos when it came to the running of the NASCAR business, a cognizance shared by Bill Jr. throughout his life and career. . . . And last but by no means least, there were journalists – Larry Roller of the International News Service; Jimmy Quisenberry of *Speed Age* magazine; and the eventual local legend Benny Kahn, who covered auto racing for years at the *Daytona Beach News-Journal* and was honored by having the old media center at Daytona International Speedway named after him."

Vogt, generally credited with being the first of the truly great NASCAR mechanics, is also credited with coming up with the new organization's name at the Streamline – the National Association for Stock Car Auto Racing. This came after a Red Byron suggestion of National Stock Car Racing Association (NSCRA) was actually voted on and approved but then ruled out because a Georgia-based organization was using the same acronym.

The iconic photograph from the Streamline is partnered in history by an iconic address given to the attendees by Bill France Sr. in which he outlined his vision for the future of stock car racing, a vision based on several platforms:

- Racing that would appeal to the average American, with stock-appearing automobiles – street cars turned into race cars;
- Rules and structure that would be part of a tightly run organization to govern the sport equitably;
- Rules that would be aimed at keeping competition close and costs down.

"My father," Bill France Jr. would say years later, "founded NASCAR on the simple idea that lots of people loved revved-up engines and fast cars as much as he did."

Bill Sr.'s 10-minute Streamline talk underscored all of that. The speech was stock car stream of consciousness but it continued to come back to his basic themes. It was powerful stuff then and remains so, in large part because an abridged version of the speech lives on a large wall at the NASCAR Research and Development Center in Concord, North Carolina.

Read on.

"Stock car racing has got distinct possibilities for Sunday shows and we do not know how big it can be if it's handled properly. . . . It can go the same way as big-car racing (Indianapolis). I believe stock car racing can become a nationally recognized sport by having a National Point Standing. Stock car racing as we've been running it is not, in my opinion, the answer. . . . We must try to get track owners and promoters interested in building stock car racing up. We are all interested in one thing, that is improving the present conditions. The answer lies in our group right here today to do it."

Well, they did it, and it all started during those three days at the Streamline that resulted in Bill France Sr. being the first president of NASCAR, Bill Tuthill its first secretary, and a former open-wheel competitor from Indianapolis, E.G. "Cannonball" Baker its first commissioner.

Bill Sr. had immediately claimed leadership of the new organization, with that status emphasized when the first shares of NASCAR stock were divvied up. Tuthill got 40 shares. A Daytona Beach lawyer, Louis Ossinsky, hired to handle the new company's legal work, got 10 shares. Bill Sr. got 50 shares – and the control he sought.

"He knew it had to be a dictatorship to work," Ed Hinton says.

On February 21, 1948, NASCAR would officially become incorporated. But first, there was a race to run.

Bill Sr.'s vision of an auto racing series with "Strictly Stock" automobiles was delayed in 1948.

Repeat: Not derailed, just delayed.

Due to World War II, relatively few cars were built from 1942–46, and the automobile manufacturers were playing "catch up" to meet post-war consumer demands. Which meant a surplus of cars simply wasn't available to go from showroom to race track just yet.

The season started with NASCAR sanctioning three divisions, and Bill Sr.'s prized concept of "Strictly Stock" was advertised as the premier division, the forerunner to today's NASCAR Sprint Cup Series.

It didn't work. There were merely a handful of stock autos – but plenty of Modifieds. Bill Sr. put all the cars together, ran a 52-race schedule and ended up crowning the Modified-driving Byron as NASCAR's first champion. Byron won 11 races, including the very first in the history of the new organization – February 15, 1948, at the Daytona Beach-road course.

At this point, Bill Sr. was just starting to discuss locally the inevitable end-game of the beach-road course. The idea of a permanent Daytona Beach facility was on low heat but heat nonetheless. It was not only Bill Sr.'s ambitions at work, but the realities of a growing Daytona Beach populace on the beachside that forced him to abandon the original 3.2-mile layout at the

end of 1947. He was running out of room to both race and provide space – both ample and safe – for spectators. The growth was
coming. The visionary knew this would alter the racing landscape
in Daytona Beach.

There were 62 entries for NASCAR's first event – 50 actually
started – on a new 2.2-mile beach-road layout, a full mile shorter
than the previous course and farther south of Daytona Beach in
the quaint seaside community of Ponce Inlet. (The course's North
Turn is now marked by a popular establishment called, appropri-
ately, Racing's North Turn Beach Bar and Grill.)

A crowd estimated at 14,000 by Bill Sr. – ticket prices were
$2.50 – watched Byron win and history being made. The Daytona
race was the start of a year that featured further highlights but
also a couple of worst-case scenario setbacks for the first-year
organization.

On July 4, Bill France came out of retirement to race at half-
mile Martinsville Speedway in Martinsville, Virginia – the only
race track from 1948 that remains on the current NASCAR Sprint
Cup Series schedule. He finished eighth.

As for the bad news . . .

The 25th of July, 1948, was a date lost in NASCAR time –
which is just as well, as separate accidents, both resulting in fatal-
ities, occurred at the two races held that day, in Columbus,
Georgia, and Greensboro, North Carolina. The regional double-
header was designed to ease the travel grind for both staff and
competitors, but whatever relief that was afforded was forgotten.
At Columbus Speedway, Red Byron lost control late in the race
when a right-front tire blew; his car went into the crowd, resulting in the death of seven-year-old Roy Brannon the next day,

and injuries to numerous others. At the Greensboro Fairgrounds track, Bill "Slick" Davis of Concord, North Carolina, fell out of his Chevrolet as it flipped over. Davis and his car were struck by oncoming traffic. He died that night.

The racing went on, as it always does, with Byron and Fonty Flock waging a spirited championship battle, and Byron claiming the championship by a scant 2.75 points – 2,966.5 to Flock's 2,963.75.

On to 1949, and a renewed Bill France Sr. commitment to make "Strictly Stock" viable for the present and a template for the future.

1948 Inaugural NASCAR Season

RACE RESULTS

Location	Date	Winning Driver	Winning Car Owner
Daytona Beach, FL	Feb 15	Red Byron	Raymond Parks
Jacksonville, FL	Feb 24	Fonty Flock	H.B. Babb/Elmer Fields
Atlanta, GA	March 27	Fonty Flock	H.B. Babb/Elmer Fields
Macon, GA	April 4	Fonty Flock	H.B Babb/Elmer Fields
Augusta, GA	April 11	Bob Flock	Raymond Parks
Jacksonville, FL	April 18	Skimp Hersey	Mac Richardson
Greensboro, NC	April 18	Fonty Flock	H.B. Babb/Elmer Fields
North Wilkesboro, NC	April 25	Red Byron	Raymond Parks
Lexington, NC	May 2	Red Byron	Raymond Parks
Wadesboro, NC	May 9	Red Byron	Raymond Parks
Richmond, VA	May 16	Red Byron	Raymond Parks
Macon, GA	May 23	Gober Sosebee	Gober Sosebee
Danville, VA	May 23	Bill Blair	Bill Blair
Dover, NJ	May 23	Johnny Rogers	N/A

Location	Date	Winning Driver	Winning Car Owner
Greensboro, NC	May 29	Bob Flock	Raymond Parks
North Wilkesboro, NC	May 30	Marshall Teague	Marshall Teague
Jacksonville, FL	May 30	Paul Pappy	N/A
Danville, VA	June 4	Bob Flock	Raymond Parks
Greensboro, NC	June 5	Red Byron	Raymond Parks
Lexington, NC	June 6	Bob Flock	Raymond Parks
Wadesboro, NC	June 13	Fonty Flock	H.B. Babb/Elmer Fields
Birmingham, AL	June 20	Fonty Flock	H.B. Babb/Elmer Fields
Columbus, GA	June 20	Bob Flock	Raymond Parks
Greensboro, NC	June 20	Tim Flock	Charlie Mobley
Occoneechee, NC	June 27	Fonty Flock	H.B. Babb/Elmer Fields
Martinsville, VA	July 4	Fonty Flock	H.B. Babb/Elmer Fields
Charlotte, NC	July 11	Red Byron	Raymond Parks
North Wilkesboro, NC	July 18	Curtis Turner	Bob Smith
Greensboro, NC	July 25	Curtis Turner	Bob Smith
Columbus, GA	July 25	Billy Carden	N/A
Lexington, NC	Aug 1	Curtis Turner	Bob Smith
Daytona Beach, FL	Aug 8	Fonty Flock	H.B. Babb/Elmer Fields
Langhorne, PA	Aug 15	Al Keller	N/A
Columbus, GA	Sept 5	Gober Sosebee	Gober Sosebee
North Wilkesboro, NC	Sept 5	Curtis Turner	Bob Smith
North Wilkesboro, NC	Sept 5	Curtis Turner	Bob Smith
Charlotte, NC	Sept 12	Curtis Turner	Bob Smith
Charlotte, NC	Sept 12	Buddy Shuman	Shuman-Thompson
Occoneechee, NC	Sept 19	Fonty Flock	H.B. Babb/Elmer Fields
Occoneechee, NC	Sept 19	Fonty Flock	H.B. Babb/Elmer Fields
Lexington, NC	Sept 26	Fonty Flock	H.B. Babb/Elmer Fields
Lexington, NC	Sept 26	Gober Sosebee	Gober Sosebee
Elkin, NC	Oct 3	Buddy Shuman	Shuman-Thompson

RACE RESULTS (CONT.)

Location	Date	Winning Driver	Winning Car Owner
Elkin, NC	Oct 3	Curtis Turner	Bob Smith
Macon, GA	Oct 3	Billy Carden	N/A
Macon, GA	Oct 3	Red Byron	Raymond Parks
Greensboro, NC	Oct 10	Fonty Flock	Joe Wolf
Greensboro, NC	Oct 16	Fonty Flock	Joe Wolf
North Wilkesboro, NC	Oct 17	Red Byron	Raymond Parks
Charlotte, NC	Oct 24	Red Byron	Raymond Parks
Winston-Salem, NC	Oct 31	Fonty Flock	Joe Wolf
Columbus, GA	Nov 14	Red Byron	Raymond Parks

Final 1948 NASCAR Point Standings

Rank	Driver	Points	Rank	Driver	Points
1	Red Byron	2,966.5	17	Jimmy Thompson	386.0
2	Fonty Flock	2,963.75	18	Jack Smith	384.75
3	Tim Flock	1,759.5	19	Pee Wee Martin	354.0
4	Curtis Turner	1,540.5	20	Fred Mahon	353.0
5	Buddy Shuman	1,350.0	21	Ed Samples	320.5
6	Bill Blair	1,188.5	22	Swayne Pritchett	290.0
7	Bob Flock	1,181.5	23	Wally Campbell	286.0
8	Marshall Teague	1,134.5	24	Carson Dyer	246.5
9	Bill Snowden	1,092.5	25	Walt Hartman	245.0
10	Buck Baker	952.5	26	Skimp Hersey	238.5
11	Billy Carden	866.5	27	Bob Smith	225.0
12	Johnny Grubb	733.0	28	Olin Allen	220.5
13	Speedy Thompson	623.0	29	Fireball Roberts	218.5
14	Roscoe Thompson	471.0	30	Cotton Owens	218.5
15	Jimmie Lewallen	437.0	31	J.L. McMichaels	217.5
16	Al Keller	415.0	32	Jim Paschal	194.0

Rank	Driver	Points
33	Frank Mundy	183.5
34	Doug Wells	183.5
35	H.D. Trice	183.5
36	Chick DiNatale	180.0
37	June Cleveland	167.5
38	Lee Morgan	166.0
39	Pete Harris	158.0
40	Buck Clardy	155.0
41	Bill McKeehan	155.0

Rank	Driver	Points
42	Leonard Tippett	150.0
43	Hugh Lanford	149.0
44	Joe Eubanks	148.5
45	P.E. Godfrey	136.0
46	Bob Apperson	125.5
47	Jerry Wimbish	110.0
48	Frank Reynolds	109.0
49	C.E. Robinson	92.5
50	Bob Richey	87.5

After a Modified season-opening event won by Marshall Teague on an enlarged (4.2-mile) Daytona Beach-road course on January 16, 1949, Bill Sr. began demonstrating his determination to revisit the Strictly Stock concept that would produce a true national championship series. He ran two "experimental" Strictly Stock races at Broward Speedway in Fort Lauderdale, Florida, a two-mile paved race track.

Both events were headlined by Modifieds. On January 23, Lloyd Christopher won a 10-mile Strictly Stock preliminary; on February 27, Benny Georgeson won a 10-mile in a 1947 Buick. The fact that the two races were labeled exhibitions belied the attention they received by fans in attendance. Bill Sr. sensed that the attention would build – but he first needed to build the division, which would not be easy. Aside from the inherent challenges of car availability that ruined the hoped-for 1948 debut of the Strictly Stocks, the rival organization based in North Carolina, the National Stock Car Racing Association (NSCRA), was vying for entries as well. This was a clear, serious threat to the Strictly Stocks concept and, de facto, to the long-term viability of NASCAR as a whole.

The situation called for a bold move. The NSCRA was led by Bruton Smith, who now heads the Speedway Motorsports Incorporated empire, which owns eight tracks that host NASCAR Sprint Cup Series weekends: Charlotte Motor Speedway, Atlanta Motor Speedway, Bristol Motor Speedway, Kentucky Speedway, Texas Motor Speedway, New Hampshire Motor Speedway, Las Vegas Motor Speedway, and Sonoma Raceway. Smith in 1949 was establishing his own personal template of being an adversary of the France family, a role he has openly relished through the years. It is generally recognized that Smith being drafted into the Korean War in 1951 was beneficial to NASCAR's early stability, as the NSCRA ceased operations while he was gone. There also was some talk about a possible merger of NASCAR and the NSCRA before Smith was drafted.

In 1949, though, there was no such talk, only action, in the form of Bill Sr. somewhat hastily scheduling a major 150-mile Strictly Stocks race for June 19 in Charlotte on a crude three-quarters-mile dirt oval – with ambitious plans advertised for a field of 33 cars, à la the Indianapolis 500's long-standing starting field number.

NASCAR provided varying crowd estimates, some as high as 22,000. Those in attendance watched a Ford driven by Glenn Dunaway cross the finish line three laps ahead of Jim Roper's Lincoln. But several hours later, the first Strictly Stock winner in NASCAR history was disqualified due to illegal spring modifica-tions, apparently the result of the Ford also being used to haul moonshine. Spring modifications – hell, any modifications – were commonplace on trippers' cars but NASCAR's rules forbade all potential changes related to performance. Dunaway's car owner

Hubert Westmoreland had to watch as the $2,000 winner's purse was withheld. Westmoreland "howled like a coyote," according to stock car historian Greg Fielden. Once done howling, Westmoreland took a more measured approach: he sued. The case eventually was dismissed. Bill France's cherished rules structure had survived its first assault.

NASCAR Hall of Fame historian Buz McKim remembers Bill Tuthill telling him that Bill Sr. loved that penalty dispute.

"It created controversy that took a good while to sort out," McKim says. "Stories about it were in the papers for days and days. Tuthill used to say 'it was the best thing that ever happened to us.'"

Publicity was one benefit. The other had to do with credibility.

"That first race established immediately how NASCAR was going to do things," said McKim. "It let everyone know that this was NASCAR's deal, NASCAR's rules and that's the way it was going to be."

Charlotte was followed by seven more Strictly Stock races, including a July 10 Daytona Beach-road course race won by Byron.

Byron also won at Martinsville on September 25 and went on to capture the Strictly Stock title with a 117-point margin over runner-up Lee Petty.

Two years, two championships – in two completely different types of vehicles. Bill France Sr. may have been the driving force, but Red Byron had literally driven NASCAR to the doorstep of the 1950s – and the future.

1949 NASCAR Strictly Stock Series

RACE RESULTS

Location	Date	Winning Driver	Winning Car Owner
Charlotte, NC	June 19	Jim Roper	R.B. McIntosh
Daytona Beach, FL	July 10	Red Byron	Raymond Parks
Hillsboro, NC	Aug 7	Bob Flock	Frank Christian
Langhorne, PA	Sept 11	Curtis Turner	Hubert Westmoreland
Hamburg, NY	Sept 18	Jack White	Dailey Moyer
Martinsville, VA	Sept 25	Red Byron	Raymond Parks
Carnegie, PA	Oct 2	Lee Petty	Petty Enterprises
North Wilkesboro, NC	Oct 16	Bob Flock	Frank Christian

Race Winners (6)

FINAL 1949 STRICTLY STOCK POINT STANDINGS

Rank	Driver	Points	Rank	Driver	Points
1	Red Byron	842.50	16	Jim Roper	253.00
2	Lee Petty	725.00	17	Sam Rice	231.00
3	Bob Flock	704.00	18	Jack White	200.00
4	Bill Blair	567.50	19	Dick Linder	180.50
5	Fonty Flock	554.50	20	Billy Rafter	160.00
6	Curtis Turner	430.00	21	Archie Smith	145.00
7	Ray Erickson	422.00	22	Joe Littlejohn	140.00
8	Tim Flock	421.00	23	Jack Russell	140.00
9	Glenn Dunaway	384.00	24	Mike Eagan	140.00
10	Frank Mundy	370.00	25	Herb Thomas	132.00
11	Bill Snowden	315.00	26	Sterling Long	100.00
12	Bill Rexford	286.00	27	Frank Christian	100.00
13	Sara Christian	282.00	28	Frankie Schneider	100.00
14	Clyde Minter	280.00	29	Lloyd Moore	100.00
15	Gober Sosebee	265.00	30	Roy Hall	100.00

Rank	Driver	Points	Rank	Driver	Points
31	Slick Smith	99.00	41	Lou Volk	30.00
32	Al Keller	90.00	42	Buddy Helms	27.50
33	John Wright	80.00	43	Bob Apperson	25.00
34	Al Bonnell	80.00	44	Bill Bennett	24.00
35	Otis Martin	69.50	45	Ted Chamberlain	24.00
36	Jimmy Thompson	65.00	46	Buck Baker	20.00
37	Charles Muscatel	60.00	47	Jack Etheridge	20.00
38	Raymond Lewis	60.00	48	Ellis Pearce	20.00
39	Al Wagoner	60.00	49	Bobby Greene	19.50
40	George Lewis	40.00	50	Ken Wagner	19.00

CHAPTER 5

The 1950s:

From Sand and Dirt to Darlington and Daytona

W hile Bill France Sr.'s address to attendees of the December 1947 Streamline Hotel gathering is memorable for both its motivational and visionary aspects, there also is a paragraph that all these years later jumps off the page.

"A dirt track is more than necessary to make a stock car race a good show. In fact, stock car races not held on dirt are nowhere near as impressive. To look their best, stock cars need dirt. Or sand."

A little more than two years later, France was backsliding on that pronouncement.

Something was brewing up in the small community of Darlington, South Carolina – and it wasn't moonshine.

A man named Harold Brasington was the brewmaster. The former racer – he had competed against Bill Sr. in the 1940s – had quit racing to focus on his farming and construction businesses. Much like Bill, he had an affinity for the Indianapolis 500 – the pageantry, the history, the cars – and the crowds. Knowing a good bottom line when he saw one, Brasington came back from the 500 in the spring of 1948 with a pie-in-the-sky plan to create an Indy-level experience down in the Southeast.

Way down in the Southeast.

A description of Darlington:

"Imagine a small town. The kind of place where families can fully bloom. Where Southern hospitality is still a way of life. A historic town with tree-lined streets, beautiful parks, and a downtown public square. Someplace only an hour away from big city life but miles away from the daily grind. Now open your eyes because there's no need to imagine it.

"It's called Darlington."

The description does not come from 1950, although it would've been perfect at the time. It comes from 2014 and the town's official website, where on the home page there is tab, you can click to "report a street light out."

In 1940, Darlington's population was just over 5,000. Seventy years later, it was just over 6,000. In fairness, though, when talking about the populace, Darlington cannot be discussed separately from its neighboring community of Florence, which has approximately 33,000 residents, according to that city's official website. Both communities are part of the historic area known as the "Pee Dee," an eight-county swath of the northeastern part of the state that includes the 435-mile-long Pee Dee River, named after the Pee Dee Native American tribe.

To bring a race track into the Pee Dee required Brasington to purchase 70 acres of cotton and peanut farmland. And, from the "you can't make it up" department, a promise to the land's former owner to not disturb a minnow pond on the west side of the property resulted in Brasington constructing an "egg-shaped" oval: one end was tight and narrow, the other wide and sweeping. The track took a year to build and in the summer of 1950 Brasington and France agreed to run the first Southern 500 on Labor Day.

There are many historical markers attached to that first Darlington event. First NASCAR-sanctioned race on a paved track . . . record purse of $25,000 . . . a two-week qualifying format and the field of 75 arranged by rows of three, à la Indy, per Brasington's obsession with the Brickyard . . . Johnny Mantz winning in a Plymouth owned by Bill Sr.

Extra-hard, Indy-style racing tires and a methodical style won the first Southern 500, and for many of Mantz's rivals it was too much to take. Red Vogt, by this time generally recognized as the grandest of wrench-turners, was especially disbelieving after his driver Red Byron finished third and demanded a teardown, which uncovered nothing untoward. The tires were the key and since they weren't explicitly prohibited, well. . . .

Tires and "stroking" – a careful driving style that over the years came also to be called "points racing" – are what won that six-and-a-half-hour marathon in the Pee Dee. Mantz stroked while most all of the favorites hauled ass and blew tires, or kissed the wall.

Darlington's real historical marker – though no one knew this at the time – was that the Southern 500 became the first truly "major" event for NASCAR's premier series, which in 1950 had been renamed "Grand National." That status spawned a romance with both racers and their fans, a relationship strong enough to create two nicknames for Darlington Raceway: "The Track Too Tough to Tame" and "The Lady in Black." The latter nickname comes from the tire rub that gradually mars the white concrete retaining walls over the course of a race weekend, as drivers struggle to negotiate the unique layout. And Darlington black led to Darlington white, as in the "Darlington stripe" cars could unfortunately acquire when sheet metal scraped across the white paint. Black, white, rubs, stripes – whatever. The reality, the new reality of Bill Sr.'s NASCAR, was that Darlington was not only big . . . and fast . . . but also intimidating, setting a new standard in that category that traditionally went undiscussed by hard-ass drivers of the day.

"Darlington Raceway is special; she's always been special and she always will be – but of course, you have to understand, I'm partial to the place," said the late Jim Hunter, the former long-time track president. "One thing has remained constant about Darlington over the years. It is still the meanest, toughest, most unforgiving, and unpredictable old track in America. And that's what people have always liked about it. You can feel just how special it is as you walk through the gates. The drivers feel it. The crews and car owners feel it. And of course the fans feel it, also. There is nothing else like Darlington in all of motorsports.

"Darlington Raceway earned its place in NASCAR history. It was 'first.' I mean the very first. There were no other asphalt tracks conducting 500-mile races for stock cars when Darlington was built. Think about that . . . without Darlington Raceway, NASCAR might not be where it is today. And without NASCAR, Darlington Raceway would certainly not be where it is today. And also, Darlington was important to solidifying Bill Sr.'s other company, International Speedway Corporation. ISC bought Darlington in 1982, which was a landmark deal.

"NASCAR and Darlington . . . the two were a perfect match all those years ago, when that first Southern 500 was run. A perfect match indeed – who would've believed it?"

It is easy to imagine Brasington's zeal seeping into the heart and soul of Bill France Sr. and serving Senior well a few years down the road when his own seemingly far-fetched idea of building a speedway would be explored.

By 1950, when it came to conversation about Bill France Sr., memories of his talents as a race car driver were fading, replaced by the news of the day, meaning his building of NASCAR. Bill Sr.'s last race had been at Martinsville during the inaugural NASCAR season of 1948; he finished eighth. He had transitioned nicely from splitting time between competing and promoting to being a full-time businessman. Still, though, the competitive fire burned.

But a desire to race again doesn't fully explain France's decision to team with Curtis Turner and enter the Carrera Panamericana – the Mexican Road Race – in May 1950. This was a prime and perhaps foolhardy example of the competitor and promoter morphing into one. Bill Sr. recognized that the entry of NASCAR's leader and one of NASCAR's most popular drivers provided a fine chance for some out-of-the-box publicity.

Make no mistake, the *Carrera Panamericana* was out of the box.

Following the completion of the Mexican portion of the Pan-American Highway, the Mexican government organized a nine-stage event that would cross the country over a very perilous six-day stretch – approximately 2,100 miles.

The race was held for five consecutive years. (It has since been reborn as a road rally event.) During that half-decade span of mayhem, the *Carrera Panamericana* earned the unofficial distinction as the most dangerous auto race in the world, with 27 deaths.

Noted NASCAR car owner and mechanic Smokey Yunick entered cars in the event, despite his own misgivings. From his autobiography *Best Damn Garage in Town: The World According to Smokey:* "I don't know who dreamt this deal up, but if it had a main sponsor, it should have been the morticians of Mexico . . . there are a thousand stories about the Mexican Road Race."

Thankfully, there is little material resulting from the France-Turner effort in a No. 37 Nash Ambassador. France crashed relatively early and the car did not finish due to radiator damage. The race was won by future NASCAR great Hershel McGriff and Ray Elliott in an Oldsmobile 88.

Little material – and a modicum of publicity.

France and Turner raced together again in 1957 in Nassau, in what was termed "Bahamas Speed Weeks." Teamed in a Chevrolet Corvette, they finished 35th in a race won by sports car legend Stirling Moss, with Carroll Shelby and Phil Hill finishing second and third, respectively.

———

The Southern 500 at Darlington was the highlight of a 1950 season marred by a controversy that created the most obscure champion in NASCAR national series history – New Yorker Bill Rexford. A New Yorker!

Rexford is not remembered as a champion. No, instead his place in history, unfairly, is being the beneficiary of a major NASCAR ruling. Bill Sr. laid heavy point penalties on two championship contenders, Red Byron and Lee Petty, because they entered races not sanctioned by NASCAR. Byron had his entire point total erased twice, Petty once. It is no slap to Rexford to say that without those penalties, either Byron or Petty would have won the championship.

Much like the beach-road race in 1938 when Smokey Purser was disqualified, or the 1949 Strictly Stock debut in which Glenn Dunaway had his victory taken away, the 1950 season, which consisted of 19 races, was all about establishing the authority needed to govern the sport of stock car racing effectively.

"Bill Sr. always made sure you knew it was 'his show,'" says seven-time champion Richard Petty.

Auto racing journalist and historian Jonathan Ingram saw the same thing in 1981 – nine years after Bill France had turned over the NASCAR presidency to his son Bill Jr.

A question about the mid-1950s gave Ingram what he considered a glimpse at Senior's psyche.

"I went to the Daytona summer race; I was working on a Carl Kiekhaefer story at the time and I really wanted to talk to Big Bill for the story," Ingram says, "because I knew Kiekhaefer had really given him fits."

Kiekhaefer, who had made a fortune with his Mercury Outboard boat engine company, came to NASCAR in 1955, motivated partly by wanting to use automobile racing as a research tool for his boat engine production. And he came in with a revolutionary manufacturer-supported multi-car team concept, using massive, elaborate car haulers, with the words "Mercury Outboards" emblazoned on the side. This was pioneering, but it also flew in the face of the "racing for everyman" vision that was central to NASCAR's foundation only seven years earlier. In 1955, Kiekhaefer's drivers, one of which was Grand National champion Tim Flock, won 22 races and finished 1-2 four times. In one event, Kiekhaefer entered four cars. The next season, Kiekhaefer's lineup, led by series champion Buck Baker, won 40 more times. Kiekhaefer pulled out of NASCAR after the 1956 season.

"So I knew Kiekhaefer had given Big Bill fits," said Ingram. "Big Bill really had his hands full [dealing] with him. But as we talked, well, let's just say that Big Bill had a way of phrasing things sometimes that could downplay situations. So, he was saying stuff to me like, 'Kiekhaefer wasn't that big of a problem . . . he was a pretty competitive guy . . . I think his mind may have worked overtime when it came to looking at our rules as being drawn up specifically against him sometimes.' You know, that sort of thing. It was Big Bill's way of acknowledging the scenario I was suggesting but not really giving in to the idea of Kiekhaefer just giving him fits. Big Bill sometimes had this soft-spoken way of making sure NASCAR was recognized as being in charge, that it wasn't the inmates running the asylum.

"The way Big Bill handled my questions struck me, looking

back, as a guy who had been very comfortable in his role of being in charge.

"But at the same time Big Bill was always trying to be shoulder-to-shoulder with people. He understood he was in a sport that really appealed to the common man, to working class people who were competing and helping to build the sport. He had a really keen understanding of that and that's also why his vision was so broad about the importance of having a true national championship, because he knew those kinds of people were all over the United States and weren't just the crazy good ole boy moonshiners."

Ingram considers Bill Sr. as a self-cast, leading character in a real-life Horatio Alger story. Alger was a renowned 19th-century author who crafted a series of entertaining novels about boys who emerged from humble beginnings to live successful lives via their commitment to hard work, resolve, and determination. Alger's heroes were developed in rags-to-riches storylines. Ingram believes Bill Sr. propagated an image that would've fit snugly into an Alger manuscript.

"And I think it tells you something about Big Bill's sophistication that he knew a Horatio Alger type of story would play well. He was just trying to be one of the guys and he came up with a Horatio Alger type of rendition to portray himself in that manner . . . just another working guy who liked cars who got lucky, as opposed to a very ambitious, shrewd guy who thought he could make a lot of money in racing and had the ability to make big things happen in the sport."

The 1950s, following the scarred season that opened the decade, introduced a series of major stars, including some who helped distance the sport somewhat from its overt link to moonshining. The link still lived, though, perhaps best personified by Wilkes County, North Carolina's Robert "Junior" Johnson, who won five races in his first full-time season (1955) and actually served time in 1956 and '57 for running shine. (In the 1960s, Johnson was immortalized by the great writer Thomas Wolfe in an epic *Esquire* magazine piece titled "The Last American Hero Is Junior Johnson. Yes!" (In 1986 Johnson was pardoned by President Ronald Reagan for his moonshining conviction.) Johnson won 50 races as a driver but decided to quit following the 1966 season; he went on to win championships as a car owner. He joined Bill Sr., Bill Jr., Richard Petty, and Dale Earnhardt in the inaugural NASCAR Hall of Fame class of 2010.

The other stars of the decade:

- Lee Petty, NASCAR's first three-time champion, winning in 1954, '58, and '59, a driver who went kicking and screaming into the era of paved ovals but still managed to win the very first Daytona 500 in 1959.
- Tim Flock, the man who did indeed run some races with a rhesus monkey named "Jocko Flocko" alongside. The 100-mph circus act serves to unfortunately obscure the memory of his NASCAR championships in 1952 and '55, plus one of the sport's best winning percentages – 20.86. It should be noted that he came by the monkey thing honestly; his father was a tightrope walker.
- Buck Baker, another two-time champion, winning in 1956 and '57 – the first driver to take consecutive titles. This was an over-achiever that fit Bill Sr.'s "everyman" competitor

concept perfectly; prior to trying his hand at auto racing, Baker drove a bus.

- Herb Thomas, the *first* two-time champion, with titles in 1951 and '53, who would've won a third in '56 were it not for an October wreck at Charlotte that ended his season and his career as well. Thomas left the speedway on a stretcher – with a 118-point lead in the standings. In the season-ending points after the last three races of 1956, Thomas was second, 704 points behind Baker.

All of the above save Johnson owned multiple championships, but there were others who defined the decade, several with nicknames silly on the surface but apropos considering their skill levels and their chosen vocation.

Fireball Roberts.

Speedy Thompson.

Tiny Lund.

None became champions but they did become stars, with Roberts eventually turning into NASCAR's first *superstar*, a metamorphosis that began with a six-win season in 1958 in only 10 starts. Roberts – a native of Apopka, Florida, who eventually made Daytona Beach his adopted hometown, got his nickname not from racing but rather as a fireballing baseball pitcher for an American Legion team, the Zellwood Mud Hens, in Apopka.*

Today, NASCAR is in the midst of a full-fledged initiative aimed at maximizing the considerable potential of "star power"

---

* Seemingly on the cusp of winning multiple championships, Roberts would perish six years later after a fiery crash in the World 600 at Charlotte.

inherent in the current crop of national series drivers. Bill France Sr. had this initiative going on in the 1950s – minus the modern-day label. He knew that his concept of everyday automobiles, while forming the foundation for his on-track business model, was worth only so much over the long promotional haul. He needed heroes at the wheels.

"NASCAR has always been about ordinary men doing extraordinary things," legendary television broadcaster Ken Squier says, in perhaps the most succinct summary – ever – of what Bill France Sr. was tapping into in the 1950s as he sought to grow NASCAR.

As Bill Sr. went about the process of selling NASCAR first to stock car honchos and then to competitors and fans, he also had to entice manufacturers, convincing them of the value involvement in NASCAR could deliver. That enticement happened in large part organically, as the link between success on the race track and sales in the showroom manifested, resulting in the time-honored phrase, "win on Sunday, sell on Monday." Manufacturers flocked to pay drivers to drive their cars, and to supply access to replacement parts. Hence another phrase: factory backing. This was vital to growth, although it may have gotten a bit out of hand in Bill Sr.'s view when Carl Kiekhaefer went on his tear. Kiekhaefer largely backed himself financially and actually gave ideas to the factories, but that capability combined with parts support made for a daunting effort that dominated the sport, albeit briefly.

The 1955 season, says NASCAR Hall of Fame historian Buz McKim, "was a big watershed year. General Motors came out with an overhead valve V8 Chevy; up until that time Chevy had had an in-line six-cylinder that was not competitive. Ford had always run the old flatheads that worked well in Modifieds but were not competitive in stock cars. So in 1955, to compete with Chevy, Ford came out with its own overhead valve V8. At that point, things were really rolling, with the manufacturers ready to throw some serious money into NASCAR, which would enable them to show off their products.

"So while you have all of this happening, everything is taking off, cars are getting a lot faster and lot more sophisticated both on the road and on the race track," McKim said. "More high-performance parts. But you also had a problem – more accidents, high-speed accidents, on the roads."

Then, in May 1957, the apparent lifeline of manufacturer involvement dropped out, with tragedy the catalyst. An accident in Clarion, Pennsylvania, resulted in the deaths of two children, ages eight and 12, when a wheel was launched into the crowd. Then, an accident at Martinsville Speedway sent debris flying. Six spectators, including an eight-year-old boy, were injured.

On June 6, the manufacturers officially recoiled from auto racing. From a United Press International (UPI) report that day:

> The auto industry [has] in effect divorced itself from future participation in automobile racing or other events involving tests of speed. Directors of the Automobile Manufacturers Association unanimously recommended to the manufacturers that they not only withdraw from such events but also refrain from suggesting speed in passenger car advertising or publicity.
>
> In as much as the board of directors of the association is made up of the heads of the different auto companies, the

proposal has the effect of an agreement among them to halt any further participation in car racing. [This] means the auto makers will take no further part in stock car racing . . . it also means withdrawal from any other competitive events wherein speed, engine torque or acceleration tests are involved.

The closest approach to an explanation of the industry action was the statement in the association announcement that emphasis on horsepower or speed was not doing highway safety any good.

The association did not explain what would become of the contracts the car makers might have with professional race drivers or with the mechanical staffs set up at various racing centers. One industry representative said solutions to the problem thus presented would probably take some time to work out.

On the same day, Bill Sr. had his own announcement at the ready, clearly trying to shed the best possible light on the situation. Also from the UPI, headlined "'Sport' Racing Revival Seen by Bill France":

The National Association for Stock Car Auto Racing said the auto industry's withdrawal today from races "will put auto racing back as more of a sports affair than it was prior to the manufacturers entering the field."

Bill France, president of NASCAR, added however that he feels the industry "cannot divorce itself from the moral obligations which it has to mechanically minded competitive Americans."

NASCAR sanctions stock car races over much of the country and conducts speed trials for late and experimental models.

France's statement indicated he thinks stock car racing, which became a full-blown sport after World War II, will not suffer, regardless of what the manufacturers do.

France also said: "I think that while the industry was actively competing in racing it learned a lot about handling and about performance, in fact more about its own cars than it had known before, even though it had built them.

"Consequently, I think the industry's participation will reflect favorably on cars to come . . . the industry sure did play hard while it was playing."

"Suddenly, overnight, there was no factory support," McKim said. "Marvin Panch told a story about that, how when he was on the Ford team but sure didn't want to be a car owner. Marvin told me Ford's NASCAR program manager Pete DePaolo called all the Ford drivers in for a meeting, told them that he was out of a job and that all of them were now car owners. Each of the Ford drivers, Fireball Roberts, Curtis Turner, Marvin, and some others, they all became team owners. They got their car and a truckload of parts – and they were in the racing business. Same thing pretty much happened to the GM teams, too."

Manufacturers did not return in full song for five years.

France, by God, soldiered on.

"Bill Sr. was the spin-master," McKim said. "He could hit the ground running while making chicken salad out of chicken manure and never miss a beat. But the racing, you have to remember, was still first-rate. Bill Sr. was still putting the same cars on the track with the same drivers behind the wheel. And to the average fan, chances are most didn't realize any difference in what they were paying to watch."

The 1950s had seen steady, if not exponential growth. From 19 races in 1950, the schedule had been expanded to 41 events a year later, a peak of 56 in '56, and 53 events in '57. Each year there was a flagship Daytona Beach-road course race in February – the bridge between the old turn-of-the-century winter speed runs and the extravaganza that was to come.

Racing on the beach was a finite proposition when it came to contributing to NASCAR's further growth. Fueled by the success of Darlington and inspired, still, by the legacy of Indianapolis Motor Speedway (IMS), France knew a permanent facility in Daytona Beach was the next step.

He had known this for quite a while.

There was other growth coming into play as well – the growth of the beachside communities during the feel-good, economic well-being of the 1950s. Residential and commercial development was making it difficult for the race course to even exist, never mind preserving an adequate spectators' area.

The cadence was changing in the once sleepy town of Daytona Beach and racing was out of step.

But not Bill Sr.

NASCAR's leader had committed his heart and soul to a permanent facility in Daytona Beach, and he tried to make it happen as early as 1953. Heart and soul, while important, needed a financial commitment. France, shopping for investors who were also believers, got Lou Perini, then the Milwaukee Braves (now the Atlanta Braves) owner who had earned millions via the family construction business, to fly down to Daytona. Millions would be needed; an early estimate of cost for a new facility, planned for a tract of swampy, undeveloped land near the Daytona Beach Airport, was more than $1.5 million. Bill Sr. hoped to entice Perini to become a partner in terms of both funding and construction capability. But Perini's interest waned dramatically not long after his arrival. To start, the estimate soared into the $3 million area. However, it was the lack of infrastructure in Daytona Beach that really shocked the successful Boston native, and he told Bill thanks but no thanks. This was a significant setback, but France saw it as merely a delay.

Bill France Racing, Inc. had been established in 1953. It was the initial foundation for what would become the International Speedway Corporation, which is today a publicly traded motorsports facility company led by Bill Sr.'s granddaughter, CEO Lesa France Kennedy, and his son, chairman Jim France.

ISC today operates 13 facilities in the United States.

In 1953, the focus was on building the first.

"My father knew the beach racing couldn't go on forever," Bill France Jr. said in 2006. "He had long foreseen the day when NASCAR would be a sport with big, modern race tracks and he tried to get the speedway project started earlier than we did. He knew that racing on the sand was a novelty. He also knew that racing on asphalt and concrete was the future. Darlington had demonstrated that to everyone. And, the way he saw it, what better place to start realizing the future than Daytona Beach? He wanted to build his business but he also wanted his community to benefit. He went out [and] got some advice and support from local politicians and businesses on how to go about building a permanent facility."

By 1955, Bill Sr. had organized the Daytona Beach Motor Speedway Corporation; the state of Florida had created the Speedway Authority to assist in making the project a reality. Things moved methodically from that point. On October 16, 1955, the authority signed a 99-year lease on the land for the project with the city of Daytona Beach. Two years later, on November 8, 1957, Bill Sr. signed a lease with the authority to secure the 446 acres of airport-adjacent land for the construction of something called the Daytona International Speedway, beginning the Daytona Beach International Speedway Corporation – now known as International Speedway Corporation.

On November 9, 1957, Bill France Sr. made a formal announcement regarding plans to build the speedway.

"We are organizing the Daytona Beach International Speedway Corporation which will begin construction within thirty days on an automobile race track to cost an estimated $750,000.

"The first event will be a NASCAR-sanctioned 500-mile late model stock car race on George Washington's birthday, February 22.

"The track will be the fastest in the country, supporting speed up to 200 miles per hour.

"The plant will have 10,000 permanent seats plus temporary bleachers. There will be standing room in the infield – same as Indianapolis.

"The plans are designed so that the speedway can be expanded and it is my goal in the future to more than triple the seating and, correspondingly, improve the racing facilities.

"The international safety and speed trials on the beach straight-away will be continued in conjunction with the racing activities at the speedway. But the last 160-mile event on the present beach-road track will be February 23, 1958. All future races will be at the speedway.

"In addition to the annual 500-mile winter stock car classic, a summer stock car event will be at the speedway, probably on July 4.

"Plans also call for building a winding sports car course around the infield of the speedway. Target date for the sports car course is 1961."

Groundbreaking for the speedway followed on November 25. Six weeks later, on January 8, 1958, the first organizational meeting of the Daytona Beach International Speedway Corporation was held and Bill Sr. was elected the new entity's president. Now all that was needed was money and hard work – both in copious quantities.

A Dallas business magnate named Clint Murchison Jr. has received much credit for salvaging the project – with good reason. Murchison, who would go on to become founder of the Dallas Cowboys NFL franchise, had met Bill Sr. when the construction was in its early phases. Bill Sr., by then a serious airplane enthusiast and pilot, ran into Murchison at an air show in Pensacola, Florida. Bill told Murchison about his speedway plans, and Murchison, his interest piqued, offered to help.

Fair enough. But first, Bill was able to offer Murchison an assist.

During the air show, Murchison learned that a construction project of his in Cuba was in deep trouble. Make that *really* deep trouble. Rebels led by Fidel Castro were threatening to shoot

Murchison's workers if they continued the project. The Cuban dictator Fulgencio Batista countered with his own chilling directive: his soldiers were being told to shoot Murchison's crew if the work stopped.

Murchison needed to get to Cuba. Bill had a plane. That led to a flight down to Miami, which enabled Murchison to then hop over to Cuba to make sure no construction workers were gunned down. In an expression of gratitude he sent one of his right-hand men, Howard Sluyter, to Daytona Beach to see if he could return the favor. Sluyter found Bill Sr. contemplating an alteration of his grand plans, due to money problems. Quickly, a $20,000 on-the-spot loan and the use of some of Murchison's equipment – which had been hustled out of Cuba and was en route to Texas via Florida – kept the project upright. Murchison then facilitated Bill Sr. securing a $600,000 loan.

France never looked back. Approximately 300,000 shares of speedway stock, at a dollar a share, were sold. Other, smaller loans completed the financial puzzle. Bill Sr. was proud, years later, to be able to boast that all debts were paid off within 10 years of the track's February 1959 opening.

The brainstorm that became Daytona International Speedway always was linked to Indianapolis Motor Speedway. Bill Sr. had been a huge fan of IMS and the Indianapolis 500 since childhood. "Big-car racing" was the label attached to the open-wheel machines, a label that had to do not only with speed but status. Indy-style racing was by far the most popular form of auto racing in the United States in the 1950s. Bill Sr.'s motivation to build a track to rival the IMS 2.5-mile oval was understandable to begin with. But then you must factor in the potential added impetus he got during a 1954 trip to the Indy 500.

This is a story that compares favorably with the coming to Daytona tale in the unofficial book of Bill Sr. lore. Bill, accompanied by Annie B., did not have the proper credentials and reportedly was asked to leave the speedway by officials of the American Automobile Association, which sanctioned the 500. Different versions of the story have evolved, with most including a heated scene in Gasoline Alley, Indy's garage area, with profanities all around. Senior himself would come to describe the experience as disappointing for him and Annie B., but by no means ugly. He chalked it all up to the AAA's dislike for NASCAR as a growing sanctioning body based in the South. The Midwestern racing establishment's prejudice against what was viewed as a crude redneck circuit showcasing many past and present moonshiners, plus assorted others from the Deep South, cannot be exaggerated. Juxtaposed against that prejudice was the reality that the racing NASCAR was selling was damn good – and getting better – fueled by stars who, when given a closer look, could rival anyone open-wheel had. And then there was the six-foot-five aura of Big Bill France himself, all presence and personality, riding herd over the whole thing. No wonder they tossed the Southeastern interloper and his demure bride out of the Brickyard! He represented a real threat to Indianapolis' dominance of America's auto racing landscape, which could not be tolerated, at least not on the grounds of the hallowed Brickyard.

The episode strengthened Bill's resolve to return to Daytona Beach and construct his own race facility – one that would rival Indianapolis Motor Speedway. The generally accepted stance is that he and Annie B. came back to Florida more determined than ever to build their own race track.

France may have admired Indy but he also saw flaws, which helped shape his vision for Daytona. He wanted his track to be big – not necessarily bigger – but he also wanted a design that would enable stock cars to chase unprecedented speeds, and for that, the flatness of Indy would not do. Doubtless he was influenced not only by Indy but by his youthful experiences at Laurel Speedway, where the wooden-plank racing surface was banked at 48 degrees. Bill Sr. envisioned extreme banks in the Daytona turns that would keep cars on the race track. But there was another reason for the banks; Bill envisioned a gigantic "cereal bowl" effect for his speedway, enabling fans in the grandstands to actually see what was transpiring on virtually all of the race track in front of them.

The first work began on November 25, 1957, starting with basic but intensive "site prep." To call the tract undeveloped would be courteous. It was a partial swamp. Much of that prep work involved moving dirt to build the banks, which ended up at 31 degrees, which was the steepest the dirt could be piled without it falling back down.

This was an unbelievably ambitious undertaking, a reality exacerbated by the timeline. Digest this again: only 15 months were being allowed between the first shovel of dirt and the green flag waving for the very first Daytona 500.

A man named Charles Moneypenny was at the helm, and he drew upon some out-of-the-ordinary technology. Serendipity and synergy met at the back gate of the project, as they seemingly have so often in the story of NASCAR. The Great American Sport, as NBC news legend and author Tom Brokaw calls NASCAR, borrowed from another great American institution, the railroad, in the construction of Daytona International Speedway.

Bill Sr.'s desire to build unheard-of asphalt high banks required unheard-of thinking. But it was not merely the construction of the banks that challenged the project. The steepness of the turns had to work with the relative flatness of the back straightaway and the three-part, two-kink "tri-oval" that would pass for a traditional front straight. To make it work, Moneypenny drew upon an engineering approach utilized during railroad expansion in the 19th century. Early railroads featured low speeds and wide curvatures, but as train speeds increased to meet the demands of both a growing populace and burgeoning industry, a need developed for turns that could handle the churning locomotives at higher speeds. This led to more gradual increases in curvatures – an approach called a transition spiral, or a track transition curve. Daytona International Speedway was a perfect candidate for this technology; never had there been a paved race track so steeply banked.

Moneypenny was the city engineer of Daytona Beach; he sought help from Ford Motor Company's engineers, who had built a test track in Detroit for the manufacturer. Moneypenny had no problems with piling the dirt in the turns or building the banks, but he needed expertise regarding the curvature transitions that would connect the banks to the back straight and the tri-oval. While Ford's track was nowhere near the monstrous layout Bill Sr. was trying to build, it did offer up needed data regarding spiral transitioning. Moneypenny utilized that data and built turns that made sense – at least as much sense as possible. After all, we were talking about 31 degrees.

"I was in junior high school when they started the speedway project," said Bill Sr.'s youngest son, Jim. "I came out with Dad but didn't really do anything. I'd come on the weekends, hang around and basically stay out of the way, playing in the dirt, that sort of thing, you know. . . .

"But it sure was interesting to watch. They had a tremendous amount of dirt to move and a lot of swamp to fill in and stabilize, so they could build on top of it. It was really quite a process with the drainage, with the muck . . . it was a real mess. I remember we had these huge bulldozers pushing the swamp muck – gumbo or whatever they called it – out of the way."

While a young Jim France played, his older brother William Clifton France worked. Bill Jr. turned 25 years old in 1958. After graduating from Daytona Beach's Seabreeze High School in 1951, he briefly attended the University of Florida before doing a 1953–55 stint in the Navy. Returning home, he traveled with his parents throughout the Southeast, working at races, doing everything from selling concessions to scoring the events. He was immersing himself in the family business of racing, and in 1958 that meant long hours in the Florida sun helping build Daytona International Speedway.

Says Jim France: "Bill was involved in the construction from the get-go."

These were formative times for Bill Jr., not only watching his father on the cusp of making history but working alongside him toward that end. There are pictures of those all-out 15 months in the muck and sand, of Bill Jr. driving a tractor and graders, his white overalls serving as a canvas to illustrate just how challenging the work actually was; whatever Daytona International

Speedway was going to be, the Frances were going to earn it – the hard way. The lasting images of Bill Jr.'s involvement serve as historical markers in his development as the eventual successor to his father as NASCAR's leader.

And a word or two about those overalls: Betty Jane France tells a delightful story about different times, about how Bill Jr. had several identical pairs of work khakis that she would wash by hand, on a rotation, and then stretch across a board to dry in the sun.

The former Betty Jane Zachary, from Winston-Salem, North Carolina, had married Bill France Jr. on September 20, 1957 – just as the speedway project was hitting its stride. And so, she says, "I sort of 'grew up' with the project, kind of around the dinner table. The project wasn't a surprise. I knew they were going to do it, but I couldn't even imagine how big it was going to be. The whole thing, now, seems like a dream."

Immediately upon joining the family, she became a sidekick of sorts for Bill France Sr. "He took me under his wing," she says. "And I think I was the first person to ride around the track, along with Bill Sr. We were going fast, too. Way too fast, I suppose. It was cool but it was also scary because you have to realize that this was before they had the track even finished. We were just riding around on the lime rock before they even put the asphalt down on top of it.

"I remember as we were riding around, Bill Sr. was saying, 'This is really going to be something one day.' Myself, I could not visualize how big the whole thing would be when it was finished. I also remember Bill Sr. telling me as we rode around the banking, 'This is your future.' I was thinking . . . right. But when it came to Bill France Sr., everything was always going to work. It was just going to work. That's the way it was with him."

Added Bill Jr.: "There were a lot of skeptics back then – with good reason. It was a long, hard job – but we did it. And immediately, the speedway transformed NASCAR, and in the process transformed the Daytona Beach community into something special.

"All those years ago, my dad spent long hours day after day, fighting the sun and the skeptics, trying to build a two-and-a-half-mile race track in the middle of what was then called nowhere. He made something out of nothing.

"The speedway's true importance, though, has nothing to do with economic impact, race victories, or things like that. It has to do with sheer inspiration.

"It stands as a testament to what people can do if they put their minds to it and their hearts into it."

One of those skeptics was the famed stunt driver Joie Chitwood, who, after a successful racing career – he finished fifth in the Indianapolis 500 three times – organized the famed "Joie Chitwood Thrill Show," which for years was based in Tampa, Florida. Chitwood was a longtime friend of Bill Sr. but that didn't prevent him from disagreeing with the concept of Daytona International Speedway. Chitwood, whose nickname was "Chief," thought Bill Sr. was full of something other than dreams.

Today, the Chief's grandson, Joie Chitwood III, is the president of Daytona International Speedway. Previously, "Joie III" was the president at Indianapolis. He has perspective.

"In the late 1950s a lot of people had told Bill Sr. that his idea would not work," Chitwood says. "The story goes that he had a conversation with my grandfather about possibly investing in the project. My grandfather, who was as opinionated as anyone in the business, apparently said something like, 'Why in the hell would you want to build a high-bank speedway? No one is going to pay to watch taxi cabs (the derogatory term for stock cars) on a high-bank speedway.' So, obviously, my grandfather couldn't have been more wrong, but I can see him saying that considering the way auto racing was at the time. Stock cars were still racing here on the beach while Indianapolis was established, with 'big cars' – so you had big car racing vs. stock car racing. So, my grandfather was wrong and that's the only time I can say that I'm glad he was wrong.

"The irony is here we are, 50-plus years from the creation of Daytona International Speedway and with the TV ratings . . . the sponsorship . . . the Daytona 500 is maybe the biggest race in the world. And it all started because of the vision, the determination, and most importantly, the imagination to think of something bigger, better, and faster than anything else was at the time. It's truly an American success story."

Bill France Sr.'s ambitious deadline was met. The outlandish idea of needing merely 15 months to construct Daytona International Speedway proved not so outlandish after all. And so, in mid-February 1959, drivers rolled into Daytona Beach, entered the tunnel burrowed under the race track just out of Turn 4 – and recoiled. The place was massive, and with relatively few grandstands erected, it looked even bigger. Richard Petty likened it to being on the surface of the moon, even though a good ole boy from Randleman, North Carolina, had no idea what the surface of the moon looked like. Apollo 11 was still 10 years away.

Intimidation regarding the 2.5-mile monster, though, was based in fact, the closest and hardest of facts.

Bill Sr., eager to get his facility on the national sporting landscape, had scheduled an Indy-car race for April. What better way to one-up Indianapolis Motor Speedway than to have *their* stars bring *their* cars to *his* brand-spanking new speedway? To help the open-wheelers prepare while also giving his track a pre-Daytona 500 publicity boost, Bill Sr. hosted an Indy-car test session two weeks before the 500.

On February 11, 1959, the fourth day of Indy-car testing, old stock car hand and beach-road course veteran Marshall Teague, driving for Chapman Root, perished when his car lifted and flipped five times. The remainder of the test was cancelled but that did nothing to ease the trepidation of the stock car drivers facing the track for the first time. (The April Indy-car race went on as scheduled, marred by the death of polesitter George Amick; it was the first and last Indy-car race at Daytona.)

So what to make of the very first Daytona 500? There are several paths to follow when assessing what those first-ever 200 laps of superspeedway racing were all about. Whatever path is chosen, both begin with the fact there were no caution flags. And so, you can pick the high road and say the drivers immediately became highly capable at the brand new, biggest stock car race track in the world. Or you can say they drove competently but cautiously. Or you can simply assume they were scared beyond belief. If those theoretical paths could somehow intersect, you might find the truth as to why the inaugural 500 proceeded in such an incredibly routine fashion.

Clint Murchison was accorded the honor of driving the pace car. He led a field of 59 cars in '59 – 22 were convertibles. There were 33 lead changes. The race lasted three hours, forty-one minutes and twenty-two seconds. Announced attendance was nearly 42,000. The winner's average speed: 135 miles per hour.

Rex White, the 1960 NASCAR Sprint Cup Series champion, says it was an exciting day but urges revisionists to not go overboard in their excitement.

"We were just riding around the place," White said. "You could've lit a cigarette while you were driving. No, it wasn't dangerous."

The winner was Lee Petty, in spite of himself. He was one of the drivers who seemed especially spooked by the high banks.

So, you had a rather mundane race won by a driver who didn't really care for the event to begin with. What to do?

Enter the era of the photo finish.

It is an iconic photo, maybe NASCAR's most iconic of all. Three cars virtually abreast, crossing the finish line to wrap up the first Daytona 500. Lee Petty's No. 42 Oldsmobile is in the middle, Johnny Beauchamp's No. 73 Thunderbird is on the inside. High and outside is the lap-down No. 48 Chevrolet of future two-time NASCAR champion Joe Weatherly, his presence obscuring the finish from Bill Sr. and other officials..

Just before they crossed the stripe, Beauchamp appeared to have the edge. At the line, though, Petty drew even, or so it appeared. Beauchamp was declared the winner; Petty, the greatest disputer of decisions in the history of NASCAR, drove straight to Victory Lane, having of course declared himself the winner.

Bob Zeller described the frantic post-race minutes in his book *Daytona 500, An Official History*:

[Bill] France [Sr.] stood below the flag stand behind the retaining fence, one yard shy of the finish line. He leaned forward on his left knee, bent his big frame down, and peered hard as the car flashed past. "Beauchamp," France thought. But he couldn't be sure. He realized he was too close for a good view. The cars had passed in a blur. [Starter Johnny] Bruner, however, agreed that Beauchamp had won. In the control tower, Bill France Jr. wasn't sure.

Meanwhile, sportswriters in the press box were near-unanimous in thinking Petty had won. Many of the fans seated near the finish line felt the same way and voiced their disapproval loudly when Beauchamp was initially announced as the winner.

Confusion reigned.

Whereupon Bill Sr. soon put out an "all call" for photos and motion picture footage that could decide the finish once and for all. Joe Weatherly's car was serving a purpose, blocking of a clear, indisputable view of the finish.

On February 22, 1959, the first Daytona 500 had been run, but it wouldn't be complete for another three days.

And so, on the early evening of February 25, Bill Sr. announced that conclusive evidence had surfaced showing that Lee Petty had indeed won.

Another piece of NASCAR lore had been created: three days of intrigue, following nearly four hours of less-than-enthralling racing. This situation has come to be viewed as the quintessential Bill Sr. stroke of genius. The Spinmaster had surfaced again.

"That was a PR deal," Richard Petty says, smiling slyly at the memory. "Bill Sr. knew my daddy had won that race."

Daytona International Speedway had transformed NASCAR, and moving forward, the Daytona 500 would define the sport. Much later in life, when an aging, ailing Bill France Sr. would ask to be driven around the race track, he would ride quietly but occasionally say softly, looking around at the expanse, "I built this place . . . I built this place."

Yes, he did.

"Anything Bill France Sr. wanted to do, we knew he'd deliver the goods," said White. "He had the knack of putting things together and making things work."

The often-combative crew chief and mechanic Smokey Yunick concurred, albeit in his own way: "Bill France was something special. He was a world-class bullshitter and he had the balls of an elephant" when it came to financial risk-taking.

Risks had been taken. Rewards were on the way.

Daytona International Speedway: A Timeline

April 1953: Bill France Sr. proposes construction of a new speedway in Daytona Beach, Florida

August 16, 1954: Bill France Sr. signs a contract with City of Daytona Beach officials to build what would become Daytona International Speedway, "The World Center of Racing"

November 1955: Volusia County begins improvements of local roads in anticipation of speedway traffic

November 9, 1957: Bill France Sr. announces that the Daytona Beach International Speedway Corporation will build a 2.5-mile race track

November 25, 1957: Work begins on clearing the land at the proposed speedway site

April 1958: Construction begins

February 1, 1959: First practice laps are run

February 20, 1959: Two days before the Daytona 500, Daytona International Speedway holds a 100-mile convertible race. This is immediately followed by a 100-mile race for Grand National "hard-top" cars. Today, the twin qualifying races are called The Gatorade Duel At Daytona.

February 22, 1959: The inaugural Daytona 500 – also known as the "500-Mile International Sweepstakes" – is held with hard-tops and convertibles. It is the only Daytona 500 to ever run with convertibles. The finish of the caution-free inaugural Daytona 500 is too close to call. Even as the results are posted as "unofficial," Johnny Beauchamp goes to Victory Lane and savors the celebration. Sixty-one hours later, Lee Petty is declared the winner in what had appeared to be a dead heat between Petty and Beauchamp – with the lapped car of Joe Weatherly making it a three-wide finish at the checkered flag. A clip of newsreel footage proved that Petty was the winner by a few feet.

July 4, 1959: The inaugural Firecracker 250 – later increased to 400 miles – is held and won by local driver Glenn "Fireball" Roberts

1961: The Daytona 200 motorcycle classic moves from the beach to a 2.0-mile road course inside Daytona International Speedway. Roger Reiman, who specialized in Flat Track racing, wins the inaugural Daytona 200 at DIS aboard a Harley-Davidson. His average winning speed is 69.26 mph.

August 27, 1961: Art Malone drives Bob Osecki's Hemi-powered, highly modified Indy car –named "Mad Dog IV" – to a new world closed-course record speed of 181.561 mph.

February 11, 1962: The inaugural Daytona Continental, now known as the Rolex 24, is held as a three-hour race run counter-clockwise on the 3.81-mile road course. Dan Gurney, driving the No. 96 Lotus-Climax 19b S 2500 car, wins the Daytona Continental, completing 82 laps and averaging 104.101 mph in what was the fastest sports car race ever run in the United States.

February 20, 1977: Janet Guthrie becomes the first woman driver to compete in the Daytona 500. She finishes 12th.

August 1978: Daytona International Speedway is repaved for the first time in its history. The project takes several months to complete and is finished in time for the 1979 Daytona 500.

February 18, 1979: The Daytona 500 is televised live for the first time in event history by CBS Sports. On the final lap, Cale Yarborough and Donnie Allison crash in Turn 3 while battling for the lead. Richard Petty holds off Darrell Waltrip to win his sixth Daytona 500, while Yarborough and Allison began a heated debate that turns into a fist fight with Allison's brother Bobby jumping into the fray.

February 13, 1982: The inaugural event of NASCAR's new Busch Series (formerly the NASCAR Sportsman Division) is held, with Dale Earnhardt the series' first winner.

July 4, 1984: President Ronald Reagan serves as Grand Marshal for the Pepsi Firecracker 400 and gives the starting command – "Gentlemen, start your engines" – aboard Air Force One. Reagan arrives mid-race, calls the race with MRN Radio's Ned Jarrett, and witnesses Richard Petty's historic 200th NASCAR win. It is the first time in NASCAR history that a sitting President attends a race.

February 9, 1987: Dawsonville, Georgia, driver Bill Elliott sets the Daytona 500 qualifying record with a speed of 210.364 mph.

July 4, 1992: President George Bush servs as the Grand Marshal for the Pepsi 400. He gives the starting command for Richard Petty's final NASCAR race at Daytona International Speedway.

February 7, 1998: Dale Earnhardt becomes the first driver to tackle the 2.5-mile high-banked tri-oval under the newly installed lighting system in a special 20-lap test following Daytona 500 qualifying.

February 15, 1998: On his 20th attempt, Dale Earnhardt finally earns his first and only victory in the 40th annual Daytona 500.

October 17, 1998: Jeff Gordon wins the first Pepsi 400 run under the lights at Daytona. The Pepsi 400 was delayed until October because of the summer wildfires.

February 18, 2001: On his 463rd career Cup start, Michael Waltrip holds off teammate Dale Earnhardt Jr. to win the Daytona 500, his first career victory. His owner Dale Earnhardt dies in a last-lap crash in Turn 4.

July 7, 2001: Dale Earnhardt Jr. wins the Pepsi 400, his first career DIS victory coming 11 years to the day that his father won his first then-Winston Cup race at DIS.

February 15, 2004: President George W. Bush serves as Grand Marshal for the Daytona 500 and Dale Earnhardt Jr. wins "The Great American Race" on his fifth attempt. The race is also the first for new sponsor Nextel.

February 18, 2007: Kevin Harvick nips Mark Martin at the start/finish line to capture the closest Daytona 500 finish since the advent of computer scoring in 1993, with a margin of victory of .020 seconds. This finish is also the eighth closest in the NASCAR Sprint Cup Series history.

February 17, 2008: Daytona International Speedway hosts the historic 50th running of the Daytona 500 NASCAR Sprint Cup Series race. A sell-out crowd witnesses Ryan Newman make a last-lap pass of Tony Stewart to win the most anticipated event in racing history. The victory is the first Daytona 500 triumph for both Newman and his car owner, Roger Penske.

February 15, 2009: The 50th anniversary running of the Daytona 500 is won by Matt Kenseth.

February 27, 2012: Due to inclement weather, the Daytona 500 is run for the first time on a Monday night, with Matt Kenseth winning.

February 23, 2014: Dale Earnhardt Jr. wins the Daytona 500 for the second time.

CHAPTER 6

The 1960s:

From the Teamsters To Talladega

W ith the Daytona 500 as the new divining rod for NASCAR, the 1960s beckoned Bill France Sr. His superspeedway had completely altered stock car racing. The future possibilities were exhilarating as the sport raced away from its hardscrabble moon-shining roots that, while romantic, were never going to be conducive to growth, for either a sport or a business.

And NASCAR *always* was a business, first and foremost. This is something many people seem to have forgotten, as it has become vogue to long for the days of dirt, dust, and low-paying race purses. Bill Sr.'s vision for NASCAR was always based, as he said at the Streamline Hotel, on "improving the present conditions." And the overall goal was always about improving conditions for everyone.

Bill France Jr., talking about the NASCAR business model years later: "Everybody involved in this deal has to benefit, or else it won't work. That's always the way it's been. It's the way it has to be."

The business model of NASCAR was taking a turn, with Daytona's speed palace the catalyst. There would be no nine-year gap as there was between the opening of Darlington and Daytona. In 1960 two more superspeedways debuted: lightning-fast Atlanta International Raceway and Charlotte Motor Speedway, smaller in length and not as steep in banking but still representative of the changing times.

The 1960 Daytona 500 officially unveiled a phenomenon that had been a puzzle in '59: drafting, the aerodynamic effect of a trailing car being "towed" by a car in front, enabling the trailing car to at times come down the banks and emerge from the draft to "slingshot" past the car in front. In '59 Lee Petty and Johnny Beauchamp had traded the lead a number of times in that manner, more or less. Since none of the drivers truly knew what in the hell was going on in the swirling, sucking, high-speed air atop the 31 degrees of asphalt, it wasn't so much drafting that was taking place as a bunch of wide-eyed, white-knuckled guys going along for a capricious ride.

But one thing was certain: something was at work, something adding previously unseen performance boosts to stock cars.

Credited with the unveiling: Glenn Robert "Junior" Johnson, the brief hero of the 1950s, back from serving a short prison stint for moonshining, back in the thick of the racing, driving a some-what underpowered Chevrolet owned by Daytona Beach resident Ray Fox. Johnson started tucking in behind faster cars during prac-tice sessions and quickly discerned that the towing effect elimi-nated whatever inequity there was in horsepower. Junior Johnson drafted his way to victory in that second Daytona 500 and became forever known as the man who "invented" drafting. Johnson points out, even to this day, that he never invented it; he just figured it out before everyone else did.

The 1960 Daytona 500 was nothing like the first, aside from Johnson's discovery. The caution-free 1959 debut was followed by a crash-fest in '60. Two days' worth of crashing, actually. The Modified/Sportsman race the day before the 500 – the precursor to the current annual 300-mile NASCAR XFINITY Series sea-son-opening race – had what was termed the biggest accident in the history of auto racing: 37 cars piling up on the very first lap. The 500 was marred by 11 accidents that destroyed 21 cars.

In 1961 it was more of the same, although with much more frightening results, this time in the two qualifying races for the 500 held on a Friday afternoon. The first qualifier ended prema-turely when Richard Petty's car was hit by Junior Johnson's and sent sailing over the guardrail and outside the race track in the first turn. Richard's car landed on its wheels, enabling him to escape with minor cuts and bruises. The second qualifying race had a far scarier incident as Lee Petty and Johnny Beauchamp, who had battled for the win in 1959, likewise sailed out of the speedway, in the area of the fourth turn. Both drivers suffered serious injuries from which they recovered, but their racing days were effectively done.

For Lee Petty, the accident was a manifestation of his worst fears about the massive race track, or any large race track, for that matter. He was never comfortable with leaving the confines of the small ovals where he had felt at home in capturing 53 of his 54 victories in NASCAR's premier series. NASCAR's first three-time champion retired from competition to guide the family race team to becoming the most successful in the sport's history, in terms of the record books. His son Richard Petty was destined to achieve greatness and, in a fitting irony, Daytona would be where that greatness was most evident and most publicized.

Curtis Turner, the hard-drinking, fast-driving black-hat hero, would forever be a good news-bad news proposition for Bill Sr. He was daring. He was colorful. He was talented. He was also a pain in the ass.

And he was a pilot, giving him something in common with Bill Sr. But that road likely forked when stories surfaced about Turner landing his plane on a road near a liquor store, jumping out to go grab a bottle or two, and then getting back into the cockpit to take off again.

On the subject of his undeniable talent: Turner was credited with approximately 360 race victories in a variety of series, with 22 wins coming in 1956 in NASCAR's short-lived Convertible Division and another 17 in NASCAR's headlining Grand National Division. His biggest victory came in the 1956 Southern 500 at Darlington Raceway.

In 1960, Turner, partnered with Bruton Smith, sought to capitalize on the sudden appeal of bigger race tracks by building Charlotte Motor Speedway. In '61, Turner was tossed out as the track's president via a coup of sorts staged by the facility's board of directors. To get back in, Turner needed money he didn't have. He approached the Teamsters Union, which could provide large loans, albeit with significant interest charges coming down the pike. Turner's need for a loan coincided with Teamsters president Jimmy Hoffa's quest to unionize professional sports in the United States. Turner got the loan; as part of the deal he was required to recruit drivers to a union – the Federation of Professional Athletes, which promised drivers more money, a pension, and insurance. Drivers thought this sounded good, and overdue.

Bill Sr., suffice to say, did not approve.

To battle the initiative he went to the top, talking his way into a meeting with the attorney general of the United States, Robert Kennedy (a pain in the ass to Jimmy Hoffa in those days of Camelot). A young attorney named John Cassidy – Bill Sr.'s "inductor" at the NASCAR Hall of Fame in 2010 – worked in the Department of Justice for RFK. He recalls the day of Bill Sr.'s visit as if it was yesterday. It actually was 1961, only months into the Kennedy administration.

How did Bill Sr. get a meeting with Kennedy in the first place? With the passage of years, Cassidy isn't absolutely certain, but he thinks the access likely can be attributed to Bill Sr.'s relationship with the controversial South Carolina Democratic congressman Mendel Rivers, who stood alongside whatever hawkish tendencies the Kennedys had but firmly against even the slightest move toward improved civil rights. Much like Bill Sr.'s friendship with Alabama Governor George Wallace, his relationship with Rivers benefited from the relative lack of media attention accorded NASCAR at the time.

"The Teamsters were trying to organize the drivers," Cassidy said, "because they figured if they could control them and all the teams from motorsports . . . they had set up a professional athletes division of the Teamsters that was heavily committed to organizing the NBA, the NFL, and motorsports."

Motorsports – that especially made sense. The Teamsters unionized truck drivers. Auto racing was a sport that truck drivers loved.

"The Teamsters knew what they were doing," Cassidy said.

"Senior knew he was in the battle of his life, and he was really viewing it as a battle for survival because if he lost the battle [over unionization] he would have lost control of NASCAR. One of the keys to Senior's thought process was always a straight-line approach. How to solve the problem? One way was to attack Hoffa, who Senior believed to be corrupt. What better place to go for help than the U.S. Department of Justice? It just so happened that he and Bobby Kennedy were on the same wavelength."

With Cassidy advising at the behest of RFK, Bill Sr. also enlisted the help of two of his valued lieutenants, Pat Purcell and Ed Otto, to collectively beat back the beast of the Teamsters. It was a multi-level response to the threat, and it started in dramatic fashion when Bill Sr. imposed a lifetime ban from NASCAR on Turner, former champion Tim Flock, and Fireball Roberts, three central figures pushing for unionization. Turner's involvement had especially infuriated Bill Sr. because it included an additional push to have betting at race tracks. After all he had done to cleanse stock car racing of its unsavory past, Bill Sr. was not about to let NASCAR regress.

Roberts was reinstated when he pulled out of the fledgling

union after a long, Scotch-fueled come-to-Jesus discussion with Purcell. Other drivers defected following an impassioned Bill Sr. speech prior to a race in Winston-Salem, North Carolina, in which he appealed to the drivers' basic values. "Auto racing," Bill Sr. told them, "is one of the few sports which has never had a scandal. Do you want to be the ones who changed that?"

Despite the defections, Flock and Turner stood their ground. So did Bill Sr., which meant they were gone from NASCAR – permanently. They tried to have their bans overturned repeatedly in the courts, to no avail. In NASCAR's corner during these legal battles was a precedent dating to 1951, when Otto had helped a Long Island race track overturn a judgment resulting from the deaths of two drivers. The state of New York originally decreed that the drivers were in effect race track employees; the reversal placed the drivers in the category of independent contractors. That distinction provided an additional roadblock to unionization in NASCAR's case; the drivers were not employed by NASCAR but rather by the individual teams.

The footnote: Bill Sr., pressured by track promoters in 1965, would grudgingly end up lifting the bans on Turner and Flock. Turner tried a half-hearted comeback. Flock stayed away for good.

Bruton Smith's emergence in 1960 as a major speedway's owner/promoter signified the start of a truly contentious relationship with NASCAR, one that exists to this day. Smith and Bill Sr. wanted the same thing: to rule stock car racing.

"They were like two bulls in the same pasture with a bunch of cows around," said longtime Charlotte Motor Speedway president Humpy Wheeler, who had his own negative experience with Smith – an acrimonious exit as track president in 2008.

"Both strong-willed of course, their competition got started because of them being dirt-track promoters [in the early days of stock car racing] promoting on the same weekends [in the Southeast]," Wheeler said. "Bruton no doubt wanted to own NASCAR. He still does.

"In the early days, racing was so rough-and-tumble, there was a lot of skullduggery so it was inevitable they'd meet like two locomotives on the same track. Their relationship was never good. There have always been very, very hard feelings between the Frances and Bruton Smith – no question about that."

Feelings are perhaps not quite as "hard" nowadays, in part due to two level-headed descendants – NASCAR chairman and CEO Brian France, Bill Sr.'s grandson, and Bruton Smith's son, Marcus Smith, now the president and COO of Speedway Motorsports Inc. They have what has been described as a solid working relationship.

But some ill-will no doubt persists. Bruton Smith "politely declined" to be interviewed for this book, according to a public relations representative. Smith also declined to be interviewed for a 2010 biography of Bill France Jr.

Purcell, Otto, Bill Tuthill, and Louis Ossinsky – these men formed NASCAR's first "cabinet." Key advisers all, whose contributions should never be overlooked. Over the last several decades, though, various depictions of NASCAR history have cast the group as almost victims of an overpowering dictator named Bill France Sr. It has even been reported that NASCAR's "official history" gives Otto and the others short shrift. There is one problem with these reports: there is nothing that can be called an "official" comprehensive

NASCAR history. There also is the fact that no less than current NASCAR chairman and CEO Brian France has routinely credited people like Purcell and Otto with helping to build the sport, in contrast to various claims that NASCAR has actually spent time conspiring to minimize the contributions of Bill Sr.'s core leadership group in the sport's early years.

Otto's departure from NASCAR in 1963 has shed considerable light on this subject, due to a campaign by his family to have him inducted into the NASCAR Hall of Fame. In '63, Otto owned 40 per cent of NASCAR's stock, having picked up Tuthill's 20 per cent when Tuthill departed the company in 1954. That left him and Bill Sr. as near-equals; Ossinsky still had his original 10 per cent dating to 1947, while Senior of course had his 50 per cent. A falling out caused Bill Sr. to ask Otto to leave the company; the '63 split was on the surface amicable, with Bill Sr. paying Otto a quarter-million dollars for his 40 per cent share. It should be noted that Otto did not have to sell.

Brian France will be the first to recognize people like Otto, but he points out that there have been repeated waves of contributors who assisted his grandfather, his father, and now him in administering the business of NASCAR.

"All of those contributions have been important," France said, "but most of the contributions we're talking about [here] came in the formative years. There's been a lot of green grass that has grown since then, with people like [former vice presidents] Paul Brooks, Jim Hunter, Les Richter . . . and today, people like [chief marketing officer] Steve Phelps making contributions. It's not just a few people. It's a lot of people contributing, all through the cycle."

———

Wendell Scott wasn't the first African American to compete in NASCAR's premier series, but he was the most successful by far, becoming the first African American to race full-time at the Grand National level. His first start was in 1961. His first and only victory came December 1, 1963, at Speedway Park in Jacksonville, Florida – the race was technically part of the 1964 season.

The fact that Scott had only that one win in 495 starts has absolutely nothing to do with his importance to the sport, for obvious reasons. The significance of his trailblazing efforts, racing primarily in the Southeast, mainly during a time when Jim Crow was hanging on by the skin of his segregationist teeth, can neither be overlooked nor exaggerated. That statistic does, however, belie an overall record of success when it comes to competition. Make no mistake: Wendell Scott was no back-marker.

He had 147 top-10 finishes over his 13-year career in what is now called the NASCAR Sprint Cup Series. But here's the real yardstick by which to measure Scott strictly as a driver: he finished in the top 15 of the premier series' final standings eight consecutive seasons, from 1963–70, with his best points finish sixth in 1966. Who finished ahead of Scott that year? David Pearson, James Hylton, Richard Petty, Henley Gray, and Paul Goldsmith. Scott finished *ahead* of Bobby Allison, Ned Jarrett, Buck Baker, and Buddy Baker. It's worth noting that Scott's point total resulted from running 45 of the 49 races, the third-highest total in the series. He earned his success in 1964 – and throughout his career.

The incredible accomplishments of Wendell Scott notwithstanding, the 1964 season, by any measure, was the lowest of lows for NASCAR as an industry and Bill France Sr. personally. The inherent danger of auto racing surfaced in startling fashion, snatching away two of NASCAR's biggest stars, one already a two-time champion, the other a certain future titlist who had already become a "people's champion" of sorts with a popularity that needed no validation by a season-ending trophy.

It happened within a 167-day span, from the season's fifth event, a road race at Riverside International Raceway, California, to the 25th event of the year, the World 600 at Charlotte Motor Speedway. On January 19 at Riverside, Joe Weatherly, the Grand National champion in 1962 and '63 – the *reigning* champion – died in a single-car crash when his head was extended outside the cockpit as the car slammed into a concrete retaining wall. On May 24, NASCAR's reigning superstar, Daytona Beach hometown hero Fireball Roberts, crashed and suffered serious burns before being pulled from his car by another two-time champion, Ned Jarrett. Roberts lived until July 2.

Consider the sum effect of these twin tragedies. The modern-day equivalent would be to lose Jimmie Johnson and Dale Earnhardt Jr. within several months' time.

Unthinkable.

Both accidents served to spotlight the need for safety advancements. In Weatherly's case, it was driver-side window netting. Roberts' crash was followed only six days later by the deaths of Eddie Sachs and Dave MacDonald at the Indianapolis 500, with fire a factor as well. Collectively those incidents led to the eventual mandating of window nets, the use of new, safer fuel cells, and fire-retardant race suits.

Roberts' death hit Bill Sr. especially hard. Roberts' decision to defect from the proposed union three years earlier led other drivers to almost immediately follow suit. And even though Bill Sr. was fully prepared to stand by his ban of Roberts, he knew from the outset the damage such a ban would do. Once again, for point of reference, imagine NASCAR today tossing Dale Earnhardt Jr. or Danica Patrick out – for good.

Unthinkable.

Bill Sr. was not about to forget what Roberts had done for him – for NASCAR – by recanting on his union commitment. He would never forget.

Auto racing, in full bloom, is a force of nature, albeit mechanically driven. And so racing takes care of itself, heals itself, especially in the toughest of times.

The deaths of Weatherly and Roberts – staggering blows. Concurrent, though, came the rise of two new stars destined to surpass virtually anyone and everyone in terms of popularity and accomplishments.

Teed up by the advent of the magnificent Daytona 500, then waylaid by the deaths of Weatherly and Roberts, NASCAR was reinvigorated by a rivalry that had never been seen before – and certainly hasn't been seen since – in terms of intensity or parity.

Petty vs. Pearson.

Richard Petty – heir to the legacy of his father, Lee, a three-time NASCAR champion – won his first race on February 28, 1960, at Southern States Fairgrounds in Charlotte. David Pearson got his first victory on May 28, 1961, at the new Charlotte Motor Speedway in one of NASCAR's three "major events" – the World 600. "That's the day I became a full-time race car driver," Pearson says.

By the end of the 1960s, Petty had won two of his eventual record seven championships, the first lightening the black cloud of 1964, the second in 1967. Pearson won all three of his titles in a mercurial '60s sprint to immortality – in 1966, '68, and '69. Petty got 101 of his record 200 victories during the decade. Of Pearson's 105 wins, 57 came in the 1960s.

The rivalry continued into the 1970s but under different parameters; Pearson, driving through the years for Cotton Owens, Holman-Moody and the Wood Brothers, disdained running full-time, concentrating mainly on key events. Along the way, he developed a style of lying low for a good portion of an event only to charge to the front in the closing laps and, often, end up in Victory Lane. The slyness in the approach, along with a full head of hair that was graying prematurely, led to his nickname: "The Silver Fox." His limited schedule often took him out of championship contention but he remained in Petty's sightlines, typically on Petty's bumper or putting him into the rearview mirror.

Except in 1967, when Petty produced the most remarkable season in the history of NASCAR. Pearson again ran a partial season, making 22 starts, winning twice. Petty, starting 48 of 49 Grand National races, won 27 times – 10 in a row at one stage – with 38 top-five finishes and 40 top-10s.

How important was the Petty-Pearson rivalry? A measure: it extended into the 1970s, peaking with a classic crash-and-bang Daytona 500 finish in 1976 – won by Pearson – that is considered by many the greatest finish ever in the "Great American Race."

Further measurement was the way the two drivers dominated a sizable portion of the discussion surrounding the first two inductee classes of the NASCAR Hall of Fame in 2010 and '11.

When Pearson didn't make it the first time around, Petty immediately came to the defense of his old rival, even though it had the effect of disparaging the late Bill France Jr., who reportedly slid into the first Hall of Fame class by the slimmest of margins, over Pearson. Petty, quoted repeatedly through the years as saying "David Pearson was the best driver I ever saw," was surprisingly outspoken over Pearson not making the cut. All was good in 2011, however, when Pearson led the hall's second class of inductees.

Petty-Pearson. It saved the '60s, as far as NASCAR was concerned. But Bill France Sr. was delving into other areas during the decade – and business was good.

The fact that the word "international" was part of the title of Daytona International Speedway was no accident. Bill Sr. possessed an inherent international sensibility that could be traced to his upbringing, amid one of the United States' true internationally flavored populaces, the District of Columbia. Something else that cannot be overlooked is the international racing heritage of the Daytona Beach area, rooted in the early 1900s when moneyed daredevils from around the world came to Florida in pursuit of land speed records on the hard-packed sands. You see, the word "international" made sense, even if the first wave of racers would have names like Junior, Fireball, and Tiny.

The word also had the purpose of further distinguishing Daytona from Indianapolis. One-upmanship, remember? Indianapolis would have its 500 but Daytona would have the world. Daytona International Speedway was intended to be *just that*: a track with global cachet that attracted the world's top sports car teams on certain weekends.

Bill Sr. had always been enchanted by Le Mans' twice-around-the-clock test, and from the time the first shovel of dirt was unearthed at Daytona, he envisioned hosting major international sports car races at the site.

Enchantment led to enterprise.

Groundwork for worldwide recognition was laid from 1956–58, when Bill Sr. had led the creation of the Automobile Competition Committee for the United States – ACCUS – to join the Fédération Internationale de l'Automobile (FIA), the Paris-based organization governing auto racing throughout the world. There was a FIA spot for ACCUS because the old AAA – the organization that had tossed Bill and his wife out of Indy – had gotten out of the auto racing business. The AAA had long sanctioned the Indianapolis 500. The end game here was automatic international motorsports recognition for NASCAR, Daytona International Speedway, and, of course, Bill France Sr.

From the outset, Bill Sr. wanted road racing to be part of his track's allure – road racing for both sports cars and high-end motorcycles. This fact has been a glaring omission in so many historical accounts of both the man and his race track. A road course was in place when the speedway opened in 1959. For several years, the track hosted amateur-level sports car races. In 1960, the Daytona 200, held on the various beach-road courses since 1937, moved to the new speedway.*

In 1961, Bill Sr. was ready to take his sports car game to another level, with a major event. He picked a prime setting to

---

* The 200 continues to be held each March at the speedway, as the finale to the annual two-wheel celebration known as "Bike Week."

announce his plans: the famed 21 Club in New York City, a renowned restaurant that opened in 1930 and gained fame as a speakeasy during Prohibition, complete with a disappearing bar to enable the quick hiding of illegal liquor.*

Before just the sort of upscale clientele and international media members he wanted to impress, Bill Sr. announced that a three-hour race called the Daytona Continental would be run on February 11, 1962.

"Big Bill made a big deal of the race," recalls veteran road racer David Hobbs. "He was keen on the international aspect of racing. He wanted to open up the race to the world and show everyone it was not just a bunch of good ole boys racing [at Daytona]."

In its own realm, the first Daytona Continental proved every bit as memorable as the first Daytona 500. Legend-in-the-making Dan Gurney, driving a Lotus, won in the strangest of ways. Here's the way he described it in J.J. O'Malley's book *Daytona 24 Hours: The Definitive History of America's Great Endurance Race*:

> "As we were coming down to the end of the three hours, with about a two-minute lead, the engine blew between turns three and four of the banking. It actually stuck a rod right through the side of the engine block. I coasted to the finish line, up to the banking in front of the grandstands. I was looking at my watch and decided if I waited for a minute,

---

* The 21 Club continued to have stature for years in NASCAR, annually hosting a media luncheon with NASCAR's champion during part of the "Champion's Week" festivities, a tradition that ended in 2009 when those festivities moved to Las Vegas.

*maybe I had enough of a lead so I could go across when they
dropped the (checkered) flag.*

*"So I sat there, four or five feet short of going across the
finish line, way up near the wall. There were shadows up
there, and the guys that were coming by were moving along
pretty fast. I was pretty happy nobody was up as high as I
was. The flagman was perched just up above me, and I was
looking at my watch, and he was looking at his watch, and
I was wondering whether in fact we had the kind of lead I
thought we had. In the end, he waved the flag, and I turned
left and coasted down the banking and that was the win."*

The event was expanded to 12 hours in 1964 and 24 hours in
'66. Expansion meant elevation, placing the new 24 Hours of
Daytona alongside the 24 Hours of Le Mans and the 12 Hours of
Sebring as the world's three greatest endurance races. Bill France
Sr. was ecstatic, and it had nothing to do with the profit margin
produced by a crowd of nearly 30,000.

"We didn't make a bundle of money on the race," he said, "but
we did start building toward a race that will become one of the
great automotive events in the world."

In 1969, Bill Sr. joined forces with a disenchanted Sports Car
Club of America (SCCA) official named John Bishop to form the
International Motor Sports Association (IMSA). Bill Sr. provided
the financing, Bishop and his wife, Peggy, the expertise. This was
but one chapter in a long story of attempts to successfully organize sports car racing in North America. There has perhaps never
been a professional sport with so much potential – and so much
potential unrealized. Sports car racing has seen its ebbs and

flows, but for the most part has been a hidden gem of North American auto racing, with its spectacular competition overshadowed for years not only by NASCAR but also Indy cars and National Hot Rod Association drag racing.

But never has there been a sports car success story like the one Bill Sr. and the Bishops assembled. The story began in unlikely fashion. Bishop's "disenchantment" with the SCCA began in 1969, when the organization finally accepted his near-annual offering of his resignation as executive director. Less than a week later, Bishop got a call from Bill Sr.

A casual business relationship was about to get personal.

John Bishop died on June 6, 2014, due to complications after surgery, at the age of 87. He lived out his final years in San Rafael, California. He was a treasure. He would joke about getting old, lament about being blind in one eye. He would talk about the pain of losing his wife in 2013. "We had 66 good years so I shouldn't complain but I still miss her terribly," the old man said.

Two months prior to his death, he also talked about Bill France Sr., whom he figured came along at just the right time to save major-league sports car racing in North America.

"There has been a lot written about the founding of IMSA and most of it has been wrong," Bishop began, at the outset of a long, spirited late-spring chat.

"Let me give it to you straight.

"I had political problems with the SCCA, who I worked with for 12 years. It was a political organization and the politics just got impossible after a while. I was executive director. At the annual SCCA convention, I would always say to them that if we couldn't work together I would submit my resignation. Well, much to my surprise and chagrin in 1969 they did accept my resignation, finally.

"So I left and it couldn't have been more than a week later that the phone rang. It was Bill Sr., who I had come to know only as a [head] of a sanctioning body, from ACCUS, and from seeing him at the 24 Hours of Daytona. He said, 'I hear you're leaving the SCCA. I think it'd be a shame for you to waste all those years of experience from SCCA. I've got some ideas I'd like to talk about.'

"Well, I went down to Daytona Beach to see Bill. We drank a lot of scotch and had a nice chat. He said that with so many race tracks being built, he didn't think the current sports car sanctioning bodies that were out there could handle it. He said, 'You ought to think about setting up a new organization, and if you do decide to do that let me know and I'll help you if I can.'

"When I got home, I talked to Peggy. We had no idea how much work it was to set up a new organization. But we did it, in the middle part of 1969."

The Bishops borrowed on Bill Sr.'s experience in starting an organization but more importantly they borrowed money – a number of unsecured loans that were vital to establishing the International Motor Sports Association, headquartered in Westport, Connecticut. After two years of struggling financially, it all came together with the 1971 creation of a GT class that introduced international-style endurance racing to North America. In 1972, the R.J. Reynolds Tobacco Company, the sponsor of NASCAR's premier series, signed on to sponsor the Camel GT Series. GT success begat Prototypes – arguably the greatest Prototypes in the history of auto racing

IMSA racing peaked in the 1980s and early '90s, with the headlining Grand Touring Prototype (GTP) class showcasing a splendid mix of international driving talent and manufacturer-supported technology. The Porsche 962s of drivers such as Derek Bell, Al Holbert, and Hans Stuck, with cameos by none other than A.J. Foyt . . . the Nissans of Geoff Brabham and Chip Robinson . . . the Toyota Eagles of Gurney's All-America Racers team and drivers Juan Manuel Fangio and P.J. Jones, Parnelli's kid.

It was a glorious era, headlined by the 24 Hours of Daytona and 12 Hours of Sebring, and, for a while, the spectacular Grand Prix of Miami run in downtown Miami on Biscayne Boulevard. A trio of Florida events to kick off the sports car season, fueled by exotic prototypes and drivers from the sports cars scene plus NASCAR, Indy Car, Trans-Am, and Formula One. And for a number of years there were other Florida events in Daytona Beach, Tampa, and West Palm Beach, most notably the Paul Revere 250 that started at midnight at Daytona, during the annual Firecracker 400 NASCAR weekend.

The era evaporated due to sheer economics. Acerbating the downturn was the Bishops selling IMSA to Tampa businessmen Michael Cone and Jeff Parker in 1989. In coming years, the costs to compete, much less win, skyrocketed and led to the demise of the GTP class. In the late 1990s disarray completely splintered North American sports car racing. The result was two organizations, with opposing philosophies, a split that while not as fractious as the CART-Indy Racing League divide that basically ruined Indy-car racing, certainly did not help the sport. Fans and teams ended up with this: on one side, the American Le Mans Series (ALMS), owned by entrepreneur Don Panoz, with an emphasis on technology and a link to the 24 Hours of Le Mans and an over-all European sensibility; on the other side, GRAND-AM Road Racing, a more economic business model owned by NASCAR and led by Bill Sr.'s younger son Jim France, with the showcase event the season-opening Rolex 24 At Daytona. Meantime, IMSA was sold three more times and eventually renamed as Professional Sports Car Racing (PSCR) in 1996, an inexplicable jettisoning of a brand that represented, at least on the surface, something sports car racing sorely lacked – stability. A Panoz-led group pur-chased PSCR in 2001 and brought back the old IMSA name for sanctioning and officiating purposes, but the once-glorious brand more or less disappeared from the public consciousness.

The ALMS and GRAND-AM competed, more or less, until the fall of 2012, when it was announced that NASCAR had acquired the ALMS, with that series and GRAND-AM's Rolex Sports Car Series slated to merge starting with the 2014 season. It happened, creating the new TUDOR United SportsCar Championship sanc-tioned by IMSA, which survived the merger in new-and-improved form, headed by Jim France. The footnote here: the acquisition by NASCAR included not only the ALMS but the Road Atlanta facility in Braselton, Georgia, the lease (from the city of Sebring) to run the 12 Hours of Sebring – and IMSA. Which means that NASCAR had to buy back the organization founded by Bill Sr. and the Bishops in 1969. Jim France finds a shade of humor in that, depending on his mood.

Jim France will certainly smile, however, when talking about the 2013 trip to the 24 Hours of Le Mans where he was asked to wave the starting flag, just as his brother Bill Jr. had done in 1976. That was the year when Bill Sr., working closely with Le

Mans, arranged to have a special NASCAR division in the famed endurance event. (In 1962, Bill Sr. had worked with Le Mans officials to facilitate the entry of Fireball Roberts and Bob Grossman in a Ferrari; they finished a stunning sixth overall.)

This was a veritable coup of the highest order and fully indicative of the ever-increasing clout of Bill Sr. He was facilitating good ole boys in their own class on the Circuit de la Sarthe, a never-before-and-never-since-addition to Le Mans, happening largely because of his will and his quest to make NASCAR and Daytona International Speedway relevant beyond not only the Southeast but the U.S. as well.

John Bishop was proud of the past – and the current sports car scene as well, proud that IMSA was retained in the GRAND-AM-ALMS merger. But he sounded even more proud when talking about how he and his wife had diligently paid back every loan to Bill France Sr.

"We not only had a good partnership with Bill Sr. but we had a good partnership with Annie B., too . . . she was priceless," Bishop said. "And we had no interference from Daytona Beach in running IMSA – at all – other than what we asked for.

"During the July 1976 race at Daytona, we paid back the last pennies to Bill Sr. We called all of the France family members into Bill's office. I said, 'Here's the check for the final payment. How can we ever thank you for backing us, when we were fresh out of ideas on what to do with sports car racing?'

"I remember Annie B. wiping some tears away during the meeting . . . it was a very touching moment."

IMSA now shares a state-of-the-art, eight-floor office complex with NASCAR and the International Speedway Corporation in

Daytona Beach – directly across the street from Daytona International Speedway. The organization has a new logo, a slightly more modern version of the original from 1969. IMSA leadership, starting with Jim France, wants to keep the connection to the past while trying to move sports car racing into the future. IMSA used to be something special. There are people who are certain it will be again, people like President and Chief Operating Officer Scott Atherton, who formally headed the ALMS. Atherton is future-oriented but recognizes fully the emotional equity that comes with the connection to John Bishop and Bill Sr.

Atherton considers Bishop's importance to IMSA akin to Bill Sr.'s importance to NASCAR. Atherton also gives Bishop de facto credit for making him into a true sports car fan, via his founding and operation of IMSA and the scheduling of a popular annual event in Portland, Oregon, near Atherton's hometown of Seattle, Washington.

"Long before I had any direct involvement with the sport or with the industry career-wise, I was a kid in Seattle who would beg, borrow, or steal to try and get to Portland each year when the IMSA circus came to town, to see those cars race around that track," Atherton said. "I'm convinced that was part of an 'inoculation' at a young age that has taken me down the path I've gone career-wise and otherwise. I had heard the name [John Bishop] back in the early days but I didn't have any recognition or understanding about the role he played or how important it was to have a visionary leader behind a sanctioning body in order for it to be successful the way IMSA was at that time."

Atherton went to work for Don Panoz in 2000 at Professional Sports Car Racing. The next year, a new PSCR employee and former NASCAR employee named Dennis Huth suggested to Atherton a return to the roots, meaning a return to the IMSA brand and all the inherent history and legacy that would come with it. Panoz loved the idea and put it on the fast track. IMSA would become linked to the ALMS until the 2014 merger.

And so there you have it: a full-circle situation, with IMSA headquartered in Daytona Beach, just a few miles from where it was conceived during that scotch-fueled conversation in 1969 at Bill Sr.'s home.

Atherton's assessment: "As we like to say regarding IMSA, we are now putting it back the way God intended it to be."

Or if not God, at least John Bishop and Bill France Sr.

At the TUDOR Championship Awards season-ending celebration in October 2014, held at the famed Cipriani event facility on 42nd Street in the heart of midtown Manhattan, there was another merger. IMSA presented the inaugural Bishop-France Awards to its respective class champions. A perpetual Bishop-France trophy with all champions' names inscribed will remain on display in Daytona Beach.

"It's pretty cool," said Bill Sr.'s youngest son, Jim France, IMSA's chairman (and NASCAR vice chairman/executive vice president), several months before the awards show. "We wanted to establish a perpetual trophy that captured the history of IMSA, the history of GRAND-AM, and also the history going back to when my dad and John Bishop started the whole thing.

"John and Peggy Bishop, with the help of my dad and others, really grabbed IMSA up by the bootstraps and got it going all those years ago. They created the high-water mark, and now we're working to get IMSA back to [the level of] those glory days . . . and beyond."

As the 1960s neared an end, Daytona International Speedway was home to four major races a year covering three racing disciplines – sports cars, stock cars, and motorcycles: the 24 Hours of Daytona, the Daytona 500, the Daytona 200, and the Firecracker 400. The speedway's 1959 debut had spurred the construction of several new speedways and by the late '60s only three dirt tracks remained on the schedule of the premier series. (The last dirt race for the top series would be September 30, 1970, at the one-mile State Fairgrounds Speedway oval in Raleigh, North Carolina.)

Daytona's initial success and steady climb in relevance whetted Bill Sr.'s appetite for yet another project: a track that would be even larger and faster than Daytona, the world's largest oval track. The fact that his proposed site was in the middle of nowhere was a slight obstacle, but Bill Sr. was accustomed to overcoming obstacles.

Talladega, Alabama, 50 miles east of Birmingham, 105 miles west of Atlanta. That was the site Bill Sr. chose for a 2.66-mile monster tri-oval with 33-degree banks – two degrees steeper than Daytona's.

"You can't talk about building Talladega without asking whether at that time another 'super track' made sense," John Cassidy said. "Here's why: it made sense to Senior because of his vision of making NASCAR a national sport. Talladega was part of his planned march across the country for NASCAR. Talladega was a very friendly territory to build the next big track, since Bill Sr. had developed quite a good relationship with Alabama Governor George Wallace, who was 'king' in Alabama.

"Bill Sr. was thinking of moving NASCAR westward, and Talladega was westward. It's important to remember that along about this time Bill was having one helluva time with the government in Volusia County, which wanted to change the tax structure to derive more revenue from Daytona International Speedway. So, Bill Sr. wanted to fire a shot across their bow . . . he wanted to say that Daytona wasn't the only place to run a major race. He also took great pains to build the International Motorsports Hall of Fame at Talladega, to send another message that if NASCAR was not treated better in Volusia County they could always pick up and move to Alabama."

The back-channel add-on to the Talladega idea: Annie B. France was strongly opposed. She thought it a horrendous notion, one that rattled her already conservative business sensibilities. And so there is this story about Bill Sr. and Annie B. arguing over the viability of building Talladega Superspeedway, courtesy of Cassidy:

"Bill and Annie B. were not in agreement. The arguments about Talladega went on and on and on, frequently taking place at their breakfast table at their home in Ormond Beach. When it came to Talladega they were diametrically opposed; one of the biggest of Annie B.'s concerns was how Bill intended to get people to attend a race at Talladega, a remote area at best.

"I remember one of those debates. It was a pitched argument. Bill pointed out that Talladega was midway between Atlanta and Birmingham and besides, Governor Wallace was going to build a 16-lane entrance road to the track to help with that, which he did. There are very few 16-lane roads anywhere in the world, by the way.

"This particular, latest debate was grinding to a halt, with

Bill using all those arguments. Annie, meanwhile, said she still was having a hard time figuring out where the spectators were going to come from. At that point, Senior said, 'Anne, one thing I failed to mention to you. If you draw 100-mile circles on the map, one around Talladega and another around Daytona, it will become self-evident. You'll see you'll get more people at Talladega than in Daytona.

"Annie B said, 'I don't get it.'

"Senior replied, 'The reason is simple. Half of the circle around Daytona is in the Atlantic Ocean and fish don't buy tickets!'

"Annie said, 'For heaven's sake' and got up and left. At that point, Senior sensed victory."

Bill Sr., said the late NASCAR vice president Jim Hunter, "was ever the visionary and was bound and determined to build another big track like Daytona – only bigger and better. He originally looked around Spartanburg, South Carolina, but he wasn't going to get any breaks with taxes or anything else, so he went to Alabama and got an audience with the governor, George Wallace, and the governor told Bill Sr., 'You build the track and I'll build a road [that] will help get people in and out.' And he did."

That would be the 16-lane job, Speedway Boulevard, which runs parallel to Interstate 20, which moves traffic east-west between Atlanta and Birmingham. Speedway Boulevard, just off of I-20, delivers people to the race track's front gates and then reconnects with the interstate after several miles.

As Bill Sr. told Jim Foster, for Foster's unpublished biography: "If there are decent highways, people will come to a race."

The Talladega connection led to Bill Sr. becoming more involved with George Wallace. In 1972, Bill ran the Florida campaign for Wallace's unsuccessful bid for the Democratic presidential nomination.

Ground was broken for Talladega on May 23, 1968, and that ground was on the site of the old Anniston Air Force Base, just outside the small burg of Lincoln, Alabama. Again, as with Daytona, it was a rush job, with the Moss-Thornton Construction Company of Birmingham the builder. The target date for the first race was September 14, 1969 – the 44th race on the 54-race Grand National schedule.

Amazingly, it was built in time to host one of the most historic weekends in NASCAR history, a confluence of events that served as a collective metaphor for the changing times surrounding the sport. Old was giving way to new. Alabama International Motor Speedway – the track's name until 1989's switch to Talladega Superspeedway – was definitely new. And for many drivers, it was absolutely frightening when tires started to fail at high speeds on the high banks.

Humpy Wheeler, the former Charlotte Motor Speedway president, was with Firestone in the late 1960s. He recalls initial test runs at Talladega – and immediate trepidation.

"There had been some deaths in racing around that time and there was tremendous unrest in the sport," Wheeler said. "Guys that were supposed to be fearless weren't. Anyway, we went down to Talladega and I was worried about how the tires would hold up, right off. And I told Bill Sr. that. He said, 'It'll be all right.'

"Then I told him that I didn't think the drivers would run the race and, man, he lit up; he was hot as a pistol."

Wheeler's fears were realized. When the tires started to balk, so did the drivers, with the specter of unionization resurfacing for the second time in the decade.

As it just so happened, earlier that season, drivers had semi-organized once more, forming the Professional Drivers' Association (PDA), with Richard Petty as an especially tenuous president. The Talladega situation facilitated a coming-out party for the group.

Soon, talk of boycotting the very first Talladega event was in the air – and rapidly gaining momentum.

"Bill Sr. took the same hard line that he had back in the early '60s," Jim Hunter recalled in 2008. "When faced with the possibility of the PDA boycott, he told the drivers to basically not let the track gate hit them in the ass on their way out."

Whether that was an exact quote is uncertain, but the way the weekend transpired is well-documented:

The growing discontent among drivers; the laps run around the track by a then-59-year-old Bill Sr. and his son Bill Jr. in an attempt to assuage the drivers – an effort discounted as a publicity stunt, with the drivers pointing to the Frances' lap times as being far under what they would be turning in actual race conditions; Bill Sr. telling the drivers that if they were scared they could feel free to go home; drivers enraged at that remark and leaving en masse; and LeeRoy Yarbrough, feeling his oats during the most successful season of his career, flat-out cold-cocking Bill Sr. in the jaw, putting an end to a tumultuous meeting in the garage.

The boycott proceeded, putting Bill France Sr. in a serious bind – and Richard Petty in the middle of it all, which, he says, all these years later, happened somewhat unwittingly.

"Yeah, I wasn't really meaning to be in the middle," Petty said. "It was just one of those things. A bunch of the drivers, we had met in Michigan [that summer] and we went to Big Bill [to] say look, we at least wanted to have a say in NASCAR. We would like more safety and more money and situations where we are involved in what is going on.

"Okay, so two months later we went to Talladega and the first thing you know the track is tearing up tires completely. So we went to Big Bill and said, 'Look, we really want to run this race, it's a new race track and a big deal and all but the tires are not safe. Can we put it off until we can give Firestone and Goodyear a chance to develop a tire for 200 miles an hour?' He said absolutely not, so then all hell broke loose. He was going to run it come hell or high water and from the drivers' standpoint we had seen the tires come apart and they had seen the cars torn up and people get hurt when they did. They wanted to run the race but we wanted to be *physically* able to run the race.

"Anyhow, we had a big conflict, the deal being that the PDA had started the week before. We said we'd get together and have a vote on what we were going to do. So basically that's what happened."

A boycott was one thing. A cancellation was something altogether different, and Bill France Sr. was not about to let that happen. "We have a lot of fans who have traveled a long way to see a race – and we're going to have a race," he told media.

Bill Sr. pieced together a patchwork field of drivers who weren't involved in the boycott plus others from the Grand American Division, which raced the day before the premier series event. And so, on September 14, 1969, a crowd of 64,000 gathered at the gigantic new facility, with many fans attending thanks to free tickets France dispensed. Richard Brickhouse – who withdrew from the PDA to take advantage of what he called a "golden opportunity" – won the first Talladega 500, the triumph coming despite "competition cautions" every 25 laps to enable teams to inspect and change tires if needed. Those cautions belied the fact that competition was fierce, with 37 lead changes, and transpired without a serious incident.

Yes, by God, the race was run. The great Indy-car racer A.J. Foyt, who through the years became one of Bill Sr.'s closest friends in racing, was not surprised.

"I really admired that he told everybody to kiss his ass, that that race was going to run," Foyt said. "You could not back Bill Sr. into a corner, without him coming out swinging. That was something I really respected about him. When he made up his mind about something, that was the way it was gonna be – period, no deviation. I wish we had more people today in the world like that, like with our politicians. I think if we did, the world would be a better place."

Bobby Allison, the leader of the "Alabama Gang" that supplied NASCAR with several decades' worth of personality and performance, was in the thick of the dispute with Bill Sr., albeit with a plan of mediation that got buried under the torrent of ill will.

"I thought we could maybe postpone the race for a week, that would be good," Allison said. "Goodyear was going to make a new tire; they just couldn't get it done quick enough to solve the problem we had that weekend. Yeah, I wish we could've just put it off for a week . . . it was such a gorgeous place to race, good for everyone in racing. But I also understood the idea [Bill Sr. was committed to] of running the race no matter what.

"I got along real well with Bill Sr. almost all of the time but that weekend, well, all of us were pretty uptight."

The end game, as far as racing, was that the drivers returned only four days – FOUR DAYS ! – later to compete in Columbia, South Carolina. Bobby Isaac won the Sandlapper 200, with Petty running second. And the following year, Bill France Sr. welcomed full fields to not one but two Talladega events – April and August, both won by Pete Hamilton, also the Daytona 500 champion in 1970.

Allison says that the return to standard operating procedure so quickly, after what seemed like a potential seismic shift on the NASCAR landscape, was actually not that big of a deal.

"Bill Sr. knew we had to go racing and we knew we had to go racing," Allison said. "We knew we didn't want to have to go out and get newspaper routes or gas-station jobs, that's for sure."

And so another end game was played and won, with memories left brewing in the heart and soul of Bill France Sr. Jousting over the unionization concept while having his authority challenged so severely did not sit well with the man who had started NASCAR. He had taken a hard hit, several hard hits: professionally, personally, and publicly. One newspaper headlined the United Press International report from the event as "Brickhouse Wins Talladega as Czar's Empire Crumbles."

"France had to scrape to fill the field . . . to give the impression, at least, that there was a field on the track," the story read.

Twelve days after Richard Brickhouse became the answer to the ultimate NASCAR trivia question, Bill Sr. turned 60 years old.

It is likely that he felt much older.

CHAPTER 7

The 1970s:

Talladega Aftermath, RJR, and Bill France Jr.

N ASCAR moved into the new decade of the 1970s, its third decade after the rough-and-tumble two years' worth of kick-off seasons in 1948 and '49, and something had been altered. Completely imperceptible to those outside the inner confines of the sport and, chances are, not all that noticeable to very many within NASCAR, the man in charge was a man amid change.

Talladega Superspeedway, Bill France Sr.'s "pet project," as his longtime executive assistant Betty Faulk called it, had gone wrong in September 1969. Terribly wrong. Thing is, it could've been worse

– much worse – were it not for the sheer will and resourcefulness of Bill Sr., who saved the day the best he could. A recurring theme, wasn't it? The problem was that this time, NASCAR's latest problem illustrated a shifting tide within the sport. Granted, the PDA hadn't survived and the concept of unionization within NASCAR had been beaten back yet again, but there was a blow to his psyche this time around. The turmoil at Talladega hit too close to home, and in this case "home" meant the heart and soul of NASCAR's founder.

LeeRoy Yarbrough's haymaker? That didn't help, but it likely had no real lasting effect on Bill Sr. He could take a punch – figuratively and literally. No, Talladega was about blows more telling than those of a physical nature. Big Bill France, all six feet five inches of him, had been brought to his knees, but not by LeeRoy Yarbrough. Instead, it was the anguish of seeing the second-most anticipated event of his career fall apart right before his eyes, and of having the NASCAR garage – *his* garage – treat him with the sort of disrespect he never could've imagined back in December 1947, when he strong-armed an entire sport into buying his notion of something called the National Association for Stock Car Auto Racing.

Disarray and disrespect notwithstanding, Bill Sr. made sure his show would go on at Talladega in '69, just as he made sure NASCAR would go on, starting the very next week in Columbia, South Carolina.

Soon, though, it would be time to let someone else ensure such things. Bill had the perfect young man for the job. A changing of the guard was imminent. Bill Sr. was ready. But first, there was one more big deal to get done, a deal that would alter the landscape far more than one goddamn boycotted race ever could. Bill Sr. was about to get lucky. Of course, in business you often make your own luck. Twenty-plus years of hard work had positioned Bill Sr. – and NASCAR – for the monumental good fortune on the horizon.

By 1970, Junior Johnson had long since given up on driving race cars for a living. His last start was in 1966, a season in which he made only seven starts but captured three poles. The last of his 50 victories had come in 1965, his greatest season, with 13 wins. He ran only 36 of the 55 Grand National races that year, which removed him from championship contention; he ended 12th in points. Johnson retired from driving to become a car owner and ended up as one of the most successful in NASCAR history. In 1970, though, Junior Johnson the car owner needed money. He wasn't alone.

There was money to be had, courtesy of the R.J. Reynolds Tobacco Company (RJR). In April 1970, Congress enacted the Public Health Cigarette Smoking Act of 1969, banning cigarette advertising on television and radio. The act also required an in-your-face health warning to be printed on all packs of cigarettes. With the TV and radio ban in effect, RJR was looking for other avenues to market its products and stem the slowly rising tide against cigarette use in the United States. Somewhat quickly, tobacco had become a sort of "outlaw" product. How appropriate, then, that a former convict, Johnson, would broker a deal to match tobacco up with the outlaw sport of NASCAR, which had its heritage partially linked to moonshiners such as ole Joonyer.

Said Johnson: "It was a match made in heaven."

Junior Johnson, the Great American Deal-Maker! Yes!

Johnson, who turned 83 in June 2014, acquired a knack through the years for reciting the way it all went down as if it was yesterday, about how he approached RJR executives seeking less than a million dollars to sponsor his own race team but that they seemed almost amused at the suggestion, because they had far more money than that to spend – and they were determined, by God, to spend it . . . about how he steered RJR to Bill France Sr.

"When I told them I wanted $850,000 to run my car for a year, they just sorta laughed at me," Johnson said. "So I asked them if that was too much. That's when they told me no, that they were looking for something a lot bigger. They said that with them having to come off of TV, they had $575 million that they had to do something with . . . I said, 'Lord have mercy, you need to go to Bill France Sr. about sponsoring NASCAR's whole deal,' I still thought I was going to get some money too, but as it got down close to making the deal, RJR realized that it would be too much of a conflict of interest for them to sponsor an individual car and the series, too. So, I lost out there."

Johnson handed the ball off and Bill Sr. took it across the goal line, resulting in a deal that set the standard for sports marketing over the next 33 years.[*]

In 1971, the partnership began with RJR sponsoring races of 250 miles or longer now designated as "Winston Cup" events in support of RJR's main brand of smokes. The next year saw the full-fledged RJR commitment and the accompanying start of the "Modern Era." That label actually had nothing to do with the

---

[*] RJR and NASCAR ended their partnership after the 2003 season, with NEXTEL Communications becoming the new main sponsor of NASCAR's top series.

revolutionary new sponsorship that would pour millions of dollars into NASCAR for the next three-plus decades; it had everything to do with the shortening of the Grand National Division. Gone was the outdated old-school approach of racing virtually anywhere, anytime if a date was available. That willy-nilly arrangement was replaced by a more manageable, reasonable slate – 48 races down to 31. The reduction also featured the adjustment of making every race at least 250 miles, to give all of them a more "premium" feel that would of course facilitate the increased marketing and promotional efforts that RJR was going to lacquer on in multiple coats starting with a new name: the NASCAR Winston Cup Grand National Division.

The top series would not be called the NASCAR Winston Cup Series until 1986. Worth noting: Winston also signed on as entitlement sponsor for NASCAR's Western tour and its grassroots short-track level. The NASCAR Winston West Series operated from 1974–2003; that splendidly competitive series, which showcased many stars who did not compete on a national level, still exists in the form of the NASCAR K&N Pro Series West. As far as the grassroots short-track scene goes, the NASCAR Weekly Winston Racing Series ran from 1982–2001 and now thrives as the NASCAR Whelen All-American Series, which has given rise to many of today's top-rung stars such as Dale Earnhardt Jr., Greg Biffle, and Clint Bowyer. This relationship also facilitated the RJR sponsorship of the IMSA GT series being assembled by Bill Sr. and John Bishop.

From the 2010 biography, *Bill France Jr.: The Man Who Made NASCAR*:

Collectively, this was the most successful sponsorship in the history of motorsports, with much of NASCAR's success and growth linked to Winston's involvement – and the secure, almost family like relationship between the sponsor and the sanctioning body. That relationship, like so many other aspects of the sport, was established by Bill France Sr. – and embellished by Bill France Jr.

Added Junior Johnson: "It all just fell the right way . . . at the right time and in the right place."

There really is no way to exaggerate the importance of what RJR's involvement meant to the expansion of NASCAR, or to the expansion of the viability of Bill France Jr. as a leader of a sport that was going from old to new, dirt to asphalt, and in myriad other distinctions and directions.

Likewise, one cannot exaggerate the importance the more modern sensibility of Bill France Jr. played during this period. The RJR deal was perhaps NASCAR's first major business situation that involved Bill Jr. more than it did Bill Sr.

"RJR brought a more disciplined, business approach to the sport, for many years providing most of the marketing and public relations support for the sport," said former RJR executive Cliff Pennell.

The term missing from the above quote is "modern," and that's what it was really all about when it came to RJR entering the fray. More money brought more of everything, but mainly, front and center, was an increased media relations presence that spilled over into the sports car realm with RJR's Camel brand being attached to the IMSA GT series organized by Bill

In 1937, Bill France Sr. was both a driver and a promoter for the beach-road course stock car races in Daytona Beach, Florida.

Bill Sr. (c) worked on the pit crew for driver Joel Thorne (r) at the Indianapolis 500 in 1938 and 1939. Like most racing enthusiasts, Bill Sr. was enamored with the 500.

Bill Sr. had a tough time giving up his racing aspirations, but gradually the business side of the sport made more sense to him.

Poised – and posed – for success.

Before he founded NASCAR, the always-dapper Bill France Sr. headed the National Championship Stock Car Circuit, which operated in 1946 and 1947, prior to NASCAR's founding in December 1947.

Daytona Beach's beach-road course was extremely popular in 1941, but would soon fall dormant due to World War II and the fear of German submarines attacking Atlantic shoreline communities.

In 1956, Bill Sr. welcomed Bill Jr. home after his stint in the Navy.

Bill Sr. retained an affinity for the old days of "big-car racing," the label that was given to Indy-car open-wheel competitions for years.

Beauty queens and beach racing were a perfect fit for Bill Sr.'s promotions in the 1950s.

Bill Sr. and the legendary Curtis Turner were hell on wheels in the 1950 *Carrera Panamericana* – the "Mexican Road Race" – until their Nash broke relatively early in the event.

Big Bill France, a promoter through and through, knew the value of a good old-fashioned publicity stunt, such as hopping on an elephant to advertise upcoming events at Daytona International Speedway.

Ready to roll: Bill France Sr. sits at the wheel of the Daytona 500 pace car in 1960, the second year for the "Great American Race."

In 1954, a pinstriped Big Bill France cut a dashing figure in the middle of NASCAR's first decade.

All business: Bill Sr. at his desk at NASCAR's Daytona Beach, Florida, headquarters in 1966.

In the 1950s, Bill France Sr. was a "former" racer –
but he still looked the part.

France Sr. and John Bishop. Henceforth, NASCAR would promote its stories to media outlets throughout the country in an aggressive fashion designed to reach not only race-market media but national media. It was one more step in taking NASCAR beyond its Southeastern roots. RJR sought to grow a sport, but also in the process to sell cigarettes to millions of core stock car fans, casual stock car fans, and anyone else who got within a stone's throw of a race track hosting a NASCAR event.

There's another iconic picture, from January 10, 1972. Bill France Sr., 62 years old but looking older, handing a set of keys to his son Bill Jr., 38 years old but looking younger. The staged photo was meant to represent the symbolic passing of the torch – in this case, a passing of the keys – to the next generation of NASCAR leadership.

With the new Winston sponsorship in place, with Talladega Superspeedway entering its third season of hosting two high-drama races a year, with the Daytona 500 growing each and every year, not to mention RJR also sponsoring the new IMSA sports car venture via its Camel brand, Bill Sr. had decided to take a step back. Not really "down," mind you, but certainly into the background.

It was time. Talladega 1969 had stuck to the older man.

"That had to take some zip out of Bill Sr.," Jim Hunter said years later. "It *had* to. What a letdown . . . it had to be a tremendous letdown and it might well have triggered him to turn things over to his son when he did."

The accomplished journalist Jonathan Ingram leans toward a more "collective effect" theory to explain Bill Sr. leaving the

NASCAR presidency when he did. While Talladega does make sense as a potential catalyst, Ingram points out that "a bright man usually has more than one motivation, especially in business.

"I would suggest Bill Jr. was ready, and that Bill Sr. was confident that he had the 'horse sense,' as he called it, to do the job.

"And, I would also say that the 1960s (in general) just wore him out. He got Daytona up and running and into the black fairly quickly, which was good, but . . ."

The battles with the manufacturers, which were regular occurrences even during steady times, and the recurring threat of unionization were two more catalysts, Ingram says, adding, "and I do think it is a very good perspective to go back to the [Horatio Alger analogy] to see that Bill Sr. was an amazing man. He wanted to be shoulder-to-shoulder with everyone but he also wanted them to see him standing above them at times, as a leader. In his heart, Bill Sr. believed in himself as 'that guy' who was 'one of them,' who wanted to make the sport of stock car racing better for the people who participated and the people who bought the tickets. That's what ultimately drove him. In that respect, with Talladega, after all the effort to get the track up and going and then, when you factor in the horrors he felt over unions . . . well, you could never really break Big Bill's heart but Talladega in '69 was really a blow to the solar plexus.

"Again, with the NASCAR garage, he saw himself as a guy who really thought he was one of them and then, all of a sudden, he was on the outside looking in. Of course whenever someone wields that much power like he did, over time, that [sort of development] is not unusual [at some point]. But [yielding the presidency] said a lot about him, because we've seen a lot of examples of others in racing, that even though the environment has changed, they keep fighting, saying they're not going to give up. And in cases with people such as Darrell Waltrip, A.J. Foyt, and 'The King,' they would say they could still win races when in fact that really wasn't the case. So yes, it said a lot about Bill Sr. to say it was time to take a back seat – after being 'Big Bill' all the time. That wasn't an easy thing to do. And a lot of times in family businesses people in those situations don't often say 'it's time.' Bill Sr. did, though.

"But, it's also important to remember here that it's not like he threw the keys to NASCAR on the desk and told people he'd be back at the marina on his boat, cooking bacon and spaghetti, if they needed him. It wasn't like that at all. Bill Jr. was ready to be the decision-maker but Big Bill was ready to guide him, particularly on the technical side, with things like the politics, things like the templates! Because Bill Jr. had some things to learn there. I imagine Big Bill was involved in vetting things [in those areas] with Bill Jr. but I'm sure he did it in a way that didn't undermine Bill Jr. And I can tell you, he never did anything to undermine his son publicly. In public, it was Bill Jr. who was 'in charge.'"

So, the bummer of Talladega '69 notwithstanding, perhaps the handoff was simply a natural progression that would've transpired at approximately the same time, no matter what.

NASCAR president Mike Helton: "I don't know that anything really wore him out. I think Bill Sr. just had a sense for 'seeing around the corner,' which is something that Bill Jr. and Jim France both inherited, quite frankly. I think Bill Sr. had that sense . . . and in the 1970s, after all he had done . . .

"Launching the sport in the 1940s . . .

"Building it up in the 1950s and '60s . . .

"Organizing it and being challenged by different stakeholders along the way during that period . . .

"Accomplishing the construction of Daytona . . .

"Accomplishing the construction of Talladega . . .

"And then, with Bill Jr. coming of age . . .

"I'm sure part of it was he was worn down some, but I think he saw that Bill Jr. was going to be the right catalyst, at that moment, for the future of NASCAR."

Jim Hunter: "It was a different time in the industry, without a doubt, requiring different people skills, when Bill Jr. took over."

Translation: different meant listening, and Bill France Jr., despite an outwardly gruff manner that was regularly spiced by well-timed profanity, was a far better listener than his father. Which seems odd on the surface, because Bill Jr. was always perceived as a rough-talking, hard-ass, his-way-or-the-highway boss when in reality he was far more of a consensus-builder than his father.

In Bill Sr.'s defense, however, who needed a consensus? In his days as NASCAR's president, he was judge and jury. Remember Richard Petty: "It was his game . . . his rules . . . that's the way it was."

And starting in 1972, it was largely Bill Jr.'s game. There was the requisite outcry, including the remarkable development that many in the garage who were ready to give Bill Sr. the boot at Talladega in 1969 suddenly were talking like the sport simply could not go on without him. Much of the trepidation had to do with Bill Jr.'s age and his perceived lack of seasoning. Such fears were way off the mark. Bill Jr. had been immersed in the family business since the 1950s; he had experienced every facet of the sport of NASCAR, from ticket sales and concessions to front-office decisions that had multi-million dollar implications.

He had a good teacher.

In '72, "Bill Jr. had been given the reins by his dad to sort of fashion the sport as he was taking over," Helton said. "And at the time you had all of these new elements that were happening. You had all these 'early-on phases' the sport was going through and that Bill Jr. was working on, fashioning."

What Jonathan Ingram points out in amusing fashion, Mike Helton concurs with. Bill Sr. indeed did not hand over the NASCAR presidency and take off on an extended fishing trip. After all, he still led the International Speedway Corporation, which ran both Daytona International Speedway and Talladega Superspeedway. And, after all, he was Big Bill France.*

There is a story that colorfully illustrates the two Bills in action in those early years after Bill Jr. became NASCAR's president. It is a story made all the more interesting because the setting is Pole Day for the 1976 Daytona 500 – a race considered by many fans as the best of the 500 lot. The tale has been told and retold countless times by journalist Ed Hinton, in person and in print. It is especially showcased in Hinton's seminal NASCAR book, *Daytona*, but also in his 2013 *France Family Saga* on ESPN.com.

---

* His continued involvement in NASCAR and support of his son was not unlike what would happen in 2003 when Brian France replaced Bill Jr. as NASCAR's chairman and CEO; Bill Jr. actually switched offices with the new, third-generation leader of NASCAR, but continued to keep regular office hours and be available for counsel.

It is being told, albeit in abridged form, one more time in these pages because, well, it's too damn good of a story to leave out. It wafts from the surreal to the very real, placing both Bills at the center of a storm threatening to blow through the biggest race of the season.

On February 8, 1976, the Daytona 500 time trials ended with A.J. Foyt and Darrell Waltrip on the front row, meaning they would start on the two poles for the following week's "Twin 125s" qualifying races. Those races, which still are run these days, although at a 150-mile length, annually set the starting grid for the 500 – with the exception of the front row, which gets "locked in" on Pole Day.

A.J. and D.W. thought they were locked in – at least until the post-race inspection went south and holy hell was raised, mainly by Foyt, who Hinton says was marching through the old Daytona garage area yelling "fuck 'em" and threatening to pack up and leave town if some official decided he was going to take the pole from him due to an alleged rule violation. Post-qualifying, Foyt and Waltrip were both suspected of using nitrous oxide to provide extra horsepower boosts.

Hinton remembers an A.J. Foyt "ready to whip somebody's ass," with the prime candidate being Bill France Jr.

There in the garage, Foyt had his left arm on Bill Jr.'s shoulders, with his right index finger jabbing into the face of NASCAR's relatively new president. But Hinton also remembers something else about the scene, something that has stayed with him all these years later.

Says Hinton: "Billy France never blinked. And from that day forward I don't think he ever blinked in that kind of situation."

Hinton's recounting of the scene continues with a description of a dramatic arrival in the garage by Bill Sr., then four years removed from NASCAR's presidency but still respected. Perhaps a good way to describe the landscape was that Bill Jr. was the president and his father was the attorney general, sergeant-at-arms and de facto enforcer, if needed.

On this February afternoon, he was needed.

Bill Sr. arrived in a Pontiac Bonneville, racing through the pit gate, snaking through the too-narrow alleys of the speedway's old garage area, and finally parking right next to the steel door to the inspection bay. He left the engine to the car running and the driver's side door slung open, as if his stay would be brief.

The tale continues with the description of a surprisingly contrite Foyt emerging from the inspection bay, with Bill France Sr.'s arm snaked around his shoulders, muttering something akin to "yes sir." The disqualifications were going to stand, per Bill Sr.

Hinton says that years later when he asked Foyt why his mood had been altered so notably and so quickly by the appearance of Bill Sr., Foyt said it was out of respect for the founder of NASCAR. "He's just a good man . . . ," Foyt said.

Foyt confirms the day's events – and his personal feelings about Bill Sr. In the spring of 2014, holding court at his Indy-car hauler at the Long Beach Grand Prix, Foyt talked about what sounded like his own podium of respect, with his father at the top, flanked by Bill Sr. and the late owner of Indianapolis Motor Speedway, Tony Hulman.

"Bill Sr. calmed things down [that day]," Foyt said. "I used to be sorta hot-headed sometimes when I was young. He said some things to me, told me some things to do."

What Hinton called the "damnedest Daytona 500 week" was only beginning with Pole Day. Third-place qualifier Dave Marcis also got disqualified, which gave the pole to one Ramo Stott – trivia question material, for certain.

The 1976 Daytona 500 itself ended with arguably the most dramatic finish in the race's history. NASCAR's two great champions, Richard Petty and David Pearson, both a bit south of their primes but nonetheless engaging in a rivalry that personified the 1970s for NASCAR, locked horns in a last-lap duel that created a several-minute milestone for the sport's history.

Going into the 1976 Daytona 500, they had finished 1-2 a remarkable 57 times over a 13-year span. In the closing laps, as things sorted out with the finish approaching, the 58th looked assured.

But as far as the actual order – that was a different story.

As the last lap began, Petty led, as he had for the previous 12 laps. Utilizing the tried-and-true slingshot move of Daytona's yesteryear, Pearson's Mercury passed Petty's Dodge on the backstretch going into Turn 3. On into the fourth turn and Petty re-took the lead by going low, but then inexplicably shot to the right, pinching Pearson off. The right rear of the Dodge touched the left front of the Mercury, and . . . the rest is the best kind of NASCAR lore: real, indisputable, and incredible. The real stuff.

Pearson crashed into the wall after the contact and somehow had the presence of mind to keep his clutch-riding left foot jammed to the floor, an act that kept the Mercury running. Within seconds, Petty crashed into the wall as well. As Pearson was ricocheting backward onto pit road, Petty was spinning into the infield.

Petty's Dodge stopped, 20 yards or so from the finish line.

It was not running. And it wouldn't. But Pearson's Mercury? It puttered through the grass, just past the Dodge, turned right and crossed the finish line, giving Pearson the sole Daytona 500 victory of his career.

What a race!

What a week!

Check it out. There's something about the ninth year of a decade when it comes to NASCAR.

1949 – The first Strictly Stock race

1959 – The first Daytona 500

1969 – The first Talladega Superspeedway race

1979 – The most significant race in NASCAR history – the 1979 Daytona 500, the event that launched NASCAR into the national consciousness of America's sports fans, thanks to a combination of factors, some planned, some serendipitous.

On the planned side, '79 was the first Daytona 500 set for a full, live television broadcast. CBS was the network and legend-in-the-works Ken Squier was the voice.

Serendipity? Try a massive late-winter snowstorm that blanketed the eastern portion of the country, including many of the nation's largest metropolitan areas. This was a huge storm, its effects stretching as far south as South Carolina. Simply put, February 19, 1979, was a great day to stay inside, and since this was long before cable or satellite TV, there basically was a 25 per cent chance of people tuning in, even if accidentally.

Those who were tuned in saw the latest and one of the greatest finishes in 500 history, which had absolutely nothing to do with Richard Petty taking the checkered flag to win the 500 for the sixth time in his career.

Petty winning the Daytona 500 a footnote? Believe it.

It was "The Fight," you see.

We'll get to that shortly. First, a sidebar: Daytona Beach had its own weather problems on race day. Rain threatened to postpone the first-ever full live broadcast. Things looked dismal. This was a job for Bill France Sr.

More lore: Bill Sr. got on top of the speedway's press box/scoring tower to talk to the Lord, the sky, Thor, somebody or something to clear the skies – and it worked, adding to the legacy of Big Bill being able to conjure up "chamber of commerce" weather on the days of NASCAR's biggest events. Bocky Bockoven, for years NASCAR's race director, will confirm another story about that day, about how Bill Sr. drove north of Daytona, saw clearing skies and phoned Bockoven with the news that his personal radar looked promising. When Bockoven said it seemed to be clearing in Daytona as well, Senior said, "Let's meet in the middle and race," or something to that effect.

Bockoven, who turned 82 in February 2014, is retired and living in Ormond Beach. He chuckles at that memory. "Yeah, Bill would do that kind of thing sometimes," he says.

On to the race, which played out before the captive TV audience that ended up producing a 10.5 rating, equating to 15,140,000 viewers. That stood as the live broadcast record for viewership until 2001.

In addition to the eloquent and educational tones of Squier –

which spoke not only to core fans but also casual fans and first-time NASCAR watchers, even – CBS had veteran racer David Hobbs in the booth. Two-time NASCAR champion Ned Jarrett and Brock Yates worked the pits. CBS also used the event to debut the in-car camera and the track-level camera, the latter giving viewers a true sight-and-sound experience of the thundering stock cars.

The experience people remember, though, had nothing do with engines.

Last lap: Donnie Allison led Cale Yarborough. They had separated from the rest of the field. Up ahead, five laps down, was Bobby Allison. Yarborough went for the slingshot pass, starting in the backstretch, coming into Turn 3, down low. Allison blocked, determined to capture a career-defining victory. Their Oldsmobiles collided several times and eventually, inevitably, both race cars went careening into the outside wall before drifting back down the banking into the infield grass.

Petty, A.J. Foyt, and Darrell Waltrip motored by, with Petty winning the surprise three-man duel.

Meanwhile, all hell was about to break loose.

Bobby Allison ended his cool-down lap by pulling off the track and into the grass, *partially* to check on his brother. Donnie Allison and Yarborough were arguing, but in truth, were about argued out. Allison, involved in a Lap 32 wreck earlier in the day with Yarborough, took the window net down after pulling to a stop. Immediately Yarborough was in his face, first with words, then with his helmet. Bobby Allison exploded out of his car and, as he has described countless times, Yarborough "started beating on my fists with his nose."

Classic.

As were the images of the scuffle, which show Allison grabbing Yarborough's leg after Yarborough had attempted to kick him. Unfortunately for Donnie Allison, images also show him in the melee holding a helmet. He wasn't fighting, but it sure did look like it. And all those millions of brand-new, coveted, first-time fans of the Daytona 500? They got an ill-fated first impression of Alabama Gang member Donnie Allison, a good ole boy who got blamed for the wreck and the fight, and never won another NASCAR race.

CHAPTER 8

The 1980s:

Closing Laps

N ASCAR is a force of nature.

Seriously.

It replenishes and renews itself.

Bill Sr. begat Bill Jr.

Darlington Raceway begat Daytona International Speedway.

Lee Petty begat Richard Petty who in turn begat David Pearson, Bobby Allison, and Cale Yarborough.

Yarborough begat Darrell Waltrip and Bill Elliott.

And around that time, Dale Earnhardt came along.

Earnhardt won three of his seven NASCAR championships during the 1980s, the same as Waltrip. And the decade also saw Allison, Terry Labonte, and Rusty Wallace win titles. And Elliott, the "anti-Earnhardt" who cashed in on R.J. Reynolds' million-dollar bonus in 1985 for winning three of four designated "major" races – the Daytona 500, the Winston 500 at Talladega, and the Southern 500 at Darlington. (The other "major" was the World 600 at Charlotte Motor Speedway.).

Elliott, though, was a different cat, a guy who separated himself from his rivals off the track as well, even though he was able to win only one championship, in 1988. Between 1984 and 1998 he won NASCAR's Most Popular Driver Award five consecutive times. (After a two-year run by Darrell Waltrip, Elliott would win the award in 10 consecutive years. Dale Earnhardt won posthumously in 2001. Elliott then won for a final time in 2002; Dale Earnhardt Jr. has been the winner every year since.)

Elliott is from Dawsonville, Georgia – moonshine country. And so, his first nickname developed: "Awesome Bill from Dawsonville." The 1985 season gave him another: "Million Dollar Bill." If Mark Martin is indeed the greatest NASCAR driver to never win the premier series championship, Elliott could be the greatest to win the title only once. He finished second three times, including in 1992 when Alan Kulwicki edged him by merely 10 points.

Somewhat hard to believe is the fact that Dale Earnhardt's popularity was not universal when he was first making his mark. Fans had a love-hate relationship with Earnhardt long before he became known as "The Intimidator." Respect, though, ran well ahead of acclaim in the early part of his career, starting with the

1979 Daytona 500 when Earnhardt, a rookie, led 10 laps and spent much of the day tucked in tight behind the other leaders, showing an immediate aptitude for the art of drafting, plus the courage and nerve needed to do so for several hours at a time on the high banks of Daytona.

Earnhardt, from the hardscrabble mill town of Kannapolis, North Carolina, was the son of Ralph Earnhardt, considered one of the greatest short-track racers of any era. On September 26, 1973, Ralph Earnhardt died of a heart attack, leaving dreams – and certainly driving potential – unfulfilled, at least when it came to NASCAR's highest level. In 1956, he won the championship of the NASCAR Sportsman division – the precursor of what evolved into the Busch Series, the Nationwide Series, and now the NASCAR XFINITY series. He made 51 starts in NASCAR's premier series from 1956–64; in '61 he finished 17th in the final points. Real racers knew how good Ralph Earnhardt was – and could've been. His son benefited, getting considerable respect right out of the box due to his lineage.

Dale Earnhardt won Rookie of the Year honors in 1979 and then started the '80s by capturing the series championship, driving for Rod Osterlund. He was not the Man in Black in those days but rather the Man in Yellow and Blue, the paint scheme for his No. 2 Chevrolet with Osterlund, then for the No. 15 Ford he drove for Bud Moore, and finally for the No. 3 he started driving for Richard Childress in '84. The "3" didn't go black until '88, with the start of the eventually iconic GM Goodwrench sponsorship. After a five-year drought, Earnhardt won back-to-back titles in 1986–87, developing a rough and sometimes outlandish style that won over fans and detractors in great numbers. It was over-aggressive driving honed to a fine, good ole art. Earnhardt didn't slam you outta the way as much as nudge you, but almost invariably it didn't matter; if someone was obstructing his path to the front, they likely were going to feel Earnhardt on their rear bumper at some point.

NASCAR had its new superstar.

Fireball Roberts notwithstanding, history shows that Bill France Sr. actually was the *first* NASCAR superstar and in 1980, when he turned 71, he was slowing down, just as the sport he had founded was inexorably accelerating, arcing toward the vision he had laid out years beforehand. There were signs that something was amiss, something beyond the normal effects of aging. This exacerbated what would have been a tough period for Big Bill France even if he had been in the best of health.

"There is nothing more challenging to a highly successful person who has achieved a great deal of notoriety and is front-page copy than to all of a sudden have diminished responsibilities," said Bill Sr.'s longtime friend and legal counsel John Cassidy. "Let's consider, for sake of comparison, George W. Bush. He serves as president for two terms. Then he's no longer president. He has a personal code that says that only in exceptional instances will he comment on current events affecting his successor, and I admire him for that. He's taking lessons on portrait painting, he's playing golf. He's relaxing. He's handling the situation.

"But there's a difference between him and Bill Sr. . . . Bill Sr. wanted to be king and he always wanted to be king. He just enjoyed being king – his way or the highway! George W., I'm not that sure he wanted to be president all that badly or that he enjoyed it all that much, nor do I think he was unhappy to leave Washington. I think he's very happy and has shown a lot of restraint. He's 'off the flypaper' now and wants to stay off it. Senior fought it, though. He didn't have that same kind of mentality. But all the while he was fighting it, you saw Bill France Jr. being the ultimately gracious son, just dealing with it, dealing with it. They were in a period of transition. And yes, Bill Sr. did some things that would've been better if he didn't do, but it wasn't in Bill Jr.'s heart to 'dust him off.' He was an absolutely committed son, to his father."

Bill Sr.'s wife Anne Bledsoe France, turned 76 in 1980. She was not slowing down, destined to do important work, nearly to the end of her life. Which is why it seems appropriate to choose her last decade to fully explore everything she meant to Bill Sr.'s vision.

Their oldest son Bill Jr. put it this way: "While my dad was climbing high to reach his far-out goals, Mom held the ladder. Dad certainly had visions and dreams. Mom, however, was his reality."

She was everybody's reality – from the outset. Her propensity for running a tight financial ship never dropped off from the days in the late 1930s when she kept the books for the service station Bill Sr. opened in Daytona Beach after leaving Sax Lloyd's dealership. As NASCAR grew, so did her influence – and control, which was necessary. Bill Sr.'s propensities, shall we say, did not run parallel to his wife's in financial matters.

"Mom," Jim France says, "was the glue that held everything together. Dad was the promotional genius. Mom was in the background making sure all the bills got paid and also making sure that if any extra money came in, that Dad didn't piss it all away."

Annie B. served as the first secretary and treasurer not only of NASCAR but the International Speedway Corporation. Along the way, she also ran the ticket office at Daytona International Speedway.

"She was tough, too," said her daughter-in-law Betty Jane France. "I used to help out in the ticket office and one day, as we got down close to five o'clock, I couldn't get my ledger to balance out. I was off – like nine cents as I recall. Nine cents! So, I told her I would figure it out the next day. She told me, 'No, you'll figure it out today before you leave.' I couldn't believe it. But I stayed, and I did figure it out. I still balance my own checkbook by hand, down to the last penny. I think it's because of her . . . I really do."

NASCAR Hall of Famer Rex White says that even amid the male-dominated, old-school atmosphere of the 1950s and '60s, Annie B. commanded respect.

"She is someone who deserves a lot of the credit for what NASCAR became," said White. "And she definitely didn't let Bill Sr. get away with anything [financially]."

In 1983, old school met the new guard. Lesa France, the daughter of Betty Jane and Bill Jr., had graduated from Duke University. She chose to continue her education under the tutelage of her grandmother, in effect following the leads of her grandparents and parents, who learned the NASCAR industry first and foremost at less-than-glamorous levels. Lesa had already done an "internship" of sorts, working in the speedway ticket office when she was in high school. She knew what she was getting into.

Juanita Epton – they still call her by her nickname, Lightnin', even though she turned 94 in 2014 – worked in the ticket office with Annie B. for years before Lesa arrived. She works in the ticket office still! And her memory is sharp when recalling Annie B. in 1983.

"To think that her granddaughter was going to help carry on what the family started, it just made her so happy," Epton said. "Lesa turned out to be a true France on the job – right off the bat. And immediately she was one of the gang. She came in and just tackled her job. She did whatever she was supposed to do and never pulled rank on anybody."

The stories about Annie B. France are as legendary in their own right as any others you might come across.

She stuffed money and uncashed personal checks in shoe boxes on race days, during times when walk-up crowds comprised the vast majority of ticket sales. She had to stuff it somewhere. She refused to accept credit card sales well into the 1980s, a stance that seems inexplicable for a growing enterprise. She figured that if fans could not afford to buy tickets with cash, they needn't use credit. Didn't seem right. Think about that: Who knows how much money this cost the International Speedway Corporation over the years? In the late 1980s, her granddaughter finally convinced "Gram" to accept plastic.

"It wasn't easy," Lesa said. "Gram was a skeptic."

"Annie B. didn't think the money from the Daytona 500, or any race for that matter, was the company's to keep until the races had been run," then-NASCAR vice president Jim Hunter said in a 2008 interview. "She would always have all kinds of money and checks just sitting around. It seemed a little strange but she had a solid reason for doing things that way and you had to admire her for it, no matter what your personal feelings were about how she should've been conducting business. Annie simply would not cash the checks or spend the money until the people had been given the product they'd paid for, not until the race they had paid to see had actually been run. The way she saw it, the money still belonged to the fans until the race had been held. It was a principle thing."

She kept two sets of financial books, then urged employees to share that secret with her and not let Bill Sr. know.

Lesa France Kennedy: "He did like to enjoy."

Annie B. made her husband actually fill out forms to be reimbursed for his business expenses. Consider the image of a six-foot-five Bill Sr. sheepishly pushing a piece of paper across a desk to his wife, hoping not to catch too much hell about whatever numbers were on the page.

"That really happened," Hunter said. "She really kept an eye on Bill Sr. and all the money. She did not believe in spending money unless it had to be spent."

Lesa Kennedy and Jim France attribute Annie B.'s approach to her having experienced the Depression, to having to raise Bill Jr. during those times. There is something else to consider. The Depression years' tough times may have seemed like relatively great times to Annie B. When she was a teenager, both of her parents died within months of each other. Six siblings were left behind, but they stayed together – something that would never happen today. Annie B. and her sister Juanita Bledsoe Miller became especially inseparable.

Jim France: "Mom came out of the Depression environment and her simplistic solution was to not encourage fans to go out on a limb but rather encourage them to pay as you go when it came to buying race tickets. I think Mom's feeling was that to have fans paying for tickets with cash was a good controlling discipline that kept people from getting in trouble financially."

The more extensive the research, the more compelling is the evidence that Anne Bledsoe France not only was important to the growth of NASCAR and the International Speedway Corporation, she was absolutely vital.

Journalist Ed Hinton: "I am absolutely convinced that without Anne Bledsoe France, without her controlling the purse strings, NASCAR might not have lasted. Bill Sr., left to his own devices, might have been too extravagant and spent himself out of business. When you talk about the foundations of NASCAR, it's sort of like a ladder; Big Bill was one leg of the ladder and Annie was the other. I am real big on Annie B. being recognized as a critical force in NASCAR."

Hinton was the most vocal media supporter for Annie B. getting a general nomination for the NASCAR Hall of Fame, which happened in 2012. Then, in 2014, came another hall nomination that looked more conducive to her actually being selected. She was one of five nominees for the first Landmark Award for Outstanding Contributions to NASCAR. The other four: Martinsville Speedway founder H. Clay Earles; the old car owner and Bill Sr. financier, Raymond Parks; R.J. Reynolds impresario Ralph Seagraves; and legendary broadcaster Ken Squier. Later in the year, Annie B. was announced as the award's inaugural winner.

The insidious nature of Alzheimer's disease is such that often the effects are so gradual, so incremental, that the inevitable is somewhat obscured. But that inevitability is undeniable, especially when what once was gradual accelerates suddenly and dramatically.

In the first half of the 1980s, the France family began dealing with the inevitable: Alzheimer's was taking their patriarch – NASCAR's patriarch – from them.

Eventually it would take his life.

In 1983 and '84, Annie B. started mentioning to friends that Bill Sr. was tiring a lot quicker than in past years. She also noticed that he was having some short-term memory problems. "But I guess we all do," she said at the time.

Bill Sr. still went to the office daily, ostensibly to oversee operation of the International Speedway Corporation, but it was mostly to stay busy. With each passing year, instances like his involvement at the '76 Daytona 500 were less and less likely. And as for the office, in the late 1980s, at the behest of his two sons, Bill Sr.'s entire office was in effect reconstructed almost perfectly at NASCAR's facility on Ballough Road near down-town Daytona Beach, across the street from the Halifax River – not far from the very first place he and Annie B. lived in Daytona Beach in 1934. His office at the speedway was upstairs and had become increasingly difficult for him to access as his mobil-ity diminished. The idea was to create virtually the exact same setting so he would be comfortable day to day, being in familiar surroundings.*

Betty Faulk, once a scorer for Fireball Roberts, became Bill Sr.'s secretary in 1964 after several years of assisting Judy Jones,

---

* Years later, Bill Sr.'s office would be reconstructed – right down to the 1950s-era wood-paneled walls – a second time and put on display at the ISC Archives facility near Daytona International Speedway. The reproduction, overseen by Jim France, was done with the accuracy of a movie set. The same closet doors, an ottoman, a storage trunk used by Annie B., a hat rack with a collection of his

Bill Sr.'s first secretary. She remembers being asked by Bill Jr. to start working out of Ballough Road.

"When he called me in," Faulk said, "I thought at first that they might be trying to get rid of me, but instead, Bill Jr. told me he wanted me to be down at Ballough so his father would have someone with him all the time who he knew, someone he would have a connection [with]. I represented his life . . . before. A woman named Joy Burke took care of him physically. His personal driver Cap (a former boat captain named Don Stephanson), would help as well. Senior would come down to Ballough every day just like he was coming to work [like the old days].

"Although, when I think back, I'm not sure how often he really recognized me. But sometimes when we ate lunch and I'd have to tell him to finish, I'd yell at him kind of, you know, 'Bill, you have to finish your lunch!' In the office at the speedway he had always been the boss of course, but that point, I could do that. Well, he'd look at me, and kind of squint his eyes. He knew who it was, yelling at him. And he tried so hard to tell me . . .

"Yes . . . it was hard to see. Senior . . . well, everyone just loved him. He was just 'it.' It broke your heart to see someone with his mental capabilities in that situation. He wasn't really an old man at all; some people at 65 are older than other people at 82, but he had that condition. He had a lot still to give but just couldn't get it out."

---

unique hats – and a globe that Bill Sr. always had sitting on his desk, which opened up on the top to reveal . . . a whiskey dispenser. When the archives moved to its current location adjacent to the speedway credentials office, there wasn't room for another re-creation. There was talk for a while of the office being set again at the NASCAR Hall of Fame. Currently the office is "deconstructed," with various items locked away in a back corner of the archives.

The late 1980s were not an easy time. The man Juanita Epton described as "like meeting a mountain" was approaching his final years – the closing laps, as it were.

A series of letters Annie B. wrote to her sister Juanita Bledsoe Miller, now archived in the NASCAR Hall of Fame, serve as snapshots of her increasing concern about her husband's health and well-being as the 1980s wore on.

July 1, 1984: *"Bill fell while pushing an airplane and injured his shoulder. He is supposed to keep it immobile and the Drs. think it will heal without any pins or surgery."*

August 1, 1987: *"Bill's memory continues to get worse and there doesn't seem to be any way of improving it. – His general health is good – but it's pretty difficult to function very well when you can't remember 2 minutes."*

October 13, 1990: *"Bill gets worse all the time. His disposition is very, very good. He sleeps well and eats well. It takes him a long time to eat. There's no need for him to rush."*

No need for him to rush. . . .

Finally.

CHAPTER 9

The 1990s:
Saying Goodbye

J ohn Cassidy remembers the demise of the grand old man from his perspective as a dear friend who wasn't there day to day but still spent a good bit of time around Bill Sr., Annie B., and the family.

"Bill Sr. was able to continue being involved in NASCAR and motorsports, even after Alzheimer's struck him, because of the kindness and support of the entire France family, who stood gallantly by Senior until the end," Cassidy said. "The France family commitment was one of the greatest family commitments I have ever witnessed, and, whenever someone who did not know Bill Sr.'s condition would question the appropriateness of one of Senior's comments, Bill Jr. would not infrequently tell them to 'go piss up a rope.' The commitment to protect Senior was unconditional and a beauty to behold.

"I have seen no greater love than that which existed between Bill Sr. and Annie B., and without the efforts of both, NASCAR and Daytona International Speedway would not exist today. Bill Sr. was the 'visionary' and Annie B. made sure it all made economic sense. They were the 'A' team."

As the 1990s arrived, Bill Sr. was spending an increasing amount of time at his home bordering the Intracoastal Waterway, on John Anderson Drive in Ormond Beach.*

Cassidy marvels at the efforts the France family, starting with Bill Jr. and Jim France, put forth to ensure that Bill Sr. would travel his final road with the care and dignity he deserved. It was important, Jim France said, to minimize the pain all would feel – starting with the old man himself. Jim actually has a somewhat glass-half-full stance; he knows that many Alzheimer's patients have a much longer, rougher road than his father did. He finds a bit of solace in that. A bit.

"One of the things we found out about Alzheimer's is that different people can go different ways, and sometimes people with the disease can get pretty belligerent. Dad never had any of those tendencies."

But you did have to keep an eye on him. Jim France laughs

---

* NASCAR president Mike Helton now lives at the same address and periodically hosts gatherings that bring together friends and France family members. Says Helton: "It just feels right, that it's the place where we should be."

openly at the memory of those times. Like when Senior would drift away from a restaurant table during dinner, go over to complete strangers, introduce himself, and break into a song.

His sons took his car away when it became obvious he should no longer drive. Undaunted, Bill Sr. got his driver to take him to the Buick dealership where he had worked as a young man. He told the salesmen he was there to buy a car.

"One of the people at the dealership called me afterward to let me know, and I explained my dad was having some issues, with his mind," said Jim France. "They told me they didn't think he had any issues, because he had known where to come to buy a good car!"

His driving days were done when the sons started noticing he would treat red lights like stop signs – a brief halt and then . . . he'd take off.

"When we told him he had to wait for the light to change," Jim France said, "he told us, 'Boys, at my age, I don't have enough time to wait until the light changes to go.'

"His personality never left him."

A.J. Foyt, the rough-talking bad-ass Texan – whom writer Ed Hinton calls "the toughest sonofabitch to ever drive a race car" – will turn introspective in the blink of an eye when reminiscing about Bill Sr.'s decline.

"We got to be great friends," Foyt said. "Whenever I'd go down to Daytona he'd come see me or I'd go see him. And I'll never forget this one time at Talladega in Bill Sr.'s later years, when he was having his problems. I was sitting in the garage there with [driver] Dick Hutcherson. Bill Sr. came walking up and said 'A.J.! What are you doing down here?'

"When I told people about that they couldn't believe it because this happened at a time when he pretty much didn't recognize anybody."

Right after that recognition and greeting, Foyt gently reminded Bill Sr. of Hutcherson's presence. Bill Sr., of course, had known Hutcherson for years. In 1965, Hutcherson was the NASCAR Sprint Cup Series championship runner-up to Dale Jarrett.

Foyt: "I said to Bill, 'This is Dick Hutcherson.' He just looked at him and said, 'Oh . . . nice meeting you.'

"But he knew me, right off."

The former Charlotte Motor Speedway president Humpy Wheeler who, like Bill Sr., was a promoter first and foremost, remembers Big Bill for "having a great mind . . . he was a tremendous help to me for years. I can remember when he would come to Charlotte I'd go pick him up at the airport and when I was with him I knew I had the greatest mentor in the world, right there. Yes, it was hard to see him go down like he did."

Joy Burke, from Norwich, England, was living in Ormond Beach in the late 1980s and looking for work. "I was working at a bank at the time; I wanted something off-the-wall," she said. "I certainly got that."

Burke lived not far from the France home on Anderson Drive. But she had no idea about the Frances' significance to the area. Yet she became Bill France Sr.'s chief caregiver during the last three years of his life, via a connection with Bob Mock, a personal assistant to Bill Sr. and Annie B.

"I basically fell into the job," Burke said. "I was looking for work and I knew some of the people who worked for Bill France

Jr. and Betty Jane France at their home. Annie B. interviewed me. I ended up primarily working for her and I actually lived at their house for a while. When I started, in 1989, he was still going to his office each day. Everyone made sure that everything was done right. We were all one big happy family at the office."

Back at home, things were not as cheerful. Annie B. slipped somewhat into a state of denial over the last few years. She had a hard time accepting her husband's condition. Many evenings at their home, with the television on in the background and people visiting, Bill Sr. would sit in a chair, saying nothing. Annie B. would explain it away, saying he was tired, just like she was. Envision the knowing glances being exchanged in that room, careful not to catch Annie B.'s eye.

"One can only imagine," Betty Faulk said. "If all of that was hard on someone like me, it was 20 times worse for her."

Annie B. France died on January 2, 1992, after suffering a stroke brought on by heart problems. Her death was unexpected.

"They say people can't really die of a broken heart," Faulk said. "Well, she was broken-hearted."

Jeff Dowling can speak to that broken heart, because in 1992 his heart was broken as well. Dowling started the 2014 racing season as a public relations representative for Chip Ganassi Racing with Felix Sabates, one of auto racing's premier organizations. He is used to high-pressure, high-profile situations. Talk to Dowling about Annie B. France and Bill Sr. and the tears will come.

Dowling came to the France family in circuitous fashion. He grew up in Daytona Beach and graduated from Seabreeze High School – same as Bill Jr. and Jim France. He joined the Air Force and six years later, when that was complete, returned home, looking to attend college.

"It was strange happenstance, right place right time, if you will," Dowling said in a February 2014 interview, right across the street from Daytona International Speedway.

"I wanted to put myself through school, and needed money. Growing up in Daytona Beach, a small town, you always have a friend who knows a friend and I knew the head of security at the speedway, Tommy Galloway. So Tommy calls me up and says, 'I got something for you but it's not very glamorous.' He told me that Bill Sr. was staying at home and was at the point where he needed help. The nurses couldn't always do it alone, because of his physical stature. So I started that afternoon actually, October 3, 1990, and was with him the rest of his life, in the capacity of a kind of a personal assistant.

"With Cap and I, between the two of us we would drive him to wherever he needed to be, if he had any appointments to visit with people. We'd take him down to his boat, the *Little Kaye*. He loved to go down there and look at the boats on the river. We'd drive him around the track at the speedway. And during the races there he would make the rounds of the garage area, although toward the end he started losing his verbal skills. I remember some of the old guys like Junior Johnson would come over and talk to him but they wouldn't get much in return."

Dowling, Cap Stephanson and Joy Burke were working hard to fulfill the family's wishes, that whatever happened, Bill Sr. would retain his way of life as much as possible while also retaining his dignity.

"Just a personal opinion, but I'd say [the way it transpired] was a blessing, because I don't think Bill Sr. ever suffered," Dowling said. "It was almost blissful, I guess, in some ways. You could get a laugh out of him sometimes and he'd recognize people. He'd watch all of us. Whenever I was there I talked to him all the time. One of the maids we had at the house would tell me that when I would come in the house, he would know it.

"And Annie B. . . . she was a fascinating person to me. She was mentally just as sharp as a tack. I remember one night in particular she pulled out a picture from nursing school and she went down and told me a little bit about every person in the picture along with their names. She had her check register she always was keeping straight. She had this little notepad she kept with her, writing things down about what needed to be done. She was always aware of what was going on around her. She was like a doting wife right up until she died. When we got Bill ready to go somewhere she'd be right there, coat in hand. When we came back, she always wanted to know how everything had gone. When she died, I don't think Bill had an awareness of her death. And toward the end of his life I don't think he had much of an understanding that she was gone . . ."

Jim France wants people to know that "Mom was carrying the biggest load for a long time." He adds, "She was there every day for Dad, until she had the stroke and passed away. We were fortunate that we had some really good people who came aboard like Joy, Jeff, and Cap. Joy was a real godsend and was an important part of Mom's day-to-day team, as we worked to help Dad have as good a quality of life as possible."

Six months, five days. That's how long Bill France Sr. lived after Annie B.'s death. Dowling wasn't there. Joy Burke was, early on Sunday, June 7, 1992.

"The first call I made was to Jim France," she said.

Jim had to in turn get in touch with his brother Bill Jr., who was at Sonoma Raceway in California for one of two road race events on what was then called the NASCAR Winston Cup (now the Sprint Cup) Series.

Ernie Irvan won that afternoon. Irvan was a driver that Bill Sr. would've appreciated for his entertainment qualities: gregarious off the track, hell on wheels on the track, hence the nickname "Swervin' Irvan." Alas, Ernie swerved a bit too often, and his career was curtailed by injuries. But while he lasted he was right out of the Lloyd Seay/Junior Johnson/Curtis Turner run-at-the-front-or-blow-up-or-crash mold, a 1990s personification of Bill Sr.'s vision of an everyman's hero come Sunday afternoon when the green flag dropped. During his post-race press conference at Sonoma, Irvan paused to acknowledge NASCAR's founder, saying, "We all know that we wouldn't be here doing what we're doing if not for him. There's a lot sorrow in the racing community today."

Ken Clapp, for years a NASCAR vice president and the company's promotional and public relations impresario on the West Coast, was with Bill Jr. that weekend. The night before the fateful Sunday, Clapp, Bill Jr., and Brian France flew to Tucson Raceway, a NASCAR-sanctioned short track that Brian had previously operated as part of his on-the-job training for learning the business from the ground floor. The next morning, Clapp recalls, they were up early, heading to Sonoma.

"We were staying in San Francisco at the Huntington Hotel," Clapp said "We got up early – myself, [NASCAR vice president] Les Richter, and Bill Jr., and drove across the Golden Gate Bridge into Marin County and stopped at a place for breakfast. We were sitting there and all of a sudden Bill Jr. said, 'Father has died.' Just like that, no emotion. Of course, we all knew it was going to happen around that time. We were waiting. But man, Bill Jr. was like a rock."

Bill Jr.'s wife Betty Jane was extremely close to Big Bill. She remembers him as the ultimate "people person, who enjoyed people from all walks of life." She adds, he was friends "with politicians, presidents, ambassadors, and royalty. In his declining years, though, his dementia took over. One of the last things he had left in life was his love of Irish music and the lyrics to his beloved song, 'Galway Bay' . . . we all have wonderful, fond memories of a 'great giant.'"

NASCAR has aspired to appropriate press coverage throughout its existence. Brian France maintains that the sport is still "undercovered." On the occasion of Bill France Sr.'s death, however, the press took notice of a one-time regional sport that was showing signs of the most significant growth in its history, starting with the *New York Times*, which announced: "William France Is Dead at 82; The Father of Stock-Car Racing." The obituary was short but strong:

> *William France, the leading figure in the creation of stock-car racing and the founder of the Daytona 500 competition, died today at his home in Ormond Beach, Fla. He was 82 years old.*
>
> *He had been suffering from Alzheimer's disease for several years, according to the* Daytona Beach News-Journal *newspaper.*
>
> *The National Association for Stock Car Auto Racing was a personal dream that Mr. France, a 6-foot-5-inch,*

*broad-shouldered former mechanic known in racing as Big
Bill, turned into reality.*

*He built his first car at the age of 17, and went on to drive
cars and motorcycles in competition, but for years he made
his living working on cars in Washington, where he grew up.*

From Shav Glick of the *Los Angeles Times*, for years the dean
of motorsports print reporters:

*The mantle of stock car racing has long since been passed to
younger members of the France family, but the shadow of
Big Bill France will remain as long as race cars that look like
passenger cars run in front of hundreds of thousands of
spectators at NASCAR races. France, who died last Sunday
at 82 after a long illness, is probably the most important
man in American motor racing history. . . . France, a self-
styled "benevolent dictator," made NASCAR.*

Glick quoted Junior Johnson, Thomas Wolfe's "Last American
Hero" as saying, "Bill France is racing's greatest hero. He was the
pioneer. He's what got us here."

Under a headline stating that Bill Sr. "Built Stock Car Racing
from Scratch," Jonathan Ingram offered an eloquent obit in the
Atlanta Journal-Constitution:

*William Henry Getty France stood 6-foot-5, but he was
known as "Big Bill" because he single-handedly took the
scruffy, backwoods sport of stock car racing and turned it
into the most popular racing series in the world. The*

dominant force in American motor racing during his years at the helm of NASCAR, [he was] able to bend the will of the roughnecks and bootlegging drivers he corralled in the 1950s, able to withstand the pressure of the automobile factories that fueled the fantastic growth of stock car racing in the roaring 1960s. . . . France won the first race he promoted. Later, after founding NASCAR, France said he thought he was successful because he was a racer, too.

And, from *USA TODAY,* under the headline "Big Bill paved way for NASCAR":

Bill France Sr. got a lot of mileage out of getting people to drive in circles. The father of NASCAR and founder of the Daytona 500 saw his brainchild grow from a dream of one 100-mile race in 1946 to its present multimillion-dollar operation. . . . At 6-5 with broad shoulders, France was nicknamed "Big Bill." An auto mechanic by trade, he was a dreamer by nature – right from building his first car when he was 17. . . . France, tough-guy leader of NASCAR, got what he wanted.

Bill Sr. was buried on Wednesday, June 10, 1992, alongside his wife of nearly 61 years, in a private ceremony at Hillside Cemetery in Ormond Beach after services at First Baptist Church in Daytona Beach. First Baptist was packed – a "who's who in auto racing" crowd, primarily. The Allisons. The Pettys. The Woods. Roger Penske. It was an event that drew a significant media turnout.

"The speedway even did quote sheets for us as I recall," said longtime *Daytona Beach News-Journal* motorsports writer Godwin Kelly.

The late Reverend Hal Marchman of Daytona Beach delivered the eulogy, in full sing-song Southern Baptist cadence. He was in top form. For years, Marchman (who died in 2009) was well known to fans at Daytona International Speedway for his rousing pre-race prayers that would end with his trademark, inclusive "shalom and amen!" He was a natural choice, the only choice really, for Bill Sr.'s funeral.

And of course Marchman told the story about the one time he couldn't make his speedway commitment, which forced Bill Sr. to stand in for him at the last minute. Bill Sr. was not known for his spirituality, and so as he began the prayer in front of a sold-out crowd, he was grasping for his usual eloquence. He never really found it but he got through the prayer well enough – until the end. After the last line there was silence for at least several seconds. Murmurs from the crowd were audible.

And then came these words from Bill Sr., to end the prayer:

"Sincerely, Bill France."

The story goes that when he got back up to speedway's suite area he sought out Annie B. and asked her, "What is the word you end a prayer with?"

Whereupon she looked at him, shook her head, and muttered, "Amen, Bill, amen."

NASCAR's history always has had a Hollywood script sort of feel. A note to readers with conspiratorial musings: we're not talking about the results of any races. Rather, it's the way the watershed years and moments have fallen on the calendar. There was an uncanny run of decade-ending symmetry: the first Sprint Cup (then called Strictly Stock) season in 1949 . . . the first Daytona 500 in 1959 . . . the first Talladega Superspeedway race in 1969 . . . and the landmark Daytona 500 of 1979 that introduced NASCAR to millions via television.

There's more. Take 1972 for example. R.J. Reynolds, after sponsoring selected races in '71, went all in, sponsoring all events and helping create a new, trimmed-down schedule that ushered in what's generally called NASCAR's "Modern Era." This was arguably the biggest development in the history of NASCAR, other than the 1947 organizational meeting in Daytona Beach that resulted in the sport's creation. Of course, one could argue that what transpired on January 10, 1972, was the biggest development of them all – Bill Sr. stepping down as NASCAR's president in favor of his son.

Twenty years later, 1992 would become a year forever circled on any NASCAR timeline, because Bill France Sr. left this world in the middle of a season that has been called by many the greatest – or the most significant – in NASCAR history, a season that ended five months later with a race that likewise has been accorded best-ever status.

It's not hyperbole.

Bill Sr.'s passing coincided with NASCAR's ascension getting shoved into high gear. The image of a strictly Southeastern sport was being reshaped on a daily basis. Times were changing. Bill Sr.'s death had come in Richard Petty's final season, for Chrissakes.

The 1992 season had gone against the grain, as the NASCAR Winston Cup Series championship battle actually went down to the wire with multiple drivers involved in the chase – 12 years before the word "chase" became part of a newly branded championship format.

The "wire" was Atlanta Motor Speedway, site of the Hooters 500 on November 15. Not only would Richard Petty race for the final time, but a 21-year-old hotshot named Jeff Gordon would race for the *first* time in NASCAR's premier series. Consider those milestones against the backdrop of this point-standing reality going into that event: Six drivers mathematically eligible for the championship, a group led by Davey Allison. Alan Kulwicki was second, 30 points behind, followed by Bill Elliott (40 behind), Harry Gant (97 behind), Kyle Petty (98 back), and Mark Martin (113).

Kulwicki, the longshot owner-driver from Wisconsin with an engineering degree and the personality of a professor – the ultimate outsider – won the championship by a scant 10 points over Elliott, the margin achieved by virtue of Kulwicki leading one more lap than Elliott and thus securing the crucial five-point bonus. Elliott won the race, a small consolation. Allison wrecked mid-race and finished third in points.

Petty crashed out, his familiar STP-sponsored No. 43 red-and-blue Pontiac catching fire early. Petty was fine but the car was, literally, toast.

"It was just one of them deals," said Petty, rolling out his tried-and-true description that came to define NASCAR racing – racin' – over the years.

"Hey, if you're going to go out, you might as well go out in a blaze of glory."

It was the strangest of afternoons. The title was on the line. Six guys were battling. But for many of the media in attendance, the story was all about Richard Petty. Weird, to say the least, but perhaps indicative that NASCAR's mainstream appeal, while definitely on the rise, remained a work in progress. A grand star competing for the last time would be a sidebar in other professional sports when measured against the real news of the day – a championship being decided. But not at Atlanta. *Sports Illustrated* sent Ed Hinton to the race with the assignment to write about Richard Petty – but only if his son Kyle won the championship. Obviously that would've been huge. When it became clear that Kyle was out of contention, Hinton called the *SI* desk and was told he could leave the track whenever he wanted, since they wouldn't need a full account of the finale.

Some newspapers shuffled their typical coverage lineup, having their main beat writers focus on Richard Petty while turning over the race-coverage duties to a back-up or, maybe, a stick-and-ball reporter who was recruited for the weekend to deal with the monotony of covering a six-driver championship shootout.

A young motorsports writer from Lakeland, Florida, named Holly Cain, working for the *Tampa (Fla.) Tribune*, benefited from that approach at Atlanta. Her editors put their lead motorsports writer on the Petty story. Cain, the motorsports backup, was handed the prime opportunity to write her first major race lead, which would run on the front page of the *Tribune*. It was in many ways the real beginning of her chosen career, a launching pad of sorts toward her current status as one of the premier motorsports journalists in the country. The apparent "one-off" at Atlanta began a journey that would take her to the *Dallas Morning News*, the *Seattle Post-Intelligencer*, AOL, and now to NASCAR.COM where she is a senior writer.

"Looking back now, with all the title contenders and

championship-clinching scenarios, that race provided all the story lines that modern-day NASCAR dreams of and thrives upon," Cain said. "But on that weekend, the story that mattered was clearly about saying goodbye to the sport's legend. I figured as a 'newbie' that I must have misjudged how interesting the championship appeared to be, even though it featured names a newcomer could appreciate – Bill Elliott, Davey Allison. I was pretty excited for the opportunity to write my first race story, but resigned to the fact it would be a smaller Monday morning headline.

"Some 20 years later I vividly remember Petty's car crashing and catching fire not even halfway through the race while my storyline was increasingly difficult to track real-time. Allison crashed early and was eliminated from the title run, but Elliott won the race and Kulwicki was crowned the champion based on a technicality of leading more laps. I felt bad for Kulwicki because it seemed like such a wonderful story – the independent owner/driver winning out over the big teams and big names. But I couldn't help but feel it was really bad timing for Kulwicki.

"When Petty came into the press box for his final post-race interview, he was greeted by applause from the media despite the sportswriter creed of 'no cheering in the press box.' After Petty answered the last question, there was a rush of reporters and photographers trying to get his autograph on their paper credential, a violation of another sportswriters' creed. No one seemed to mind that evening, though. I don't recall Kulwicki being asked for a single autograph, nor do I remember any standing ovation. His accomplishment that cold Atlanta evening has taken years and decades to fully appreciate, despite being one of the most dramatic in the sport's history. I think Kulwicki is more appreciated today than during his brief reign as NASCAR champion. As NASCAR settles its championships today, that 1992 Hooters 500 finale is always cited as the gold standard in comparing drama and excitement. While I may have gotten the smaller headline, I have always felt like my story has gotten bigger and bigger as the seasons pass."

"I don't think anyone realized so much would come out of that race," said Hinton. "It was a huge thing but we didn't really know it at the time. What I was pulling for most was Kyle Petty and his outside chance at the title. That race has 'grown' way beyond what it was to begin with, in importance."

Jeff Gordon came into that race after a full season in the NASCAR Busch (now XFINITY) Series where he had a series-record 11 poles three race victories. He remembers a race morning of being "very anxious" and "wanting to run fast." Long-term historical significance involving the championship battle wasn't on his mind. Like others, he was Petty-centric.

"Over the years I've gotten more and more questions about that day," Gordon said. "As far as the significance of the day, it wasn't that significant for me [because of a 31st-place finish]. But it was definitely a very special event obviously, for me, because it was my first Cup race. As far as [Richard Petty's finale], I don't think it really hit me until I got there. To me, here was a legend calling it quits, saying the time had come. But now, I can say that I actually raced against Richard Petty; no one else in the garage today can say that! It was a heckuva day. To be part of a day like that and a race like that..."

The late *Charlotte Observer* motorsports writer David Poole chronicled the race in his book about the 1992 season, *Race with*

Destiny: The Year that Changed NASCAR Forever. Poole's book reintroduced the Atlanta finale, hindsight helping greatly in the presentation.

Perhaps the bottom line about that day is simply this: we didn't know then what we do today.

Steve Waid, at the time the editor of the immensely popular *Winston Cup Scene* weekly publication, looks back and says, "We definitely did not realize the impact of that race . . . very strange."

The impact grew incrementally and dramatically starting in 1993. That spring, Alan Kulwicki died when his team plane crashed en route to Bristol. That summer, Allison – widely considered a future multi-time champion – crashed his new helicopter in the Talladega Superspeedway infield and died the next day. Many NASCAR insiders will look you in the eye to this day and swear that if Davey Allison had lived, Dale Earnhardt never would've won seven titles to tie Petty's all-time record.

Bill Elliott, by then ensconced as NASCAR's yearly Most Popular Driver honoree, never challenged for the championship again, his prime gone with only one title produced, in 1988. Elliott won 44 NASCAR Sprint Cup races but only five after the 1992 finale. Awesome Bill was seldom awesome after that Atlanta afternoon, due mainly to a frustrating string of seasons campaigning as a driver-owner himself.

Against that grain you would have the sudden ascension of Gordon in the several seasons post-Atlanta, with him winning four championships between 1995 and 2001.

Cruel irony, that the deaths of Kulwicki and Allison attracted far more attention overall than Bill France Sr.'s passing had the previous year.

Much like the case of the '92 finale, the significance of his death was lost on many.

It is perhaps fair to say that Bill Sr. had to die to get people's attention 20 years after he had stepped away from NASCAR's leadership role.

"Because Bill Sr. had Alzheimer's, he had declined and in the process had faded from the scene," said Hinton. "He was out of circulation . . . just out of sight."

"Back then for all of us covering NASCAR, there was just so much happening all the time, every day almost . . . to be honest, we didn't give Bill France Sr. a second thought in those days," Waid said, emphasizing that such a remembrance isn't meant to be disrespectful, just honest.

"It was only after he died that many of us sat down and started realizing the impact he had had on motorsports and on sports overall."

CHAPTER 10

What Would Bill Sr. Think?

A t the time of Bill France Sr.'s death, NASCAR was in the second half of a season that many consider the greatest in the history of the sport – and certainly the greatest of the "pre-Chase" era, when the top series championship was decided by a season-long points competition. The Chase for the NASCAR Sprint Cup, instituted in 2004 – the same year the 33-year run of Winston sponsorship ended, to be replaced by NEXTEL (now Sprint) communications – created a playoff-style format contested over the course of the last 10 races, with qualification for "making the Chase" based on the drivers' performances in the 26 races preceding the "playoffs."

So, as 1992 concluded, Bill France Sr. and Annie B. France were gone.

Richard Petty was done racing.

Eras ending, everywhere.

But NASCAR had been "teed up" in many ways for a popularity boom in the 1990s and 2000s. In the process, Dale Earnhardt was usurped by Gordon. Earnhardt won championships in 1990, '91, '93, and '94. Gordon took the series over with titles in '95, '97, and '98. Attendance soared. A first-ever network television deal started at the 2001 Daytona 500, with FOX broadcasting. Dale Earnhardt died that day. Gordon won his fourth title in '01. NASCAR continued to grow.

The second decade of the new century has seen attendance throttle back somewhat, with NASCAR's core fan base hit hard by the economic challenges affecting all of professional sports. Television viewership isn't quite what it was 10 years ago, either.

But these developments are relative.

In 2013, average attendance for the Sprint Cup Series again exceeded 100,000. And on television, an average of nearly SIX MILLION people watched the series' 36 races. The high point of 2013 was the season-opening Daytona, with an average viewership of 16,652,000. The 2014 500 was expected to challenge that total, but a rain delay forced the event to be run at night, altering the ratings returns.

There is so much happening in the sport these days. Jimmie Johnson started 2014 with six series championships, closing in on the all-time record of seven held by Petty and Earnhardt, a record once thought untouchable. Dale Earnhardt Jr., the sport's most popular driver, looks like he will win a championship, after all, before he is through competing. Danica Patrick is attracting female fans. Talented drivers such as African-American Darrell Wallace Jr. and Asian-American Kyle Larson are further diversifying the sport. Facilities are upgrading, starting with Daytona International Speedway's multi-million-dollar project slated for 2016 completion. NASCAR recently announced a new television deal resulting in increased revenue, along with a revamped Chase format. NASCAR has acquired the old American Le Mans Series and re-acquired the sports car sanctioning body that Bill Sr. founded – the International Motor Sports Association. This has resulted in a new IMSA-sanctioned series, the TUDOR United SportsCar Championship.

In 2013, a new NASCAR Sprint Cup Series car was introduced, called "Gen-6." It is rejuvenating the connection between the race track and showroom with stock cars that truly resemble street cars – the basic appeal of Bill France Sr.'s Strictly Stock division, in modern-day form.

And then there's this: NASCAR is partnered with the hugely popular actor Vince Vaughn and accomplished writer Randy Brown to develop a potential feature film project about Bill France Sr. and the sport's beginnings, with Vaughn playing the part of Bill Sr.

Bill Sr.'s grandson Brian France, as the sport's third-generation boss, is running point across all fronts.

One has to ask, if Bill France Sr. were here today, what would he think of the sport he founded on a whim, a prayer, and a bottle or two of scotch?

Or better yet, what would he do, or change?

In fact, several people who might have insight to those hypotheticals *were* asked.

Read on.

- **Jim France, NASCAR vice chairman, IMSA chairman – and Bill Sr.'s son:** "He would be impressed with everything, I think. Matter-of-fact, if he was alive and well, he'd be doing a lot these things himself. Mom, now, she'd be white-knuckling it regarding what they're doing over at the speedway. But Dad? He'd be leading the charge."

The sports car situation is of special interest to Jim France, just as it was to his dad. This would result in another modern-day thumbs-up, the son said. "His view was international – global. He had the ability to look over the horizon to the future. He wasn't completely focused on NASCAR."

Moving on . . .

- **Lesa France Kennedy, NASCAR vice chairwoman and executive vice president, CEO and vice chairwoman of the International Speedway Corporation – and Bill Sr.'s granddaughter:** "He would probably say, 'Just keep it going.' I can hear him saying something kind of understated like that. I think he would recognize the need to keep trying new things and that there will always be people who are in your camp and there will always be naysayers. He would say to just do your best to get people to a consensus and move forward with people understanding your vision."
- **Betty Jane France, NASCAR executive vice president, NASCAR Foundation chairwoman – and Bill Sr.'s daughter-in-law:** "He would love [the technology available] today, the phones and everything, the iPads and computers. He would go ballistic with all of that! Good Lord, we would never be able to see him, he'd

be so busy. The racing part, he would've been right there making it grow."

- **Brian France, NASCAR chairman, chief executive officer – and Bill Sr.'s grandson:** "I think he would really like the efforts to elevate the sport. We're doing exactly what he had intended to do. He liked to do big things, liked doing hard things. He was pretty good at that. And that said a lot about his ability to pull people together. You can't do big things without a lot of help and a lot of cooperation. My sister Lesa is probably the best family member in my view when it comes to pulling things together like that. She's probably got more of the Bill Sr. approach, in building coalitions. You don't really think of Bill Sr. much in terms of building coalitions but he had to in the early days. You got tough when you had to get tough but you also had to win people over. Lesa has got a lot of that . . . more than I do."

- **Ken Clapp, former NASCAR vice president:** "I don't think he probably thought too much about [this kind of future] back when he and Annie came to Daytona Beach in 1934 but I think he'd be very, very pleased. Senior was always very, very pleased with the progression of Bill Jr. Jim France always sort of flew under the radar but I think everybody [including Bill Sr.] spotted early on just how bright of a guy Jim France was – and is."

- **John Cooper: former NASCAR and International Speedway Corporation executive:** "I'll tell you this: Bill Sr. was the most important man in my life, other than my family. And I mean that sincerely. . . . He would be enormously pleased that the sport went the way it did and grew to what it is. And while it's vastly different than it was in the early years, I think he'd be proud that his family and the key people who worked for him at ISC have gotten it to where it is. If there is anybody who thinks he would be frustrated or disappointed with [the sport today] they're crazy. Everybody is entitled to their own opinion, but in my opinion – and I knew him as well as anybody – he would be proud, happy, and pleased."

- **Darrell Waltrip, three-time NASCAR Sprint Cup Series champion and NASCAR Hall of Fame member:** "Big Bill would say that 'This is exactly the way I wanted it to be, exactly how I planned it.' . . . Big Bill was building something in his day. Brian is trying to build on that. It's hands-on, a family sport. That's what Bill Sr. wanted."

- **Ned Jarrett, two-time NASCAR Sprint Cup Series champion and NASCAR Hall of Fame member:** "I've said for a long time that I don't know any other person who had the vision Bill Sr. had for seeing where the sport could go, and I feel like he would say today, 'Okay, this is doing what I thought it would do.' I really feel like he had the vision of seeing where NASCAR is today."

    Count Jarrett among those thinking Brian France's style is reminiscent of Big Bill. "I agree with that idea and I applaud Brian for the way he is going about it. I think there's a lot in common between those two and I think it's good for the sport."

- **Joie Chitwood III, Daytona International Speedway president:** "You can only hope Bill Sr. would be proud that we've lived up to his challenge to represent stock car racing, Daytona, and the speedway the right way. What it took back in the late 1950s to build the speedway, it's truly an American success story. . . . The place has such a unique legacy . . . our team drinks the Kool-Aid; Daytona is a special place; we treat it as a special place. There's no doubt that Bill Sr., if he was here, would have a lot of input on what we could do better – and we would put that input at the top of our list."

- **Judy Jones, Bill France Sr.'s former secretary:** "I don't think he'd be a bit surprised. He was always thinking that if it could be made better, yes, we'll make it better. Of course, he always thought he hung the moon, and he [may have]."*

- **Ed Hinton, author and motorsports journalist for ESPN.com:** "If we could move Bill Sr. in time . . . I think Bill France Sr. would've initiated change probably even before his descendants have. I seriously doubt he would've resisted anything. He was always cognizant of 'the show.' I think he would approve of the changes that have come to the sport, if he had not already initiated changes himself, years earlier."

- **Richard Childress, six-time NASCAR Sprint Cup Series champion owner at Richard Childress Racing:** "Bill Sr. was a man whose life was built around this sport and the word 'NASCAR.' I think he would be very, very happy and pleased . . . He was a visionary 100 per cent – Talladega, Daytona . . . but if he could see where we are today with the television contracts, some of the big race tracks where we race . . . the France family has carried the legacy he started and taken it to another level.

  "He's smiling down at us, these days."

- **Junior Johnson, NASCAR Hall of Fame member:** "I think he'd be proud of everything, but I also don't think NASCAR would have

---

* Judy Jones passed away in September 2014.

a lot of the stuff it has now [if he was still running the sport]. I think he'd want the racing to be more like the way we started out with. He didn't want anyone to dominate because he thought it would hurt the sport. His rules were 'run what you brung and we'll see if we can let you run it.' He wanted the best team to win; the best driver, the best car, the best crew.

"But I also think he'd be proud of how big NASCAR's gotten, all the success it's had because of his ideas. I can remember when Bill Jr. was taking over for him and he'd tell people that NASCAR was going to get bigger and a lot better. Bill Sr. was not the kind of guy who thought he'd be around forever [running things]."

- **Bobby Allison, NASCAR Sprint Cup Series champion and NASCAR Hall of Fame member:** "I think Bill Sr. would say, 'I did a good job [getting this started]. This thing today is really, really good.'

  "I do think that if Bill Sr. was still alive and running NASCAR, we wouldn't have what people call 'one-of-a-kind cars.' No, I think we'd have Chevys, Fords, and Toyotas [off the showroom floor] running, because Bill Sr. thought the guy with the car in the driveway [that was the same as the race car] was the guy who bought the tickets to the races."

- **A.J. Foyt, Daytona 500 winner and four-time Indianapolis 500 champion:** "You gotta take your hat off to Bill Sr. He was the foundation of NASCAR today. I don't think NASCAR would be anything like it is today without Bill Sr.

  "I think he'd be very proud of what his boys and the [grandkids] have done . . . very proud. But I also think he would have kept things [under his control] more. I guarantee you, he put manners on everybody. He was the type of guy who, if things got out of hand, he would put a lid on it real quick."

- **Scott Atherton, president and chief operating officer, International Motor Sports Association:** "Sometimes through the years when I've been on a trans-Atlantic flight, I've thought about what Charles Lindbergh might think if he was somehow able to come back and witness how we do it today. Would he be impressed? I have to believe that today's IMSA is the equivalent of a modern-day jet compared to the earliest forms of IMSA when John Bishop and Bill France Sr. founded [it] way back when.

  "If Bill Sr. could see IMSA now, I would hope and expect he would be very proud to have been there at the start and see it come full circle . . . to see the iconic International Motorsports Center building in Daytona Beach have IMSA branding on it, right alongside NASCAR and the International Speedway Corporation brandings in equal stature . . . to see what the IMSA brand stands for today as the benchmark not only for professional sports car racing in North America but, many would say, on a global scale . . . and to see that we have maintained close ties with all the international constituents like the ACO [Automobile Club de l'Ouest] and Le Mans.

  "I think we are fulfilling against what his original vision was but probably at a level beyond what he could've imagined at that time."

- **Humpy Wheeler, former Charlotte Motor Speedway president:** "If he was here, I think he would bring the sport back to its roots real quick. One thing he definitely would have done was address this aero-push problem we have in racing today [that affects the ability to pass]. He would have done whatever he needed to, to get rid of that. Bill Sr. knew that passing for the lead is what the people pay to see. . . . Bill Sr. knew the race fan better than anyone. He had a knack of getting to them, serving what they wanted.

"He would've been proud of NASCAR's [network] television contracts because he chased after that for a long time. His timing just wasn't right.

"And he'd also be proud of how far the sport has grown nationally which is something we all fought for, for so long. He'd also be proud of how nationwide the publicity is now for NASCAR compared to the way it was when he started out.

"As far as the [growth in] sponsorship is concerned I think he would've taken a different look, a different path. I'm not sure he would've 'corporatized' the sport as much as it is today."

- **Ken Squier, legendary NASCAR television broadcaster:** "I think he'd be thrilled, not even a question, with this 'Sweet 16' (the new Chase for the NASCAR Sprint Cup). This is his kind of promotion that builds up to something. He totally understood what motivated the public and what would motivate the competitors and [he would understand] that those two things would come together with this new deal.

"He tried new stuff all the time and this new thing fits right in, with his sense of what you need to do to ensure at the end you have one helluva finish. Running [the championship battle] through to the [end of the season], eliminating competitors, causing all kinds of media evaluation – the media upset with NASCAR, drivers upset about not making the next round – will keep the plot stirring until the last show. And when the guys roll out at the last race the gloves will be off. It's absolutely perfect. This [Chase] would have been a Bill France Sr. creation. He was an old-time promoter. He was just a piece of work. There wasn't anybody else like him.

"Here's a line from the 1960s he gave me one time. Senior got me aside and said, 'You know, we're going to be a big-league sport by turn of century, right up there with football, baseball, and basketball. We'll be major league.' Well, everybody attributed that statement to his hyperbole. As far as I'm concerned he was totally wrong. He missed [his prediction] by six months.

"Actually, he nailed it."

- **Steve Waid, longtime motorsports journalist:** "I think Bill Sr. would approve of NASCAR today, because of one reason – it has far transcended what he created. I don't think he ever fathomed something like we have today.

"Now, as far as the politics, the rules and regulations . . . I'm not so sure. He was an iron-willed man. I'm not so sure he would approve of this Race Team Alliance thing very much at all.*

---

* Editor's Note: The Race Team Alliance came into existence in the summer of 2014, an organization comprised of various team owners competing in NASCAR's highest levels.

"And . . . I don't think he would disagree with the idea of the Chase for the NASCAR Sprint Cup. Bill France Sr. was a smart man and he would've recognized that the racing had to change [in these times] to keep fans interested. He would've seen the need to try something different."

- **Winston Kelley, NASCAR Hall of Fame executive director:** "As big a visionary as Bill France Sr. was, if he was here he would probably still acknowledge that NASCAR had grown beyond his expectations. I go back to his quote – 'if we manage it right there's no telling what the sport can grow into.' I think even he would admit that while he had lofty expectations and huge vision, the growth may have exceeded even his expectations – and I mean that as a compliment.

"Bill Jr. may have seen it getting this big because he [operated] in a different era. It's hard to say that someone from the 1940s and 1950s could've seen something growing this big. Bill Jr. may have in the 1980s and '90s.

"I would love to walk both of them through the NASCAR Hall of Fame to get their reactions, what they like, what they would do differently. Going through the hall with Richard Petty has been an experience. Going through it with Junior Johnson has been very special. But to see it through the eyes of Bill Sr. and Bill Jr., because of how they started the business and grew the business, to get their perspectives . . . would just be priceless. You hope they would be pleased, at the end of the day.

EPILOGUE

s the 2014 auto racing season unfolded, the finger-prints of the France family were everywhere – a multi-faceted manifestation not only of Bill France Sr.'s dreams and vision, but of the origins of auto racing in the Daytona Beach area that dated back 111 years.

- NASCAR's third-generation leader, Chairman and Chief Operating Officer Brian Zachary France, looking and acting more like his grandfather with each passing year, was instituting a revolutionary change to the already-revolutionary Chase for the NASCAR Sprint Cup.

- Brian's sister Lesa France Kennedy, the chief executive officer of the International Speedway Corporation, was leading the way on a multi-million-dollar facelift of Daytona International Speedway, labeled "Daytona Rising." She is also vice chairwoman and executive vice president at NASCAR.

- Bill Sr.'s younger son, James Carl France, was presiding as chairman of the board of the directors running a new-and-improved International Motor Sports Association, the organization his father helped found back in 1969. IMSA had been acquired in 2013 and returned to the Daytona Beach fold, and in 2014 started sanctioning the new TUDOR United SportsCar Championship and seven other ancillary series. And of course, Jim France was also operating in his usual under-the-public-radar style as NASCAR's vice chairman and executive vice president – and as chairman at ISC.

- Bill Sr.'s daughter-in-law Betty Jane France was serving proudly as chairwoman of The NASCAR Foundation, NASCAR's charitable arm that she founded in 2006, while also maintaining her unofficial title of "First Lady of NASCAR."

- And his great-grandson, Lesa Kennedy's son Ben, was racing at the NASCAR national series level, in the NASCAR Camping World Truck Series – while also finishing up his degree at the University of Florida.

Let's take a closer look at each.

In September 2003, Brian France took over as NASCAR's chairman and CEO from his father Bill Jr. Within several months he rolled out two major announcements: replacing Winston as sponsor of NASCAR's top series with NEXTEL (now Sprint) Communications and modifying the long-standing point system to create what became known as NASCAR's "playoffs."

This was straight out of the Book of Bill Sr.; that is, if there had been a Book of Bill Sr. before this one.

It was forward-thinking to say the least: After 26 races, the top 10 drivers in the points qualified for the "Chase for the NASCAR Sprint Cup." They then had their point totals reset, with the points leader starting atop the top 10. Those 10 would then compete in a separate competition over the last 10 races on the schedule; hence the "playoffs."

Prior to the 2014 season, Brian took things to another level. Fed up with the notion of "points racing" that was perceived by fans – and reinforced by drivers' post-race comments – to be endemic to NASCAR's top series, he announced a revamped Chase that has come to be known as "win and you're in," which is a slight over-simplification but still puts the main point across. Gone are the days when drivers in the NASCAR Sprint Cup Series would be satisfied with anything other than a trip to Victory Lane.

The new world order in Sprint Cup:

- A victory in the first 26 races likely guarantees a driver a berth in the 10-race Chase.
- The Chase field is expanded from 12 to 16 drivers.
- The number of Chase drivers in contention for the championship now decreases after every three Chase races, from 16 to start the Chase, to 12 after Chase race No. 3; eight

after Chase race No. 6; and four after Chase race No. 9. Those final four drivers will enter the "NASCAR Sprint Cup Championship" with a chance for the title.

- The top 15 drivers with the most wins over the first 26 races will earn a spot in the Chase Grid – provided they have finished in the top 30 in points and attempted to qualify for every race (except in rare instances, such as injury or illness). The 16th Chase position will go to the points leader after race No. 26, if they do not have a win. In the event that there are 16 or more different winners over 26 races, the only winless driver who can earn a Chase spot would be the points leader after 26 races.

- If there are fewer than 16 different winners in the first 26 races, the remaining Chase positions will go to those winless drivers highest in points. If there are 16 or more different winners in the first 26 races, the ties will be broken first by number of wins, followed by NASCAR Sprint Cup Series driver points.

Not exactly "win and you're in" but pretty close. But again, it's the message that counts and that message is "winning is what matters."

"We have arrived at a format that makes every race matter even more, diminishes points racing, puts a premium on winning races, and concludes with a best-of-the-best, first-to-the-finish-line showdown race – all of which is exactly what fans want," Brian France said the day the changes were announced.

"We have looked at a number of concepts for the last three years through fan research, models, and simulations, and also maintained extensive dialogue with our drivers, teams, and partners. The new Chase for the NASCAR Sprint Cup will be thrilling, easy to understand, and help drive our sport's competition to a whole new level."

Lesa Kennedy, named as the Most Powerful Woman in Sports in October 2009 by *Forbes* magazine, is making Daytona International Speedway the model for the entire motorsports industry, with efforts to upgrade facilities to standards that serve an evolving fan base. "Daytona Rising" does Bill Sr.'s legacy proud. It's a $400 million renovation targeted for 2016 completion that will make the somewhat aging track a true event destination for modern-day sports fans who demand more than a seat, a view, and a hot dog.

Some specifics:

- Plans call for five expanded and redesigned fan entrances, or injectors, taking fans to three different concourse levels, each featuring spacious and strategically-placed social "neighborhoods."
- A total of 11 neighborhoods, each the size of a football field, will enable fans to socialize during events without missing any of the on-track action.
- Every seat in the speedway front stretch will be replaced with wider and more comfortable seating.
- At the conclusion of the redevelopment, the speedway will have approximately 101,000 permanent seats with the potential to increase permanent seating to 125,000.
- The new front stretch will include 53 suites that will offer

superb views of the track, and a totally different concept for hospitality.

"Motorsports is among the other large sports across the country that have continued to upgrade, improve, and diversify their event venues," Kennedy said. "Our industry is well aware of the need to take it to the next level. Today's sports fans – especially younger fans – demand more out of their experience, and their investment. They want a multi-faceted entertainment experience.

"To say we are excited about this project would be a massive understatement. It will redefine the overall approach to motorsports entertainment in North America. I can only imagine what my granddad and dad would say about these plans, if they were here today. Chances are they both would say 'press on.'"

Accompanying the Daytona Rising project is a venture involving ISC and Atlanta-based Jacoby Development, Inc. to develop a multi-faceted entertainment destination directly across from the speedway. The "ONE DAYTONA" project encompasses 181 acres owned by ISC. Initial designs include 1.1 million square feet of world-class shopping, fine dining, hotel, theater, and other entertainment. Bass Pro Shops and Cobb Theatres both signed early letters of intent to become high-profile tenants.

The Jim France–headed IMSA season started 2014 the way it used to years ago, before North American sports car racing split into two factions, France's GRAND-AM Road Racing and the Braselton, Georgia–based American Le Man Series. For years, the Rolex 24 At Daytona and the Mobil 1 Twelve Hours of Sebring were the first two major sports car events of the year, while also being the biggest on the calendar. Those two races led off the new

TUDOR United SportsCar Championship schedule but were also part of a separate competition called the Tequila Patrón North American Endurance Cup (NAEC) – a championship within a championship, in layman's terms – encompassing the season's four endurance races. Completing the NAEC lineup were the Sahlen's Six Hours of the Glen at Watkins Glen International in upstate New York and the season-ending Petit Le Mans Powered by Mazda at Road Atlanta in Braselton. For the first time in 13 years, sports car racing in North America began a season united, as the series title prominently notes. And although there were considerable initial growing pains, the combination of Jim France's resolve and a stunning schedule that travels to virtually every iconic road circuit on the continent means the future looks bright.

Betty Jane France started becoming involved in community-oriented activities years ago, in the process carving her own niche in both Daytona Beach and the NASCAR industry. Since her husband's death in June 2007, she has become even more visible, not only as the chairwoman of The NASCAR Foundation but also as its chief spokesperson. In 2011, the foundation started the Betty Jane France Humanitarian Award, given annually to a NASCAR fan who has done extraordinary work for charitable and community causes, especially as they pertain to enriching the lives of children. The award is presented annually at the NASCAR Sprint Cup Series Awards show, held at Wynn Las Vegas each December. Since the award was created, it has been utilized by the foundation to donate more than half a million dollars to charities. Overall, the foundation has raised more than $18 million.

Ben Kennedy, who turned 24 in December 2014, advanced to the NASCAR Camping World Truck Series 10 months earlier, which meant a season-opening race at Daytona International Speedway – the race track his great-grandfather and grandfather built. And, then, when qualifying for that race got rained out, the starting grid was set according to practice times – which put Kennedy on the pole. Whereupon he ran like the wind, leading 52 of the 100 laps and finishing 15th. Kennedy is a bright young man whom employees at NASCAR and ISC routinely refer to as "their future boss." With each day he more resembles his late father, the highly respected Dr. Bruce Kennedy, who died in a June 2007 plane crash, only two weeks after the death of Ben's grandfather Bill Jr. The young man is the pride of the family and seems destined for greatness either on or off the race track.

"All the pieces that Bill Sr. saw possibilities around . . . after 65 years, those possibilities [are reality]," says NASCAR President Mike Helton. "Nobody could be any prouder than Bill Sr. and Annie B. would be.

"Yes, he would be a happy man right now."

And ultimately, is there any better way to measure the life and legacy of Bill France Sr.? He died in 1992, but he has never left us.

He remains larger than life, still.

Bill France Sr. and Anne Bledsoe France – Big Bill and Annie B. – with his beach-road race car in Daytona Beach, 1940. The two remained NASCAR's "First Couple" until their respective deaths in 1992.

Talladega Superspeedway opened in 1969; Bill Sr. and Annie B. loved returning to the massive track through the years.

NASCAR's first office, at 42 Peninsula Drive in Daytona Beach, Florida.

An old-fashioned family Christmas morning at the France home in Daytona Beach, Florida, circa 1950, with Bill Sr. helping his son Jim assemble an electric train set while Bill Jr. looks on.

A 1973 classic on Daytona International Speedway's pit road: sons Bill France Jr. (l) and Jim France (r) with their mother Anne and father Bill Sr.

In 1990, the France family gathered for a portrait. Top row, from left: Jim France, J.C. France, Brian France, Lesa France Kennedy, Bruce Kennedy, Bill France Jr. Bottom row, from left: Jennifer France, Sharon France, Anne France, Bill France Sr., Betty Jane France, Amy France.

The early success of Bill France Sr. (l) and NASCAR was aided greatly by Big Bill's right-hand men Ed Otto (c) and Bill Tuthill (r).

Bill Sr. (l), with help from Ed Otto (r) and others, studied film and photographs of the inaugural Daytona 500's close finish for several days in February 1959, before declaring Lee Petty the winner over Johnny Beauchamp – 72 hours after the checkered flag flew. Richard Petty thinks this was a classic Bill Sr. promotional ploy to keep the buzz going about his new speedway beyond race day.

The 24 Hours of Daytona sports car endurance race – now called the Rolex 24 At Daytona – was always a key component in Bill Sr.'s vision of creating a worldwide reputation for Daytona International Speedway. Here, he presents the 1968 championship trophy to Porsche co-drivers Hans Hermann (l) and Jo Siffert (r).

The controversial Alabama governor George C. Wallace, shown here in 1973, was a longtime benefactor of Bill Sr.'s friendship and political support, and reciprocated by facilitating construction of a 16-lane access road leading into Talladega Superspeedway.

Bill France Sr. was like a proud father when Talladega Super-speedway opened in 1969. Attempting to allay drivers' concerns about safety, the nearly 60-year-old France took to the 2.66-mile tri-oval and ran some laps himself. Drivers were not impressed.

President Ronald Reagan was greeted warmly by Bill Sr. during a July 4, 1984, visit to Daytona International Speedway – the day Richard Petty got his 200th and final NASCAR victory.

President George Bush, flanked by Bill France Sr. and Bill Jr., visited Daytona International Speedway in February 1992 for the Daytona 500.

Big Bill, early 1960s

FROM THE ARCHIVES

This section is a compilation of speeches, interview excerpts, sayings, slogans, and archival documents and statistics that provide additional insight into the life and times of NASCAR founder Bill France Sr. All speech text is presented in the form – as much as possible – that speakers used, including pauses and emphasis on particular phrases, to give the reader as much authenticity as possible.

Bill France Sr. 1938 Pit Pass for the Indianapolis 500

THIS IS NOT A STAY IN PASS
AND
IS NOT GOOD FOR GATE ADMISSION

1938

MR. *Bill France*

has permission to work in Garages
the night of May 29, 1938.

SAFETY DIRECTOR

FRONT

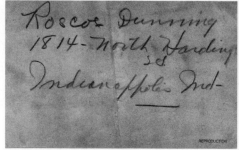

*Roscoe Dunning
1814 - North Harding
st
Indianapolis Ind -*

REPRODUCTION

BACK

Bill France Sr. may have founded NASCAR, but long before that he was enamored with what was called big-car racing: the open-wheel monsters that raced in the "Great Spectacle in Motorsports" – the Indianapolis 500.

The 500 was sanctioned by the American Automobile Association, which also sanctioned the first beach-road course race in Daytona Beach, in 1936. Bill Sr., a pioneer in motorsports "networking," got to know a number of the officials and his fellow racers from the 1936 event. That led to him working on the pit crew for a number of teams at the Indianapolis 500 that year and a number of years after that. The highlight of this slice of Bill Sr.'s life was the 1946 500, when he was part of the crew for the race's winner, George Robson.

The lowlight of the France-Indy connection seemingly took place in 1954, although the following tale has been discounted at times as part of NASCAR lore. The story goes that Bill Sr. and his wife were basically tossed out of the Gasoline Alley garage area at Indy because they didn't have the proper passes, and that Bill Sr. blamed the AAA and an increasingly combative relationship that had developed since NASCAR was founded in 1947.

From the 2010 book *The Man Who Made NASCAR: Bill France Jr.*:

Legend has it that Bill Sr. told people that he and his wife decided they would go on back to Florida and build their own damn speedway. And from there perhaps sprang the true impetus to rival Indianapolis – and try to outdo the hallowed ground of auto racing in America. The banking planned for Daytona [International Speedway] would best Indy in two ways: the aforementioned benefit to fans' sight lines but also by enabling stock cars to go faster than they ever had anywhere.

Through the years, whenever the original or reproductions have been seen, the conversation starter often has been the reverse side of the pass, where Bill Sr. had scrawled the address of the noted Indy Car builder Roscoe Dunning – 1814 North Harding Street, Indianapolis, Indiana.

Bill France Sr. Address at NASCAR Organizational Meeting, Streamline Hotel

DECEMBER 14, 1947

DAYTONA BEACH, FLORIDA

Nothing stands still in the world. Things get better or worse, bigger or smaller.

Stock car racing has been my whole life. I've gone to other territories; I've left home, and I've always tried to develop

something as I was going. I've tried to build up instead of tear-ing down.

The first stock car racing that I became associated with was here in 1936. After the old speed trials on the beach were taken away, Daytona was looking for something else to take their place, so they came up with a strictly stock car race, and they lost $22,000, so they pulled out.

An average man in a fast automobile can still win races. It's just like Ted Horn in his Indianapolis racer against a boy in a cheap Ford. Horn could run off and hide from him, because the average boy doesn't have the money to improve his equipment.

A dirt track is more than necessary to make a stock car race a good show. In fact, stock car races not held on dirt are nowhere near as impressive. To look their best, stock cars need dirt. Or sand.

Oh, I was associated with Bill Tuthill at Lonsdale, Rhode Island, and it was pretty good [racing] on asphalt. It was almost dark when the race was over, and if the boys would have put on an extra lap or two, we could have seen how the lights worked for stock cars. But nobody left. I guess it proved that even on asphalt, nobody wanted their money back.

We have to think about the image. If you get a junky old automobile, it's a jalopy in the average person's mind. Even if you take a new Cadillac and pull the fenders off and let it get real dirty, it would be a jalopy to most people.

Stock car racing has got distinct possibilities for Sunday shows. It would allow race-minded boys that work all week, who don't have the money to afford a regular racing car, to be competitive with a rich guy. It would allow them the opportunity to go to a race track on Sunday and to show their stuff, and maybe win a prize, and not make it their full-time job.

We don't know how big it can be; I doubt if anyone here knows that, but I do know that if stock car racing is handled properly, it can go the same way big-car racing has gone. [The same goes for] bicycle racing, or any racing.

And if you have an event where you can publicize talent, then there is much better cooperation from the newspapers.

There are a whole lot of things to be straightened out here. We've got to get track owners and promoters interested in building up stock car racing. I would like to get all of us in accord on as many different subjects as we can bring up. Tomorrow morning (December 15, 1947), I would like to appoint some committees for laying down rules and regulations which can be followed by the majority of the promoters and drivers. That will keep the whole thing on more or less a fair basis.

Stock car racing as we've been running it is not, in my opinion, the answer. If it were, I wouldn't worry about anybody else. I would like to see to it that the average American boy, say, in Miami, if he runs according to the rules, is going to be able to [also] run if he goes to Fort Lauderdale or Atlanta or even Trenton.

The main purpose of the technical committee will be to get a uniform automobile over the circuit. I believe stock car racing can become a nationally recognized sport by having a national point standing which will embrace the majority of large stock car events. Regardless of whether you win a race in New Zealand or Florida, the points would apply in a national championship bracket. What it would amount to is we'd have a national champion who had won his spurs on a national championship basis.

And we should have a national benevolent fund that protects the boys who are laid up. There are things that come up from time to time, like the mechanic who gets hurt working on a car or the new driver who makes up his mind the day before the race to compete. They don't have to get insurance, so we should be able to protect them.

This touches just about everything I had in mind. Right here within our group rests the outcome of stock car racing in the country today. We have the opportunity to set it up on a big scale.

I don't mean we can convert all of the men in the association; they have their own minds; but if the picture is bright enough and the boys have some goal in mind, or at the end of the year, when this thing is over, they've got some national recognition or a little money out of a point fund, and if everybody puts on races according to rules, and contributes money to the point fund, then it will mean something, and the boys in Ohio will want to have their own cars fixed up where they can come over and compete.

We are all interested in one thing: improving present conditions.

First NASCAR Rule Book

PUBLISHED FEBRUARY 1948

The 2014 NASCAR Sprint Cup Series rule book was 208 pages.
The very first one was four pages.

Check out the reproduction of those pages in the photo insert.
One has to love the page 4 footnote at the bottom:

. . . Retain These Rules For Future Reference . . .

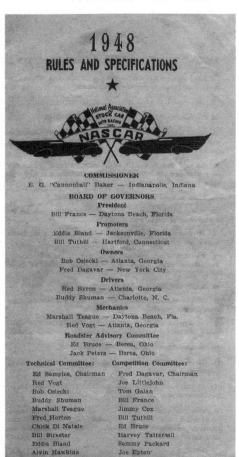

1948

RULES AND SPECIFICATIONS

★

NASCAR

COMMISSIONER
E. G. "Cannonball" Baker — Indianapolis, Indiana

BOARD OF GOVERNORS
President
Bill France — Daytona Beach, Florida

Promoters
Eddie Bland — Jacksonville, Florida
Bill Tuthill — Hartford, Connecticut

Owners
Bob Osiecki — Atlanta, Georgia
Fred Dagavar — New York City

Drivers
Red Byron — Atlanta, Georgia
Buddy Shuman — Charlotte, N. C.

Mechanics
Marshall Teague — Daytona Beach, Fla.
Red Vogt — Atlanta, Georgia

Roadster Advisory Committee
Ed Bruce — Berea, Ohio
Jack Peters — Berea, Ohio

Technical Committee:	Competition Committee:
Ed Samples, Chairman	Fred Dagavar, Chairman
Red Vogt	Joe Littlejohn
Bob Osiecki	Tom Galan
Buddy Shuman	Bill France
Marshall Teague	Jimmy Cox
Fred Horton	Bill Tuthill
Chick Di Natale	Ed Bruce
Bill Streeter	Harvey Tattersall
Eddie Bland	Sammy Packard
Alvin Hawkins	Joe Epton

1948 RULES and SPECIFICATIONS

1. Cars eligible—1937 models and up through 1948. '37 and '38 models must have 4-wheel hydraulic brakes.

2. Later models must be run in the same model chassis.

3. Foreign-manufactured cars will not be permitted.

4. If car is a convertible type, it must be run with top up and in proper place and must be equipped with safety hoops mounted to frame.

5. All cars must have full stock fenders, running boards and body if so equipped when new, and not abbreviated in any way other than reinforcement.

6. Stock bumpers and mufflers must be removed.

7. Crash bars may be used no wider than frame, protruding no farther than 12 inches from body.

8. All doors must be welded, bolted or strapped shut. Doors blocked will not be permitted.

9. Fuel and oil capacities may be increased in any safe manner. Any extra or bigger tanks must be concealed inside car or under hood.

10. Wheel base, length and width must be stock.

11. All cars must have safety glass. All head light and tail light glass must be removed.

12. All cars must have full windshield in place and used as windshield. No glass or material other than safety glass may be used.

13. Cars must be equipped with rear view mirror.

14. All cars must be subject to safety inspection by Technical Committee at any time.

15. All cars must have 4-wheel hydraulic brakes or any brake manufactured after 1947.

16. Piston displacement in any car is limited to 300 cu. in. except where motor is used in same body and chassis it was designed and catalogued for. Under 300 cu. in. motors may be interchanged in same manufacturer's line.

The Committee recommends for the 1949 season

★　　★

1948 RULES and SPECIFICATIONS

17. Any block can be oversize. The only truck blocks permitted to be used in any Stock Car will be 100 H. P. Ford Blocks which are fundamentally same as passenger car. These may only be used in models up to 1947 Fords. (Stock interchangeable passenger car blocks must be used in all cars through 1947.)

18. Cars may be run with or without fan or generator.

19. Any fly wheel may be used.

20. Any part may be reinforced.

21. Any interchangeable wheel or tire size may be used.

22. Any rear end arrangement may be used.

23. Any radiator may be used providing stock hood will close and latch properly. Hoods must have safety straps. All cars must have hoods on and must be stock hood for same model car.

24. Any type battery ignition may be used, excluding magnetos.

25. Any type of manufactured spark plug may be used.

26. Any model manufactured flat type cylinder heads may be used. Cylinder heads may be machined to increase compression.

27. Heads allowed with overhead valves only when coming as standard or optional equipment from factory.

28. Any valve springs may be used.

29. Multiple carburetion will be permitted. Any type carburetion may be used.

30. Superchargers allowed only when optional on stock equipment by manufacturer.

31. Water pump impellers may be cut down.

32. Altered cam shafts will be permitted.

33. Altered crank shafts may be used.

34. All drivers must be strapped in and must wear safety helmets. Belt must be bolted to frame at two points and must be aviation latch type quick release belt.

35. Regulation crash helmets must be used.

that 1937 Models be dropped from competition

All tracks must be inspected by NASCAR or its representative before a sanction will be granted.

NASCAR or its representative reserves the right to reject any entry for failure to comply with any rules or regulations.

In all NASCAR sanctioned races, when checkered flag is given to winning car, the race is officially over and all cars will stop on that lap. Finishing positions will be paid according to distance run, whether car is still running or not.

No race shall be run over 5 laps on the caution flag without stopping the race. This is to be at the discretion of the steward.

In the event of a protest, $500.00 must be deposited with NASCAR representative by driver making his protest within 10 minutes after completion of event. Protest fee will be forfeited and applied to hospital fund if judges and scorers rule against protest. The decision of judges and scorers is final. Appeal of any protest can be made in writing to the NASCAR Board of Governors for consideration at the annual convention but appeal will not change above rules on day of race and all positions will be paid according to the decision rendered.

These rules are subject to change on recommendations of the Committee.

Notice of any rule changes or additions will be sent to NASCAR members from national headquarters.

... Retain These Rules For Future Reference ...

First NASCAR Race Report — Daytona Beach-Road Course

FEBRUARY 15, 1948

Just four weeks after NASCAR's historic organizational meeting at the Streamline Hotel, and one week before becoming incorporated, NASCAR held its inaugural race on the Daytona Beach-road course.

Red Byron, who would become NASCAR's first national series champion, won the event, which had 67 cars and a total purse of $3,500.

Some class names in this first event: runner-up Marshall Teague, Bob and Fonty Flock, and one female driver, Louise Taylor, who finished 16th.

REPRESENTATIVE'S RACE REPORT

Name of Track *Daytona Beach Road Course* Date *2/15* 19*48*

City or Town *Daytona Beach* State *Fla.*

Name of Promoter or Manager *Bill France*

NASCAR Representative in Charge of Event *Lucky Sauer*

Amount of Prize Money $*3,500 00* Championship Point Fund $ *175 00*

Benevolent Fund $ *235 00* Total Number of Cars Entered *67*

Approximate Attendance _____ Approximate Paid Attendance $_____

List here the finishing positions of all drivers in the feature race regardless of whether they finished or not. The number of laps completed shall determine positions of non-finishers. Number of finishers shall be according to the purse involved as listed here: $1,000—14; $1,500—15; $2,000—16; $2,500—17; $3,000—18; adding one position for each additional $500 of prize money.

1st *Red Byron* 2nd *Marshall Teague* 3rd *Bob Flock* 4th *Buddy Shuman*

5th *J. L. McMickol* 6th *Swayne Pritchett* 7th *Lee Morgan* 8th *Ed Samples*

9th *Howard Farmer* 10th *John Gulb* 11th *Dick O'Brien* 12th *Fonty Flock*

13th *Roscoe Thompson* 14th *Glenn Law* 15th *Frank Mc* 16th *Louise Taylor*

17th *Gober Sosebe* 18th *Paul Sanborn* 19th *Red Croft* 20th _____

Signature of Representative _____

This report shall be mailed to NASCAR headquarters within 48 hours of completion of race meet. Included with this report shall be Accident Report form, New Membership Blanks, copy of payoff sheet, checks or money order for Championship Point Fund money and Benevolent Fund money.

Announcement of Plans to Build
Daytona International Speedway and Form the
International Speedway Corporation

NOVEMBER 9, 1957

ANNOUNCEMENT BY BILL FRANCE SR.

We are organizing the Daytona Beach International Speedway Corporation, which will begin construction within 30 days on an automobile race track to cost an estimated $750,000.

The first event will be a NASCAR-sanctioned 500-mile late model stock car race in 1959 on George Washington's birthday, February 22. The track will be the fastest in the country, supporting speeds up to 200 miles per hour. The plant with have 10,000 permanent seats plus temporary bleachers. There will be standing room in the infield – same as in Indianapolis.

The plans are designed so that the speedway can be expanded and it is my goal in the future to more than triple the seating and, correspondingly, improve the racing facilities.

The international safety and speed trials on the beach straightaway will be continued in conjunction with the racing activities at the speedway. But the last 160-mile event on the present 3.2-mile beach-road track will be February 23, 1958. All future races will be at the speedway.

In addition to the annual 500-mile winter stock car classic, a summer stock car event will be at the speedway, probably on July 4.

Plans also call for building a winding sports car course around the infield of the speedway. Target date for the sports car course is 1961.

Bill France Sr. Interview with WNDB Radio

FEBRUARY 1986

Announcer: Speedweeks 1986 is well underway. . . . Thousands of people were in town last week. . . . This week thousands more for Busch Clash. . . . Millions on television. . . . Millions coming in to the total economy. . . . Years ago there was racing on the beach. Later the speedway was built. . . . Today we take a walk back in history. . . . We will talk about how the cars were on the beach and how the speedway came to be. . . . We will talk to a gentleman. . . . A leader in the community. . . . A founder of NASCAR, the founder of the speedway. . . . Central to the modernization of worldwide racing. . . . Bill France Sr.

Bill France Sr.: I was born in Washington, D.C., and lived there until I was married. And while I was going to school up there, there was a speedway out at Laurel, Maryland, a board speedway between Baltimore and Washington . . . and I used to go out there and watch the cars go around that track. Then when I got myself a job, I was mechanically inclined, I got a job in the summertime at a filling station and we had to work on a lot of cars in the snow and ice of the winter. So I decided if I was going to work on cars in the winter I'd come down to Florida for the rest of my life.

My wife Annie and I came to Florida and I got a job working for Sax Lloyd, the Cadillac dealer in town, in 1934. In 1935 I saw Sir Malcolm Campbell make the fastest run he ever made on the beach, about 256 miles per hour I believe . . . but that was his last time here because he went to the Bonneville Salt Flats after that to run. The next year there was a fellow named Sig Haugdahl who teamed up with the city and helped design the first stock car race on the beach. I didn't help put the race on but I raced in it. I finished fifth.

The following year the city decided they weren't going to have a race. But by this time I had my own gas station over on Main Street and one of my customers had the best restaurant in town. His name was Charlie Reese. So Charlie was interested in keeping racing here and asked me if I knew how to put the race on. I told him yeah, but I don't have any dough. So he said I'll bankroll it and we'll go partners. So that's how I got into the race promoting business.

Announcer: What was it like racing on the beach?

Bill France Sr.: I enjoyed it. It was pretty much fun for me. When we'd come up the beach, of course you had to figure some way to keep your windshield clean. If you were driving up behind somebody the salt water and sand would cloud your windshield. But it wasn't bad.

But I pointed out to the city eventually that if they wanted to continue races here and keep motorsports as a function in the community they should have a big permanent facility. And I help design the one we have now (Daytona International Speedway).

I asked how steep a bank could be paved with asphalt. That's how come we have the track banked the way it is. It hasn't been all bad. Were other tracks banked steep at that time? The only ones with steep banks were wooden tracks. The problem was there was no way to stop the wood from rotting so they went out of business. The banking made new speeds possible. And I felt that if we had the right kind of facility, we could race on and people could also see what's going on. I did keep in mind the spectators. I never considered making it a traditional oval track because people couldn't see as good as they can see now. Talladega Superspeedway, we built that the same as Daytona except it's a little steeper and longer and a little faster. Daytona and Talladega have had a lot of influence on what cars and tires are doing today. I think we've been helpful in the development of motor vehicles. I don't regret the fact that I have been involved.

Announcer: What is Bill France Sr. doing these days?

Bill France Sr.: Keeping up with the motorsports world, not only here but in other parts of the country. I've turned the management over to my two sons, Bill and Jim, and they are doing a commendable job. I do some boating in the summer time.

Announcer: How would you like to be remembered?

Bill France Sr.: I think if people would remember me as being not too bad a guy, I'd like that. I've tried to be a good guy all of my life. If I tell somebody I'm going to do something, well that's what I intend to do. I've been honest about things.

Announcer: When I've travelled across the country and I tell someone I live in Daytona Beach, Florida, they often bring up two subjects, the beach and the racing events at Daytona International

Speedway . . . the Daytona 500. Looking at the history of our area and our nation it is obvious that Bill France Sr. has made a major impact not only on automobile development and racing itself, but people throughout the world.

Sport Magazine 40th Anniversary Special Collectors Edition: Bill France Sr.

DECEMBER 1986

Sixty years [after building his first race car] he is an old king, a blue, bearish silhouette against the lavender Florida sky. He is far from the early days of looking for a ride (meaning backers), of saving dimes and nickels, of borrowing from friends as poor as himself for just enough gas to get to the track.

Senior, as he is known around the office, has turned over the empire to his son Bill France Jr., conveniently known as Junior here at headquarters [in Daytona Beach]. Yet, the old man is here every day. He is 77, still way over 200 pounds, his 6-5 frame unstooped by the tentacles of time. As he stood and motioned to a picture of an ancient Dodge, I was conscious of the fact that here indeed was Abner Doubleday, the Rutgers-Princeton game, and the Marquis of Queensbury in one being. In short, he is the last living man to have founded a major sport.

"How'd you end up in Daytona?" I asked.

The old man chuckled. "Easy. I ran out of money."

Birmingham News Column, by Clyde Bolton

FEBRUARY 19, 1997

I think Bill France Sr. is the only authentic genius I ever met. Certainly he was the smartest person and that includes three presidents of the U.S.

He asked me to write his biography. "We'll go out on my boat," he said, "and you can take your tape recorder and we'll stay a couple of days at a time, and I'll tell you some stories."

They would have been marvelous stories . . . I looked forward with tingling anticipation to writing that book. And then, one day I strolled into France's office at Talladega Superspeedway, as I had done scores of times, and he had no idea who I was. That great mind was under bombardment by Alzheimer's disease.

Years before, France had told me he never planned to retire. "Victor Hugo said when you stop fighting the battles of life you start to die; I believe that."

I'm glad he couldn't foresee the final battle that awaited him.

Interview with Bill France Sr. (author unknown)

I realized that during the interview with Big Bill I wasn't getting information.

I was getting advice.

International Motorsports Hall of Fame of America
Bill France Jr. Induction

MAY 2004

TALLADEGA, ALABAMA

ACCEPTANCE SPEECH GIVEN BY BILL FRANCE JR.

It's a great honor to be here tonight on a professional level and even more so on a personal level. Tonight, I get to see my name listed next to the man who laid the groundwork for everything I've been able to accomplish, Bill France Sr., who was inducted here in 1990.

NASCAR is moving fast these days, on and off the track.

Our sport has grown tremendously, to the point where sometimes it's hard to imagine the days, many years ago, when NASCAR was basically a two-man operation run by my father and his right-hand man at the time, Pat Purcell.

They did it all. And they did it well.

When I think of how they forged on, in the face of adversity and uncertainty, I'm reminded of a poem by a fellow named Edward Sill.

It's called "Opportunity."

The poem is about a great battle, and how a brave soldier was wounded and lost his weapon. On the edge of the battlefield, a coward had given up the fight, snapped his sword in two, flung it to the ground and run away.

The coward's sword was crude and blunt, nothing like the precision blue-steel blade the brave soldier had lost. But when the brave soldier came upon that sword half-buried in the dirt, he snatched it up and carried on the fight.

Here's how the writer put it:

"With battle-shout, lifted afresh, he hewed his enemy down . . . and saved a great cause that heroic day."

In simple terms, the soldier saw an opportunity, and made the most of it.

That was the way my father approached things. Decisively – and bravely.

We need to remember those days, the battles fought and the opportunities sought. And we should acknowledge how important those days were to building what we enjoy today.

You can't build anything successful without a solid foundation – be it a house or a business. My father made sure that NASCAR would have a solid foundation.

He knew the importance of that because he knew we were headed toward something big.

He knew that from the beginning.

At the December 1947 meeting in Daytona that created NASCAR, this is what he told those in attendance:

"Stock car racing has got distinct possibilities for Sunday shows and we do not know how big it can be if it's handled properly. . . . I believe stock car racing can become a nationally recognized sport."

Through the years, so many factors have contributed to the foundation of NASCAR and later the growth of NASCAR. We've been fortunate to be involved with outstanding drivers, great race tracks, companies like Champion, Pure Oil, and R.J. Reynolds. A lot of good people, working together.

There are a lot of good people here tonight.

Let me take a moment to congratulate the other inductees.

I know they all feel the same gratitude I do, about being honored this evening.

This is a great night, not only for me but also for all the people who came before me. They made it all possible.

In many cases I simply followed the lead of others.

There is no one I followed more than Bill France Sr.

Bill Sr. had a lot of favorite sayings. Here's one of those: "On the Plains of Hesitation lie the bleached bones of countless millions. Who, when within the grasp of victory, sat and waited . . . and waiting died."

Bill Sr., as some of you here tonight remember, was not real big on waiting.

He knew what he wanted for the great sport of stock car racing. He went out and made it happen, and didn't wait.

I think I'm here tonight because I've tried to follow his style along the way. That being the case, I feel like I've served his memory well.

I hope that in the process, I've also served our sport well.

Thank you.

United States Business Hall of Fame Induction Speech

APRIL 9, 2008

NASHVILLE, TENNESSEE

SPEECH GIVEN BY J.C. FRANCE, GRANDSON OF BILL FRANCE SR.

It's truly an honor to be with you tonight and be part of this event.

This is really a proud moment for the France family and the

sport of NASCAR overall, to see my grandfather's name listed next to so many giants of industry in this country.

It's also very humbling, when you look at the list of past inductees into the U.S. Business Hall of Fame.

One name on that list I found especially interesting: Henry Flagler, the man who helped put Daytona Beach, Florida on the map – literally – with his revolutionary Florida East Coast Railway, in 1890.

Not long after that, the Daytona area became famous for fast cars.

Starting in 1903, drivers came from all over to chase the land speed record on what would become known as the world's most famous beach.

Forty-four years after Flagler's railroad rolled into Daytona, in 1934, the France family arrived. At the wheel of the family Ford was a man who, like Henry Flagler, was a visionary, a man who made dreams come to life by the sheer force of his will . . .

My grandfather, William Henry Getty France.

They called him Big Bill and not only because he was 6-foot-5.

He had big ideas.

And big dreams.

[PAUSE]

Not long after moving to Daytona Beach, he got involved in the promotion of races that used both the beach and a stretch of the A1A coastal road. He also raced himself in those days, but his concerns for the welfare of the sport turned his interest to the business side.

Aiming to shift that business into high gear, in 1947 he assembled a group of leaders of what was then the very unorganized sport of stock car racing.

He wanted organization – and he got it, with the founding of NASCAR.

Twelve years later, another dream of his became realized, with the opening of the 2.5-mile Daytona International Speedway. What's especially impressive is that he actually helped build that facility with his own two hands.

From that point on, he never looked back – only forward.

Through the years, his vision included other forms of racing, and eventually brought the world's greatest drivers to his city, for the creation of the famed 24 Hours of Daytona.

He was also responsible for the inclusion of many NASCAR stars into the 24 Hours of Le Mans, in 1976, as they competed in a special stock car class that year.

[PAUSE]

Every successful business needs a solid foundation. My grandfather made sure NASCAR would have that.

He knew how important that was right from the outset, because he knew NASCAR was headed toward something big.

His success had a lot in common with another member of the U.S. Business Hall of Fame – Henry Ford.

Henry Ford didn't invent the automobile but he invented a process, a way to make the automobile a healthy business endeavor.

Likewise, Bill France Sr. didn't invent the sport of stock car racing, but he too developed a process that resulted in a thriving business.

[PAUSE]

My grandfather was a creative man – and a colorful man.

He was a large man, in terms of stature, but in many other ways, he was larger than life.

[PAUSE]

Big Bill France knew what he wanted for the sport of stock car racing. And he went out and made it happen.

In closing, I just want to again thank everyone who made tonight happen.

Everyone in the France family is extremely grateful and so very proud of this induction.

My grandfather was a great man, and this is a great honor.

We are very appreciative.

Thank you – and enjoy the rest of your evening.

NASCAR Hall of Fame Induction Speech for Bill France Sr.

MAY 25, 2010

CHARLOTTE, NORTH CAROLINA

SPEECH GIVEN BY JOHN CASSIDY

Good afternoon everyone.

No one deserves to be in the NASCAR Hall of Fame more than Bill France Sr., since there would not have been a NASCAR without Bill.

[PAUSE]

Bill France Sr. first became a part of my life almost 50 years ago, in 1961, when I was working in Washington as a special assistant to another great man, Robert Kennedy . . . the attorney general at that time.

Kennedy called me and gave me what you would call a "warning."

He said a man named Bill France was coming down the hall . . . to my office.

"This fellow has something to do with auto racing," said Kennedy, who obviously knew very little about motorsports.

He went on to say, "Jimmy Hoffa is giving him a hard time and WE must help him."

Shortly after Kennedy's call, the door to my office opened and, filling the doorway, was one of the biggest men I had ever seen. It was Bill France, Sr., whose first words to me were, "SON, we have a problem, and Mr. Kennedy says you have the answer."

[PAUSE]

Bill pulled up a chair and proceeded to educate me over several hours on the history of motorsports, the history of "racing on the beach," stock car racing, and NASCAR.

He explained that NASCAR was created to bring order to the sport, to guarantee prize money would be paid, and to adopt and enforce the rules of competition . . . he also emphasized NASCAR-sanctioned events would someday become a recognized professional sport.

Little did I know then how much that first encounter with Big Bill France would change my life's work . . . for it led to a career in the practice of law focused in large part on motorsports.

I witnessed first-hand the growth of NASCAR and stock car racing to a level of public acceptance beyond Bill Sr.'s wildest dreams.

My experience was not unlike that which many of you here today have enjoyed . . . whether you are a fan, a competitor, a sponsor, or a track operator . . . we all have experienced the joy of being associated with NASCAR . . . because NASCAR stands for EXCELLENCE in motorsports.

People frequently say Bill Sr. was a "visionary." I don't dispute that, but I prefer to call him a "dreamer" who was also "a man of action" . . . someone who turned dreams into reality.

Not only did Bill follow his dreams . . . he expected the rest of us to do likewise.

Senior relished a challenge . . . the bigger the better.

He once quoted George Bernard Shaw to me, saying:

"Some look at things that are, and ask . . . Why?

"I dream of things that never were and ask . . . Why not?"

When I left the Department of Justice to start a law firm, Bill Sr. and his wife, Annie B., saw to it that NASCAR and ISC were our first clients.

I soon found myself in Daytona, working with them on many NASCAR projects.

I lived with them while in Daytona and was involved in many "breakfast table" discussions that were primarily devoted to expansion projects, such as whether to build Talladega.

It was during those discussions, that frequently included their oldest son Bill – Jim was in the military in those days – that the significance of Annie B.'s role in NASCAR and ISC became apparent.

Annie B. had a fine sense of business and finance.

She was a full-fledged partner with Bill Sr. on every significant business issue that confronted NASCAR and ISC.

While Bill Sr. created NASCAR and built two superspeedways . . . he did far more.

Bill Sr. championed the effort that gained national and worldwide recognition for NASCAR's brand of stock car racing.

His efforts attracted some of the world's finest competitors and corporate sponsors – many of whom are substantial supporters of this Hall of Fame.

Bill Sr.'s efforts led to the creation of NASCAR's fan base, which is second to none in the professional sports world.

To attract this kind of attention, Bill Sr. knew his sport needed an annual national champion, if it was going to be recognized on the same level as other professional sports.

Needless to say, the NASCAR champion today is mentioned in the same breath as World Series champions, and the champions of other professional sports. In fact, four-time NASCAR champion Jimmie Johnson was named "Male Athlete of the Year" in 2009 by The Associated Press . . . a recognition of NASCAR's sports prominence.

Bill Sr. not only nurtured a major professional sport from infancy to adulthood, but he and Annie B. raised a wonderful family, who have followed in their footsteps, with the help of the very talented NASCAR family . . . taking NASCAR to the next plateau, a plateau of great popularity.

Bill Sr. never forgot the humble beginnings from which both he and NASCAR sprung, and . . . while he walked with ease in the corridors of power in Washington and elsewhere . . . he walked with equal grace through the infields and garages during NASCAR events.

A walk with Bill Sr. through an infield was truly a walk among good friends . . . most of them greeting him as "Bill."

While he could be tough as nails, especially when dealing with race competition issues, Senior was always fair and compassionate to those faced with adversity.

And, when a race driver or car owner was down on his luck, Bill Sr. was always there to help him out.

Bill was loyal and especially interested in those who shared the early days of racing with him.

And, he could be the consummate diplomat and politician when the occasion demanded.

Bill had a forceful personality combined with a reputation for integrity.

The word "big" was always on Bill's mind.

One autumn night many years ago . . . Bill Sr. and I were driving on the beach at Daytona when the moon rose over the ocean . . . It was a huge golden "Harvest Moon."

Bill turned to me and said, "Son, that's a pretty big moon for a small town like this."

Bill's dreams of growth for NASCAR were only exceeded by his desire that stock car racing become a recognized and respected professional sport in America. If he were here today he would be the first to acknowledge NASCAR has exceeded his dreams.

I can think of no better way to close than to reference one of Bill Sr.'s favorite songs.

Suffice it to say that Bill France Sr. . . . . INDEED . . . did it his way.

[PAUSE]

Please join me now in welcoming to the stage Bill France Sr.'s son, the chairman of the International Speedway Corporation and NASCAR's vice chairman, Jim France.

NASCAR Hall of Fame Bill France Sr. Induction Acceptance Speech

MAY 25, 2010

CHARLOTTE, NORTH CAROLINA

SPEECH GIVEN BY JIM FRANCE

On behalf of everyone in our family, thank you for that introduction and great tribute to my father.

Let me begin by saying that our family is very proud to be involved in this memorable afternoon for the induction of my father and my brother Bill. We would like to thank the Hall of Fame voting panel for including them in this inaugural class with Junior, Richard, and Dale, truly the iconic heroes of NASCAR.

If Dad were here today, he would be proud, as well, but in a different way. He would be proud mostly for NASCAR. He would be proud of this Hall of Fame, a commitment made to honor our past and to recognize the individuals who are responsible for making NASCAR what it is today, for their great accomplishments.

The NASCAR Hall of Fame in many ways is the ultimate tribute to my father, the hopes and dreams that he had for our sport.

In closing, I would like to offer the donation of this ring back to the hall for display wherever they would choose to place it.

Thank you.

The Quotes

"I knew that we – me and my partners – were on to something. We had stock bodies and engines racing. A fellow could actually see something that he owned race at over a hundred miles an hour. That made the sport different." – Talking about the early days of NASCAR

"I feel that automobiles are really not the problem. I think they've been kicked around principally because they can't talk back." – Regarding the late-1960s nationwide debate about highway safety

"Don't forget, the Ten Commandments were written on stone – and they've lasted a long time." – Describing the importance of newspaper coverage to NASCAR's growth in popularity

"We also have a bathroom in the back, but it doesn't work." – Conveying some unfortunate news to passengers on his private plane, prior to a several-hour flight in 1982, to the NASCAR Sprint Cup awards ceremony in New York

"One of the strongest factors in stock car racing's success has been the way that plain, ordinary people can associate with the cars and drivers." – 1950s assessment

From the Bible – Proverbs 31:6

Bill France Sr. was not an outwardly religious man, but he retained a deep spirituality developed in his childhood when church attendance was mandated by his parents, as was Bible study. Although Bill found excuses to sometimes avoid church services, he memorized many of the Bible lessons, especially from the book of Proverbs.

His favorite Bible verse was Proverbs 31:6.

"Give strong drink unto him that is ready to perish, and wine unto those that be of heavy hearts. Let him drink, and forget his poverty, and remember his misery no more."

It is easy to imagine this scripture being at the core of one of Bill Sr.'s most recognizable traits – generosity.

The Statistics: 1949–92

In 1949, NASCAR's second season of existence but the first for what would evolve into today's NASCAR Sprint Cup Series, series champion Red Byron collected a total of $5,800 in race winnings. In 1992, the year Bill France Sr. died, series champion Alan Kulwicki won a total of $2,322,561. Following is a recap of each of those seasons. Combined, they encompass the leadership – and a good portion of the life – of Big Bill France.

NASCAR Cup Champions 1949-1992

Year	Driver	Winnings	Year	Driver	Winnings
1949	Red Byron	$5,800	1971	Richard Petty	$309,225
1950	Bill Rexford	$6,175	1972	Richard Petty	$227,015
1951	Herb Thomas	$18,200	1973	Benny Parsons	$114,345
1952	Tim Flock	$20,210	1974	Richard Petty	$299,175
1953	Herb Thomas	$27,300	1975	Richard Petty	$378,865
1954	Lee Petty	$26,706	1976	Cale Yarborough	$387,173
1955	Tim Flock	$33,750	1977	Cale Yarborough	$477,499
1956	Buck Baker	$29,790	1978	Cale Yarborough	$530,751
1957	Buck Baker	$24,712	1979	Richard Petty	$531,292
1958	Lee Petty	$20,600	1980	Dale Earnhardt	$588,926
1959	Lee Petty	$45,570	1981	Darrell Waltrip	$693,342
1960	Rex White	$45,260	1982	Darrell Waltrip	$873,118
1961	Ned Jarrett	$27,285	1983	Bobby Allison	$828,355
1962	Joe Weatherly	$56,110	1984	Terry Labonte	$713,010
1963	Joe Weatherly	$58,110	1985	Darrell Waltrip	$1,318,735
1964	Richard Petty	$98,810	1986	Dale Earnhardt	$1,783,880
1965	Ned Jarrett	$77,966	1987	Dale Earnhardt	$2,099,243
1966	David Pearson	$59,205	1988	Bill Elliott	$1,574,639
1967	Richard Petty	$130,275	1989	Rusty Wallace	$2,247,950
1968	David Pearson	$118,842	1990	Dale Earnhardt	$3,083,056
1969	David Pearson	$183,700	1991	Dale Earnhardt	$2,416,685
1970	Bobby Isaac	$121,470	1992	Alan Kulwicki	$2,322,561

1949

FINAL CHAMPIONSHIP STANDINGS TOP 10

Rank	Driver	Points
1	Red Byron	842.50
2	Lee Petty	725.00
3	Bob Flock	704.00

FINAL CHAMPIONSHIP STANDINGS TOP 10 (CONT.)

Rank	Driver	Points
4	Bill Blair	567.50
5	Fonty Flock	554.50
6	Curtis Turner	430.00
7	Ray Erickson	422.00
8	Tim Flock	421.00
9	Glenn Dunaway	384.00
10	Frank Mundy	370.00

RACE WINNERS

Race	Location	Date	Winning Driver
1	Charlotte, NC	June 19	Jim Roper
2	Daytona Beach, FL	July 10	Red Byron
3	Hillsboro, NC	Aug 7	Bob Flock
4	Langhorne, PA	Sept 11	Curtis Turner
5	Hamburg, NY	Sept 18	Jack White
6	Martinsville, VA	Sept 25	Red Byron
7	Carnegie, PA	Oct 2	Lee Petty
8	North Wilkesboro, NC	Oct 16	Bob Flock

1950

FINAL CHAMPIONSHIP STANDINGS TOP 10

Rank	Driver	Points
1	Bill Rexford	1,959.00
2	Fireball Roberts	1,848.50
3	Lee Petty	1,590.00
4	Lloyd Moore	1,398.00
5	Curtis Turner	1,375.50
6	Johnny Mantz	1,282.00

Rank	Driver	Points
7	Chuck Mahoney	1,217.50
8	Dick Linder	1,121.00
9	Jimmy Florian	801.00
10	Bill Blair	766.00

RACE WINNERS

Race	Location	Date	Winning Driver
1	Daytona Beach, FL	Feb 5	Harold Kite
2	Charlotte, NC	April 2	Tim Flock
3	Langhorne, PA	April 16	Curtis Turner
4	Martinsville, VA	May 21	Curtis Turner
5	Canfield, OH	May 30	Bill Rexford
6	Vernon, NY	June 18	Bill Blair
7	Dayton, OH	June 25	Jimmy Florian
8	Rochester, NY	July 2	Curtis Turner
9	Charlotte, NC	July 23	Curtis Turner
10	Hillsboro, NC	Aug 13	Fireball Roberts
11	Dayton, OH	Aug 20	Dick Linder
12	Hamburg, NY	Aug 27	Dick Linder
13	Darlington, SC	Sept 4	Johnny Mantz
14	Langhorne, PA	Sept 17	Fonty Flock
15	North Wilkesboro, NC	Sept 24	Leon Sales
16	Vernon, NY	Oct 1	Dick Linder
17	Martinsville, VA	Oct 15	Herb Thomas
18	Winchester, IN	Oct 15	Lloyd Moore
19	Hillsboro, NC	Oct 29	Lee Petty

1951

FINAL CHAMPIONSHIP STANDINGS TOP 10

Rank	Driver	Points
1	Herb Thomas	4,208.45
2	Fonty Flock	4,062.25
3	Tim Flock	3,722.50
4	Lee Petty	2,392.25
5	Frank Mundy	1,963.50
6	Buddy Shuman	1,368.75
7	Jesse James Taylor	1,214.00
8	Dick Rathmann	1,040.00
9	Bill Snowden	1,009.25
10	Joe Eubanks	1,005.50

RACE WINNERS

Race	Location	Date	Winning Driver
1	Daytona Beach, FL	Feb 11	Marshall Teague
2	Charlotte, NC	April 1	Curtis Turner
3	Mobile, AL	April 8	Tim Flock
4	Gardena, CA	April 8	Marshall Teague
5	Hillsboro, NC	April 15	Fonty Flock
6	Phoenix, AZ	April 22	Marshall Teague
7	North Wilkesboro, NC	April 29	Fonty Flock
8	Martinsville, VA	May 6	Curtis Turner
9	Canfield, OH	May 30	Marshall Teague
10	Columbus, GA	June 10	Tim Flock
11	Columbia, SC	June 16	Frank Mundy
12	Dayton, OH	June 24	Curtis Turner
13	Gardena, CA	June 30	Lou Figaro
14	Grand Rapids, MI	July 1	Marshall Teague

Race	Location	Date	Winning Driver
15	Bainbridge, OH	July 8	Fonty Flock
16	Carnegie, PA	July 15	Herb Thomas
17	Weaverville, NC	July 29	Fonty Flock
18	Rochester, NY	July 31	Lee Petty
19	Altamont, NY	Aug 1	Fonty Flock
20	Detroit, MI	Aug 12	Tommy Thompson
21	Toledo, OH	Aug 19	Tim Flock
22	Morristown, NJ	Aug 24	Tim Flock
23	Greenville, SC	Aug 25	Bob Flock
24	Darlington, SC	Sept 3	Herb Thomas
25	Columbia, SC	Sept 7	Tim Flock
26	Macon, GA	Sept 8	Herb Thomas
27	Langhorne, PA	Sept 15	Herb Thomas
28	Charlotte, NC	Sept 23	Herb Thomas
29	Dayton, OH	Sept 23	Fonty Flock
30	Wilson, NC	Sept 30	Fonty Flock
31	Hillsboro, NC	Oct 7	Herb Thomas
32	Thompson, CT	Oct 12	Neil Cole
33	Shippenville, PA	Oct 14	Tim Flock
34	Martinsville, VA	Oct 14	Frank Mundy
35	Oakland, CA	Oct 14	Marvin Burke
36	North Wilkesboro, NC	Oct 21	Fonty Flock
37	Hanford, CA	Oct 28	Danny Weinberg
38	Jacksonville, FL	Nov 4	Herb Thomas
39	Atlanta, GA	Nov 11	Tim Flock
40	Gardena, CA	Nov 11	Bill Norton
41	Mobile, AL	Nov 25	Frank Mundy

1952

FINAL CHAMPIONSHIP STANDINGS TOP 10

Rank	Driver	Points
1	Tim Flock	6,858.50
2	Herb Thomas	6,752.50
3	Lee Petty	6,498.50
4	Fonty Flock	5,183.50
5	Dick Rathmann	3,952.50
6	Bill Blair	3,499.00
7	Joe Eubanks	3,090.50
8	Ray Duhigg	2,986.50
9	Donald Thomas	2,574.00
10	Buddy Shuman	2,483.00

RACE WINNERS

Race	Location	Date	Winning Driver
1	West Palm Beach, FL	Jan 20	Tim Flock
2	Daytona Beach, FL	Feb 10	Marshall Teague
3	Jacksonville, FL	March 6	Marshall Teague
4	North Wilkesboro, NC	March 30	Herb Thomas
5	Martinsville, VA	April 6	Dick Rathmann
6	Columbia, SC	April 12	Buck Baker
7	Atlanta, GA	April 20	Bill Blair
8	Macon, GA	April 27	Herb Thomas
9	Langhorne, PA	May 4	Dick Rathmann
10	Darlington, SC	May 10	Dick Rathmann
11	Dayton, OH	May 18	Dick Rathmann
12	Canfield, OH	May 30	Herb Thomas
13	Augusta, GA	June 1	Gober Sosebee
14	Toledo, OH	June 1	Tim Flock

Race	Location	Date	Winning Driver
15	Hillsboro, NC	June 8	Tim Flock
16	Charlotte, NC	June 15	Herb Thomas
17	Detroit, MI	June 29	Tim Flock
18	Niagara Falls, ON, Canada	July 1	Buddy Shuman
19	Oswego, NY	July 4	Tim Flock
20	Monroe, MI	July 6	Tim Flock
21	Morristown, NJ	July 11	Lee Petty
22	South Bend, IN	July 20	Tim Flock
23	Rochester, NY	Aug 15	Tim Flock
24	Weaverville, NC	Aug 17	Bob Flock
25	Darlington, SC	Sept 1	Fonty Flock
26	Macon, GA	Sept 7	Lee Petty
27	Langhorne, PA	Sept 14	Lee Petty
28	Dayton, OH	Sept 21	Dick Rathmann
29	Wilson, NC	Sept 28	Herb Thomas
30	Hillsboro, NC	Oct 12	Fonty Flock
31	Martinsville, VA	Oct 19	Herb Thomas
32	North Wilkesboro, NC	Oct 26	Herb Thomas
33	Atlanta, GA	Nov 16	Donald Thomas
34	West Palm Beach, FL	Nov 30	Herb Thomas

1953

FINAL CHAMPIONSHIP STANDINGS TOP 10

Rank	Driver	Points
1	Herb Thomas	8,460
2	Lee Petty	7,814
3	Dick Rathmann	7,362
4	Buck Baker	6,713

FINAL CHAMPIONSHIP STANDINGS TOP 10 (CONT.)

Rank	Driver	Points
5	Fonty Flock	6,174
6	Tim Flock	5,011
7	Jim Paschal	4,211
8	Joe Eubanks	3,603
9	Jimmie Lewallen	3,508
10	Curtis Turner	3,373

RACE WINNERS

Race	Location	Date	Winning Driver
1	West Palm Beach, FL	Feb 1	Lee Petty
2	Daytona Beach, FL	Feb 15	Bill Blair
3	Spring Lake, NC	March 8	Herb Thomas
4	North Wilkesboro, NC	March 29	Herb Thomas
5	Charlotte, NC	June 5	Dick Passwater
6	Richmond, VA	June 19	Lee Petty
7	Macon, GA	June 26	Dick Rathmann
8	Langhorne, PA	May 3	Buck Baker
9	Columbia, SC	May 9	Buck Baker
10	Hickory, NC	May 16	Tim Flock
11	Martinsville, VA	May 17	Lee Petty
12	Columbus, OH	May 24	Herb Thomas
13	Raleigh, NC	May 30	Fonty Flock
14	Shreveport, LA	June 7	Lee Petty
15	Pensacola, FL	June 14	Herb Thomas
16	Langhorne, PA	June 21	Dick Rathmann
17	High Point, NC	June 26	Herb Thomas
18	Wilson, NC	June 28	Fonty Flock

Race	Location	Date	Winning Driver
19	Rochester, NY	July 3	Herb Thomas
20	Spartanburg, SC	July 4	Lee Petty
21	Morristown, NJ	July 10	Dick Rathmann
22	Atlanta, GA	July 12	Herb Thomas
23	Rapid City, SD	July 22	Herb Thomas
24	North Platte, NE	July 26	Dick Rathmann
25	Davenport, IA	Aug 2	Herb Thomas
26	Hillsboro, NC	Aug 9	Curtis Turner
27	Weaverville, NC	Aug 16	Fonty Flock
28	Norfolk, VA	Aug 23	Herb Thomas
29	Hickory, NC	Aug 29	Fonty Flock
30	Darlington, SC	Sept 7	Buck Baker
31	Macon, GA	Sept 13	Speedy Thompson
32	Langhorne, PA	Sept 20	Dick Rathmann
33	Bloomsburg, PA	Oct 3	Herb Thomas
34	Wilson, NC	Oct 4	Herb Thomas
35	North Wilkesboro, NC	Oct 11	Speedy Thompson
36	Martinsville, VA	Oct 18	Jim Paschal
37	Atlanta, GA	Nov 1	Buck Baker

1954

FINAL CHAMPIONSHIP STANDINGS TOP 10

Rank	Driver	Points
1	Lee Petty	8,649
2	Herb Thomas	8,366
3	Buck Baker	6,893
4	Dick Rathmann	6,760
5	Joe Eubanks	5,467

FINAL CHAMPIONSHIP STANDINGS TOP 10 (CONT.)

Rank	Driver	Points
6	Hershel McGriff	5,137
7	Jim Paschal	3,903
8	Jimmie Lewallen	3,233
9	Curtis Turner	2,994
10	Ralph Liguori	2,905

RACE WINNERS

Race	Location	Date	Winning Driver
1	West Palm Beach, FL	Feb 7	Herb Thomas
2	Daytona Beach, FL	Feb 21	Lee Petty
3	Jacksonville, FL	March 7	Herb Thomas
4	Atlanta, GA	March 21	Herb Thomas
5	Savannah, GA	March 28	Al Keller
6	Oakland, CA	March 28	Dick Rathmann
7	North Wilkesboro, NC	June 4	Dick Rathmann
8	Hillsboro, NC	June 18	Herb Thomas
9	Macon, GA	June 25	Gober Sosebee
10	Langhorne, PA	May 2	Herb Thomas
11	Wilson, NC	May 9	Buck Baker
12	Martinsville, VA	May 16	Jim Paschal
13	Sharon, PA	May 23	Lee Petty
14	Raleigh, NC	May 29	Herb Thomas
15	Charlotte, NC	May 30	Buck Baker
16	Gardena, CA	May 30	John Soares
17	Columbia, SC	June 6	Curtis Turner
18	Linden, NJ	June 13	Al Keller
19	Mechanicsburg, PA	June 17	Herb Thomas
20	Hickory, NC	June 19	Herb Thomas

Race	Location	Date	Winning Driver
21	Rochester, NY	June 25	Lee Petty
22	Spartanburg, SC	July 3	Herb Thomas
23	Weaverville, NC	July 4	Herb Thomas
24	Willow Springs, IL	July 10	Dick Rathmann
25	Grand Rapids, MI	July 11	Lee Petty
26	Morristown, NJ	July 30	Buck Baker
27	Oakland, CA	Aug 1	Danny Letner
28	Charlotte, NC	Aug 13	Lee Petty
29	San Mateo, CA	Aug 22	Hershel McGriff
30	Corbin, KY	Aug 29	Lee Petty
31	Darlington, SC	Sept 6	Herb Thomas
32	Macon, GA	Sept 12	Hershel McGriff
33	Charlotte, NC	Sept 24	Hershel McGriff
34	Langhorne, PA	Sept 26	Herb Thomas
35	LeHi, AK	Oct 10	Buck Baker
36	Martinsville, VA	Oct 17	Lee Petty
37	North Wilkesboro, NC	Oct 24	Hershel McGriff

1955

FINAL CHAMPIONSHIP STANDINGS TOP 10

Rank	Driver	Points
1	Tim Flock	9,596
2	Buck Baker	8,088
3	Lee Petty	7,194
4	Bob Welborn	5,460
5	Herb Thomas	5,186
6	Junior Johnson	4,810
7	Eddie Skinner	4,652
8	Jim Paschal	4,572

FINAL CHAMPIONSHIP STANDINGS TOP 10 (CONT.)

Rank	Driver	Points
9	Jimmie Lewallen	4,526
10	Gwyn Staley	4,360

RACE WINNERS

Race	Location	Date	Winning Driver
1	High Point, NC	Nov 7	Lee Petty
2	West Palm Beach, FL	Feb 6	Herb Thomas
3	Jacksonville, FL	Feb 13	Lee Petty
4	Daytona Beach, FL	Feb 27	Tim Flock
5	Savannah, GA	March 6	Lee Petty
6	Columbia, SC	March 26	Fonty Flock
7	Hillsboro, NC	March 27	Jim Paschal
8	North Wilkesboro, NC	April 3	Buck Baker
9	Montgomery, AL	April 17	Tim Flock
10	Langhorne, PA	April 24	Tim Flock
11	Charlotte, NC	May 1	Buck Baker
12	Hickory, NC	May 7	Junior Johnson
13	Phoenix, AZ	May 8	Tim Flock
14	Tucson, AZ	May 15	Danny Letner
15	Martinsville, VA	May 15	Tim Flock
16	Richmond, VA	May 22	Tim Flock
17	Raleigh, NC	May 28	Junior Johnson
18	Winston-Salem, NC	May 29	Lee Petty
19	New Oxford, PA	June 10	Junior Johnson
20	Rochester, NY	June 17	Tim Flock
21	Fonda, NY	June 18	Junior Johnson
22	Plattsburg, NY	June 19	Lee Petty

Race	Location	Date	Winning Driver
23	Charlotte, NC	June 24	Tim Flock
24	Spartanburg, SC	July 6	Tim Flock
25	Columbia, SC	July 9	Jim Paschal
26	Weaverville, NC	July 10	Tim Flock
27	Morristown, NJ	July 15	Tim Flock
28	Altamont, NY	July 29	Junior Johnson
29	Syracuse, NY	July 30	Tim Flock
30	San Mateo, CA	July 31	Tim Flock
31	Charlotte, NC	Aug 5	Jim Paschal
32	Winston-Salem, NC	Aug 7	Lee Petty
33	LeHi, AK	Aug 14	Fonty Flock
34	Raleigh, NC	Aug 20	Herb Thomas
35	Darlington, SC	Sept 5	Herb Thomas
36	Montgomery, AL	Sept 11	Tim Flock
37	Langhorne, PA	Sept 18	Tim Flock
38	Raleigh, NC	Sept 30	Fonty Flock
39	Greenville, SC	Oct 6	Tim Flock
40	LeHi, AK	Oct 9	Speedy Thompson
41	Columbia, SC	Oct 15	Tim Flock
42	Martinsville, VA	Oct 16	Speedy Thompson
43	Las Vegas, NV	Oct 16	Norm Nelson
44	North Wilkesboro, NC	Oct 23	Buck Baker
45	Hillsboro, NC	Oct 30	Tim Flock

1956

FINAL CHAMPIONSHIP STANDINGS TOP 10

Rank	Driver	Points
1	Buck Baker	9,272
2	Herb Thomas	8,568
3	Speedy Thompson	8,328
4	Lee Petty	8,324
5	Jim Paschal	7,878
6	Billy Myers	6,920
7	Fireball Roberts	5,794
8	Ralph Moody	5,548
9	Tim Flock	5,062
10	Marvin Panch	4,680

RACE WINNERS

Race	Location	Date	Winning Driver
1	Hickory, NC	Nov 13	Tim Flock
2	Charlotte, NC	Nov 20	Fonty Flock
3	Lancaster, CA	Nov 20	Chuck Stevenson
4	West Palm Beach, FL	Dec 11	Herb Thomas
5	Phoenix, AZ	Jan 22	Buck Baker
6	Daytona Beach, FL	Feb 26	Tim Flock
7	West Palm Beach, FL	March 4	Billy Myers
8	Wilson, NC	March 18	Herb Thomas
9	Atlanta, GA	March 25	Buck Baker
10	North Wilkesboro, NC	April 8	Tim Flock
11	Langhorne, PA	April 22	Buck Baker
12	Richmond, VA	April 29	Buck Baker
13	Columbia, SC	May 5	Speedy Thompson
14	Concord, NC	May 6	Speedy Thompson

Race	Location	Date	Winning Driver
15	Greenville, SC	May 10	Buck Baker
16	Hickory, NC	May 12	Speedy Thompson
17	Hillsboro, NC	May 13	Buck Baker
18	Martinsville, VA	May 20	Buck Baker
19	New Oxford, PA	May 25	Buck Baker
20	Charlotte, NC	May 27	Speedy Thompson
21	Portland, OR	May 27	Herb Thomas
22	Eureka, CA	May 30	Herb Thomas
23	Syracuse, NY	May 30	Buck Baker
24	Merced, CA	June 3	Herb Thomas
25	LeHi, AK	June 10	Ralph Moody
26	Charlotte, NC	June 15	Speedy Thompson
27	Rochester, NY	June 22	Speedy Thompson
28	Portland, OR	June 24	John Kieper
29	Weaverville, NC	July 1	Lee Petty
30	Raleigh, NC	July 4	Fireball Roberts
31	Spartanburg, SC	July 7	Lee Petty
32	Sacramento, CA	July 8	Lloyd Dane
33	Chicago, IL	July 21	Fireball Roberts
34	Shelby, NC	July 27	Speedy Thompson
35	Montgomery, AL	July 29	Marvin Panch
36	Oklahoma City, OK	Aug 3	Jim Paschal
37	Elkhart Lakes, WI	Aug 12	Tim Flock
38	Old Bridge, NJ	Aug 17	Ralph Moody
39	San Mateo, CA	Aug 19	Eddie Pagan
40	Norfolk, VA	Aug 22	Billy Myers
41	Spartanburg, SC	Aug 23	Ralph Moody
42	Myrtle Beach, SC	Aug 25	Fireball Roberts
43	Portland, OR	Aug 26	Royce Haggerty

RACE WINNERS (CONT.)

Race	Location	Date	Winning Driver
44	Darlington, SC	Sept 3	Curtis Turner
45	Montgomery, AL	Sept 9	Buck Baker
46	Charlotte, NC	Sept 12	Ralph Moody
47	Langhorne, PA	Sept 23	Paul Goldsmith
48	Portland, OR	Sept 23	Lloyd Dane
49	Columbia, SC	Sept 29	Buck Baker
50	Hillsboro, NC	Sept 30	Fireball Roberts
51	Newport, TN	Oct 7	Fireball Roberts
52	Charlotte, NC	Oct 17	Buck Baker
53	Shelby, NC	Oct 23	Buck Baker
54	Martinsville, VA	Oct 28	Jack Smith
55	Hickory, NC	Nov 11	Speedy Thompson
56	Wilson, NC	Nov 18	Buck Baker

1957

FINAL CHAMPIONSHIP STANDINGS TOP 10

Rank	Driver	Points
1	Buck Baker	10,716
2	Marvin Panch	9,956
3	Speedy Thompson	8,580
4	Lee Petty	8,528
5	Jack Smith	8,464
6	Fireball Roberts	8,268
7	Johnny Allen	7,068
8	L.D. Austin	6,532
9	Brownie King	5,740
10	Jim Paschal	5,136

RACE WINNERS

Rank	Location	Date	Winning Driver
1	Lancaster, CA	Nov 11	Marvin Panch
2	Concord, NC	Dec 2	Marvin Panch
3	Titusville, FL	Dec 30	Fireball Roberts
4	Daytona Beach, FL	Feb 17	Cotton Owens
5	Concord, NC	March 3	Jack Smith
6	Wilson, NC	March 17	Ralph Moody
7	Hillsboro, NC	March 24	Buck Baker
8	Weaverville, NC	March 31	Buck Baker
9	North Wilkesboro, NC	April 7	Fireball Roberts
10	Langhorne, PA	April 14	Fireball Roberts
11	Charlotte, NC	April 19	Fireball Roberts
12	Spartanburg, SC	April 27	Marvin Panch
13	Greensboro, NC	April 28	Paul Goldsmith
14	Portland, OR	April 28	Art Watts
15	Shelby, NC	May 4	Fireball Roberts
16	Richmond, VA	May 5	Paul Goldsmith
17	Martinsville, VA	May 19	Buck Baker
18	Portland, OR	May 26	Eddie Pagan
19	Eureka, CA	May 30	Lloyd Dane
20	New Oxford, PA	May 30	Buck Baker
21	Lancaster, SC	June 1	Paul Goldsmith
22	Los Angeles, CA	June 8	Eddie Pagan
23	Newport, TN	June 15	Fireball Roberts
24	Columbia, SC	June 20	Jack Smith
25	Sacramento, CA	June 22	Bill Amick
26	Spartanburg, SC	June 29	Lee Petty
27	Jacksonville, NC	June 30	Buck Baker

RACE WINNERS (CONT.)

Rank	Location	Date	Winning Driver
28	Raleigh, NC	July 4	Paul Goldsmith
29	Charlotte, NC	July 12	Marvin Panch
30	LeHi, AK	July 14	Marvin Panch
31	Portland, OR	July 14	Eddie Pagan
32	Hickory, NC	July 20	Jack Smith
33	Norfolk, VA	July 24	Buck Baker
34	Lancaster, SC	July 30	Speedy Thompson
35	Watkins Glen, NY	Aug 4	Buck Baker
36	Bremerton, WA	Aug 4	Parnelli Jones
37	New Oxford, PA	Aug 10	Marvin Panch
38	Old Bridge, NJ	Aug 16	Lee Petty
39	Myrtle Beach, SC	Aug 26	Gwyn Staley
40	Darlington, SC	Sept 2	Speedy Thompson
41	Syracuse, NY	Sept 5	Gwyn Staley
42	Weaverville, NC	Sept 8	Lee Petty
43	Sacramento, CA	Sept 8	Danny Graves
44	San Jose, CA	Sept 15	Marvin Porter
45	Langhorne, PA	Sept 15	Gwyn Staley
46	Columbia, SC	Sept 19	Buck Baker
47	Shelby, NC	Sept 21	Buck Baker
48	Charlotte, NC	Oct 5	Lee Petty
49	Martinsville, VA	Oct 6	Bob Welborn
50	Newberry, SC	Oct 12	Fireball Roberts
51	Concord, NC	Oct 13	Fireball Roberts
52	North Wilkesboro, NC	Oct 20	Jack Smith
53	Greensboro, NC	Oct 27	Buck Baker

1958

FINAL CHAMPIONSHIP STANDINGS TOP 10

Rank	Driver	Points
1	Lee Petty	12,232
2	Buck Baker	11,588
3	Speedy Thompson	8,792
4	Shorty Rollins	8,124
5	Jack Smith	7,666
6	L.D. Austin	6,972
7	Rex White	6,552
8	Junior Johnson	6,380
9	Eddie Pagan	4,910
10	Jim Reed	4,762

RACE WINNERS

Race	Location	Date	Winning Driver
1	Fayetteville, NC	Nov 3	Rex White
2	Daytona Beach, FL	Feb 23	Paul Goldsmith
3	Concord, NC	March 2	Lee Petty
4	Fayetteville, NC	March 15	Curtis Turner
5	Wilson, NC	March 16	Lee Petty
6	Hillsboro, NC	March 23	Buck Baker
7	Fayetteville, NC	April 5	Bob Welborn
8	Columbia, SC	April 10	Speedy Thompson
9	Spartanburg, SC	April 12	Speedy Thompson
10	Atlanta, GA	April 13	Curtis Turner
11	Charlotte, NC	April 18	Curtis Turner
12	Martinsville, VA	April 20	Bob Welborn
13	Manassas, VA	April 25	Frankie Schneider
14	Old Bridge, NJ	April 27	Jim Reed

Race	Location	Date	Winning Driver
15	Greenville, SC	May 3	Jack Smith
16	Greensboro, NC	May 11	Bob Welborn
17	Roanoke, VA	May 15	Jim Reed
18	North Wilkesboro, NC	May 18	Junior Johnson
19	Winston-Salem, NC	May 24	Bob Welborn
20	Trenton, NJ	May 30	Fireball Roberts
21	Riverside, CA	June 1	Eddie Gray
22	Columbia, SC	June 5	Junior Johnson
23	Bradford, PA	June 12	Junior Johnson
24	Reading, PA	June 15	Junior Johnson
25	New Oxford, PA	June 25	Lee Petty
26	Hickory, NC	June 28	Lee Petty
27	Weaverville, NC	June 29	Rex White
28	Raleigh, NC	July 4	Fireball Roberts
29	Asheville, NC	July 12	Jim Paschal
30	Busti, NY	July 16	Shorty Rollins
31	Toronto, ON, Canada	July 18	Lee Petty
32	Buffalo, NY	July 19	Jim Reed
33	Rochester, NY	July 25	Cotton Owens
34	Belmar, NJ	July 26	Jim Reed
35	Bridgehampton, NY	Aug 2	Jack Smith
36	Columbia, SC	Aug 7	Speedy Thompson
37	Nashville, TN	Aug 10	Joe Weatherly
38	Weaverville, NC	Aug 17	Fireball Roberts
39	Winston-Salem, NC	Aug 22	Lee Petty
40	Myrtle Beach, SC	Aug 23	Bob Welborn
41	Darlington, SC	Sept 1	Fireball Roberts
42	Charlotte, NC	Sept 5	Buck Baker
43	Birmingham, AL	Sept 7	Fireball Roberts

Race	Location	Date	Winning Driver
44	Sacramento, CA	Sept 7	Parnelli Jones
45	Gastonia, NC	Sept 12	Buck Baker
46	Richmond, VA	Sept 14	Speedy Thompson
47	Hillsboro, NC	Sept 28	Joe Eubanks
48	Salisbury, NC	Oct 5	Lee Petty
49	Martinsville, VA	Oct 12	Fireball Roberts
50	North Wilkesboro, NC	Oct 19	Junior Johnson
51	Atlanta, GA	Oct 26	Junior Johnson

1959

FINAL CHAMPIONSHIP STANDINGS TOP 10

Rank	Driver	Points
1	Lee Petty	11,792
2	Cotton Owens	9,962
3	Speedy Thompson	7,684
4	Herman Beam	7,396
5	Buck Baker	7,170
6	Tom Pistone	7,050
7	L.D. Austin	6,519
8	Jack Smith	6,150
9	Jim Reed	5,744
10	Rex White	5,526

RACE WINNERS

Race	Location	Date	Winning Driver
1	Fayetteville, NC	Nov 9	Bob Welborn
2	Daytona Beach, FL	Feb 20	Bob Welborn
3	Daytona Beach, FL	Feb 22	Lee Petty

RACE WINNERS (CONT.)

Race	Location	Date	Winning Driver
4	Hillsboro, NC	March 1	Curtis Turner
5	Concord, NC	March 8	Curtis Turner
6	Atlanta, GA	March 22	Johnny Beauchamp
7	Wilson, NC	March 29	Junior Johnson
8	Winston-Salem, NC	March 30	Jim Reed
9	Columbia, SC	April 4	Jack Smith
10	North Wilkesboro, NC	April 5	Lee Petty
11	Reading, PA	April 26	Junior Johnson
12	Hickory, NC	May 2	Junior Johnson
13	Martinsville, VA	May 3	Lee Petty
14	Trenton, NJ	May 17	Tom Pistone
15	Charlotte, NC	May 22	Lee Petty
16	Nashville, TN	May 24	Rex White
17	Los Angeles, CA	May 30	Parnelli Jones
18	Spartanburg, SC	June 5	Jack Smith
19	Greenville, SC	June 13	Junior Johnson
20	Atlanta, GA	June 14	Lee Petty
21	Columbia, SC	June 18	Lee Petty
22	Wilson, NC	June 20	Junior Johnson
23	Richmond, VA	June 21	Tom Pistone
24	Winston-Salem, NC	June 27	Rex White
25	Weaverville, NC	June 28	Rex White
26	Daytona Beach, FL	July 4	Fireball Roberts
27	Pittsburgh, PA	July 21	Jim Reed
28	Charlotte, NC	July 26	Jack Smith
29	Myrtle Beach, SC	Aug 1	Ned Jarrett
30	Charlotte, NC	Aug 2	Ned Jarrett

Race	Location	Date	Winning Driver
31	Nashville, TN	Aug 9	Joe Lee Johnson
32	Weaverville, NC	Aug 16	Bob Welborn
33	Winston-Salem, NC	Aug 21	Rex White
34	Greenville, SC	Aug 22	Buck Baker
35	Columbia, SC	Aug 29	Lee Petty
36	Darlington, SC	Sept 7	Jim Reed
37	Hickory, NC	Sept 11	Lee Petty
38	Richmond, VA	Sept 13	Cotton Owens
39	Sacramento, CA	Sept 13	Eddie Gray
40	Hillsboro, NC	Sept 20	Lee Petty
41	Martinsville, VA	Sept 27	Rex White
42	Weaverville, NC	Oct 11	Lee Petty
43	North Wilkesboro, NC	Oct 18	Lee Petty
44	Concord, NC	Oct 25	Jack Smith

1960

FINAL CHAMPIONSHIP STANDINGS TOP 10

Rank	Driver	Points
1	Rex White	21,164
2	Richard Petty	17,228
3	Bobby Johns	14,964
4	Buck Baker	14,674
5	Ned Jarrett	14,660
6	Lee Petty	14,510
7	Junior Johnson	9,932
8	Emanuel Zervakis	9,720
9	Jim Paschal	8,968
10	Banjo Matthews	8,458

RACE WINNERS

Race	Location	Date	Winning Driver
1	Charlotte, NC	Nov 8	Jack Smith
2	Columbia, SC	Nov 26	Ned Jarrett
3	Daytona Beach, FL	Feb 12	Fireball Roberts
4	Daytona Beach, FL	Feb 12	Jack Smith
5	Daytona Beach, FL	Feb 14	Junior Johnson
6	Charlotte, NC	Feb 28	Richard Petty
7	North Wilkesboro, NC	March 27	Lee Petty
8	Phoenix, AZ	April 3	John Rostek
9	Columbia, SC	April 5	Rex White
10	Martinsville, VA	April 10	Richard Petty
11	Hickory, NC	April 16	Joe Weatherly
12	Wilson, NC	April 17	Joe Weatherly
13	Winston-Salem, NC	April 18	Glen Wood
14	Greenville, SC	April 23	Ned Jarrett
15	Weaverville, NC	April 24	Lee Petty
16	Darlington, SC	May 14	Joe Weatherly
17	Spartanburg, SC	May 28	Ned Jarrett
18	Hillsboro, NC	May 29	Lee Petty
19	Richmond, VA	June 5	Lee Petty
20	Hanford, CA	June 12	Marvin Porter
21	Concord, NC	June 19	Joe Lee Johnson
22	Winston-Salem, NC	June 26	Glen Wood
23	Daytona Beach, FA	July 4	Jack Smith
24	Heidelburg, PA	July 10	Lee Petty
25	Montgomery, NY	July 17	Rex White
26	Myrtle Beach, SC	July 23	Buck Baker
27	Hampton, GA	July 31	Fireball Roberts

Race	Location	Date	Winning Driver
28	Birmingham, AL	Aug 3	Ned Jarrett
29	Nashville, TN	Aug 7	Johnny Beauchamp
30	Weaverville, NC	Aug 14	Rex White
31	Spartanburg, SC	Aug 16	Cotton Owens
32	Columbia, SC	Aug 18	Rex White
33	South Boston, VA	Aug 20	Junior Johnson
34	Winston-Salem, NC	Aug 23	Glen Wood
35	Darlington, SC	Sept 5	Buck Baker
36	Hickory, NC	Sept 9	Junior Johnson
37	Sacramento, CA	Sept 11	Jim Cook
38	Sumter, SC	Sept 15	Ned Jarrett
39	Hillsboro, NC	Sept 18	Richard Petty
40	Martinsville, VA	Sept 25	Rex White
41	North Wilkesboro, NC	Oct 2	Rex White
42	Concord, NC	Oct 16	Speedy Thompson
43	Richmond, VA	Oct 23	Speedy Thompson
44	Hampton, GA	Oct 30	Bobby Johns

1961

FINAL CHAMPIONSHIP STANDINGS TOP 10

Rank	Driver	Points
1	Ned Jarrett	27,272
2	Rex White	26,442
3	Emanuel Zervakis	22,312
4	Joe Weatherly	17,894
5	Fireball Roberts	17,600
6	Junior Johnson	17,178
7	Jack Smith	15,186
8	Richard Petty	14,984

FINAL CHAMPIONSHIP STANDINGS TOP 10 (CONT.)

Rank	Driver	Points
9	Jim Paschal	13,922
10	Buck Baker	13,746

RACE WINNERS

Race	Location	Date	Winning Driver
1	Charlotte, NC	Nov 6	Joe Weatherly
2	Jacksonville, FL	Nov 20	Lee Petty
3	Daytona Beach, FL	Feb 24	Fireball Roberts
4	Daytona Beach, FL	Feb 24	Joe Weatherly
5	Daytona Beach, FL	Feb 26	Marvin Panch
6	Spartanburg, SC	March 4	Cotton Owens
7	Weaverville, NC	March 5	Rex White
8	Hanford, CA	March 12	Fireball Roberts
9	Hampton, GA	March 26	Bob Burdick
10	Greenville, SC	April 1	Emanuel Zervakis
11	Hillsboro, NC	April 2	Cotton Owens
12	Winston-Salem, NC	April 3	Rex White
13	Martinsville, VA	April 9	Fred Lorenzen
14	North Wilkesboro, NC	April 16	Rex White
15	Columbia, SC	April 20	Cotton Owens
16	Hickory, NC	April 22	Junior Johnson
17	Richmond, VA	April 23	Richard Petty
18	Martinsville, VA	April 30	Junior Johnson
19	Darlington, SC	May 6	Fred Lorenzen
20	Concord, NC	May 21	Richard Petty
21	Concord, NC	May 21	Joe Weatherly

Race	Location	Date	Winning Driver
22	Riverside, CA	May 21	Lloyd Dane
23	Los Angles, CA	May 27	Eddie Gray
24	Concord, NC	May 28	David Pearson
25	Spartanburg, SC	June 2	Jim Paschal
26	Birmingham, AL	June 4	Ned Jarrett
27	Greenville, SC	June 8	Jack Smith
28	Winston-Salem, NC	June 10	Rex White
29	Norwood, MA	June 17	Emanuel Zervakis
30	Hartsville, SC	June 23	Buck Baker
31	Roanoke, VA	June 24	Junior Johnson
32	Daytona Beach, FL	July 4	David Pearson
33	Hampton, GA	July 9	Fred Lorenzen
34	Columbia, SC	July 20	Cotton Owens
35	Myrtle Beach, SC	July 22	Joe Weatherly
36	Bristol, TN	July 30	Jack Smith
37	Nashville, TN	Aug 6	Jim Paschal
38	Winston-Salem, NC	Aug 9	Rex White
39	Weaverville, NC	Aug 13	Junior Johnson
40	Richmond, VA	Aug 18	Junior Johnson
41	South Boston, VA	Aug 27	Junior Johnson
42	Darlington, SC	Sept 4	Nelson Stacy
43	Hickory, NC	Sept 8	Rex White
44	Richmond, VA	Sept 10	Joe Weatherly
45	Sacramento, CA	Sept 10	Eddie Gray
46	Hampton, GA	Sept 17	David Pearson
47	Martinsville, VA	Sept 24	Joe Weatherly
48	North Wilkesboro, NC	Oct 1	Rex White
49	Concord, NC	Oct 15	Joe Weatherly

RACE WINNERS (CONT.)

Race	Location	Date	Winning Driver
50	Bristol, TN	Oct 22	Joe Weatherly
51	Greenville, SC	Oct 28	Junior Johnson
52	Hillsboro, NC	Oct 29	Joe Weatherly

1962

FINAL CHAMPIONSHIP STANDINGS TOP 10

Rank	Driver	Points
1	Joe Weatherly	30,836
2	Richard Petty	28,440
3	Ned Jarrett	25,336
4	Jack Smith	22,870
5	Rex White	19,424
6	Jim Paschal	18,128
7	Fred Lorenzen	17,554
8	Fireball Roberts	16,380
9	Marvin Panch	15,138
10	David Pearson	14,404

RACE WINNERS

Rank	Location	Date	Winning Driver
1	Concord, NC	Nov 5	Jack Smith
2	Weaverville, NC	Nov 12	Rex White
3	Daytona Beach, FL	Feb 16	Fireball Roberts
4	Daytona Beach, FL	Feb 16	Joe Weatherly
5	Daytona Beach, FL	Feb 18	Fireball Roberts
6	Concord, NC	Feb 25	Joe Weatherly
7	Weaverville, NC	March 4	Joe Weatherly

Rank	Location	Date	Winning Driver
8	Savannah, GA	March 17	Jack Smith
9	Hillsboro, NC	March 18	Rex White
10	Richmond, VA	April 1	Rex White
11	Columbia, SC	April 13	Ned Jarrett
12	North Wilkesboro, NC	April 15	Richard Petty
13	Greenville, SC	April 19	Ned Jarrett
14	Myrtle Beach, SC	April 21	Jack Smith
15	Martinsville, VA	April 22	Richard Petty
16	Winston-Salem, NC	April 23	Rex White
17	Bristol, TN	April 29	Bobby Johns
18	Richmond, VA	May 4	Jimmy Pardue
19	Hickory, NC	May 5	Jack Smith
20	Concord, NC	May 6	Joe Weatherly
21	Darlington, SC	May 12	Nelson Stacy
22	Spartanburg, SC	May 19	Ned Jarrett
23	Concord, NC	May 27	Nelson Stacy
24	Hampton, GA	June 10	Fred Lorenzen
25	Winston-Salem, NC	June 16	Johnny Allen
26	Augusta, GA	June 19	Joe Weatherly
27	Richmond, VA	June 22	Jim Paschal
28	South Boston, VA	June 23	Rex White
29	Daytona Beach, FL	July 4	Fireball Roberts
30	Columbia, SC	July 7	Rex White
31	Asheville, NC	July 13	Jack Smith
32	Greenville, SC	July 14	Richard Petty
33	Augusta, GA	July 17	Joe Weatherly
34	Savannah, GA	July 20	Joe Weatherly
35	Myrtle Beach, SC	July 21	Ned Jarrett
36	Bristol, TN	July 29	Jim Paschal
37	Chattanooga, TN	Aug 3	Joe Weatherly

Rank	Location	Date	Winning Driver
38	Nashville, TN	Aug 5	Jim Paschal
39	Huntsville, AL	Aug 8	Richard Petty
40	Weaverville, NC	Aug 12	Jim Paschal
41	Roanoke, VA	Aug 15	Richard Petty
42	Winston-Salem, NC	Aug 18	Richard Petty
43	Spartanburg, SC	Aug 21	Richard Petty
44	Valdosta, GA	Aug 25	Ned Jarrett
45	Darlington, SC	Sept 3	Larry Frank
46	Hickory, NC	Sept 7	Rex White
47	Richmond, VA	Sept 9	Joe Weatherly
48	Moyock, NC	Sept 11	Ned Jarrett
49	Augusta, GA	Sept 13	Fred Lorenzen
50	Martinsville, VA	Sept 23	Nelson Stacy
51	North Wilkesboro, NC	Sept 30	Richard Petty
52	Concord, NC	Oct 14	Junior Johnson
53	Hampton, GA	Oct 28	Rex White

1963

FINAL CHAMPIONSHIP STANDINGS TOP 10

Rank	Driver	Points
1	Joe Weatherly	33,398
2	Richard Petty	31,170
3	Fred Lorenzen	29,684
4	Ned Jarrett	27,214
5	Fireball Roberts	22,642
6	Jimmy Pardue	22,228
7	Darel Dieringer	21,418
8	David Pearson	21,156
9	Rex White	20,976
10	Tiny Lund	19,624

RACE WINNERS

Rank	Location	Date	Winning Driver
1	Birmingham, AL	Nov 4	Jim Paschal
2	Tampa, FL	Nov 11	Richard Petty
3	Randleman, NC	Nov 22	Jim Paschal
4	Riverside, CA	Jan 20	Dan Gurney
5	Daytona Beach, FL	Feb 22	Junior Johnson
6	Daytona Beach, FL	Feb 22	Johnny Rutherford
7	Daytona Beach, FL	Feb 24	Tiny Lund
8	Spartanburg, SC	March 2	Richard Petty
9	Weaverville, NC	March 3	Richard Petty
10	Hillsboro, NC	March 10	Junior Johnson
11	Hampton, GA	March 17	Fred Lorenzen
12	Hickory, NC	March 24	Junior Johnson
13	Bristol, TN	March 31	Fireball Roberts
14	Augusta, GA	April 4	Ned Jarrett
15	Richmond, VA	April 7	Joe Weatherly
16	Greenville, SC	April 13	Buck Baker
17	South Boston, VA	April 14	Richard Petty
18	Winston-Salem, NC	April 15	Jim Paschal
19	Martinsville, VA	April 21	Richard Petty
20	North Wilkesboro, NC	April 28	Richard Petty
21	Columbia, SC	May 2	Richard Petty
22	Randleman, NC	May 5	Jim Paschal
23	Darlington, SC	May 11	Joe Weatherly
24	Manassas, VA	May 18	Richard Petty
25	Richmond, VA	May 19	Ned Jarrett
26	Concord, NC	June 2	Fred Lorenzen
27	Birmingham, AL	June 9	Richard Petty

Rank	Location	Date	Winning Driver
28	Hampton, GA	June 30	Junior Johnson
29	Daytona Beach, FL	July 4	Fireball Roberts
30	Myrtle Beach, SC	July 7	Ned Jarrett
31	Savannah, GA	July 10	Ned Jarrett
32	Moyock, NC	July 11	Jimmy Pardue
33	Winston-Salem, NC	July 13	Glen Wood
34	Asheville, NC	July 14	Ned Jarrett
35	Old Bridge, NJ	July 19	Fireball Roberts
36	Bridgehampton, NY	July 21	Richard Petty
37	Bristol, TN	July 28	Fred Lorenzen
38	Greenville, SC	July 30	Richard Petty
39	Nashville, TN	Aug 4	Jim Paschal
40	Columbia, SC	Aug 8	Richard Petty
41	Weaverville, NC	Aug 11	Fred Lorenzen
42	Spartanburg, SC	Aug 14	Ned Jarrett
43	Winston-Salem, NC	Aug 16	Junior Johnson
44	Huntington, WV	Aug 18	Fred Lorenzen
45	Darlington, SC	Sept 2	Fireball Roberts
46	Hickory, NC	Sept 6	Junior Johnson
47	Richmond, VA	Sept 8	Ned Jarrett
48	Martinsville, VA	Sept 22	Fred Lorenzen
49	Moyock, NC	Sept 24	Ned Jarrett
50	North Wilkesboro, NC	Sept 29	Marvin Panch
51	Randleman, NC	Oct 5	Richard Petty
52	Concord, NC	Oct 13	Junior Johnson
53	South Boston, VA	Oct 20	Richard Petty
54	Hillsboro, NC	Oct 27	Joe Weatherly
55	Riverside, CA	Nov 3	Darel Dieringer

1964

FINAL CHAMPIONSHIP STANDINGS TOP 10

Rank	Driver	Points
1	Richard Petty	40,252
2	Ned Jarrett	34,950
3	David Pearson	32,146
4	Billy Wade	28,474
5	Jimmy Pardue	26,570
6	Curtis Crider	25,606
7	Jim Paschal	25,450
8	Larry Thomas	22,950
9	Buck Baker	22,366
10	Marvin Panch	21,480

RACE WINNERS

Race	Location	Date	Winning Driver
1	Concord, NC	Nov 10	Ned Jarrett
2	Augusta, GA	Nov 17	Fireball Roberts
3	Jacksonville, FL	Dec 1	Wendell Scott
4	Savannah, GA	Dec 9	Richard Petty
5	Riverside, CA	Jan 19	Dan Gurney
6	Daytona Beach, FL	Feb 21	Junior Johnson
7	Daytona Beach, FL	Feb 21	Bobby Isaac
8	Daytona Beach, FL	Feb 23	Richard Petty
9	Richmond, VA	March 10	David Pearson
10	Bristol, TN	March 22	Fred Lorenzen
11	Greenville, SC	March 28	David Pearson
12	Winston-Salem, NC	March 30	Marvin Panch
13	Hampton, GA	April 5	Fred Lorenzen
14	Weaverville, NC	April 11	Marvin Panch

RACE WINNERS (CONT.)

Race	Location	Date	Winning Driver
15	Hillsboro, NC	April 12	David Pearson
16	Spartanburg, SC	April 14	Ned Jarrett
17	Columbia, SC	April 16	Ned Jarrett
18	North Wilkesboro, NC	April 19	Fred Lorenzen
19	Martinsville, VA	April 26	Fred Lorenzen
20	Savannah, GA	May 1	LeeRoy Yarbrough
21	Darlington, SC	May 9	Fred Lorenzen
22	Hampton, VA	May 15	Ned Jarrett
23	Hickory, NC	May 16	Ned Jarrett
24	South Boston, VA	May 17	Richard Petty
25	Concord, NC	May 24	Jim Paschal
26	Greenville, SC	May 30	LeeRoy Yarbrough
27	Asheville, NC	May 31	Ned Jarrett
28	Hampton, GA	June 7	Ned Jarrett
29	Concord, NC	June 11	Richard Petty
30	Nashville, TN	June 14	Richard Petty
31	Chattanooga, TN	June 19	David Pearson
32	Birmingham, AL	June 21	Ned Jarrett
33	Valdosta, GA	June 23	Buck Baker
34	Spartanburg, SC	June 26	Richard Petty
35	Daytona Beach, FL	July 4	A.J. Foyt
36	Manassas, VA	July 8	Ned Jarrett
37	Old Bridge, NJ	July 10	Billy Wade
38	Bridgehampton, NY	July 12	Billy Wade
39	Islip, NY	July 15	Billy Wade
40	Watkins Glen, NY	July 19	Billy Wade
41	New Oxford, PA	July 21	David Pearson

Race	Location	Date	Winning Driver
42	Bristol, TN	July 26	Fred Lorenzen
43	Nashville, TN	Aug 2	Richard Petty
44	Myrtle Beach, SC	Aug 7	David Pearson
45	Weaverville, NC	Aug 9	Ned Jarrett
46	Moyock, NC	Aug 13	Ned Jarrett
47	Huntington, WV	Aug 16	Richard Petty
48	Columbia, SC	Aug 21	David Pearson
49	Winston-Salem, NC	Aug 22	Junior Johnson
50	Roanoke, VA	Aug 23	Junior Johnson
51	Darlington, SC	Sept 7	Buck Baker
52	Hickory, NC	Sept 11	David Pearson
53	Richmond, VA	Sept 14	Cotton Owens
54	Manassas, VA	Sept 18	Ned Jarrett
55	Hillsboro, NC	Sept 20	Ned Jarrett
56	Martinsville, VA	Sept 27	Fred Lorenzen
57	Savannah, GA	Oct 9	Ned Jarrett
58	North Wilkesboro, NC	Oct 11	Marvin Panch
59	Concord, NC	Oct 18	Fred Lorenzen
60	Harris, NC	Oct 25	Richard Petty
61	Augusta, GA	Nov 1	Darel Dieringer
62	Jacksonville, NC	Nov 8	Ned Jarrett

1965

FINAL CHAMPIONSHIP STANDINGS TOP 10

Rank	Driver	Points
1	Ned Jarrett	38,824
2	Dick Hutcherson	35,790
3	Darel Dieringer	24,696

Rank	Driver	Points
4	G.C. Spencer	24,314
5	Marvin Panch	22,798
6	Bob Derrington	21,394
7	J.T. Putney	20,928
8	Neil Castles	20,848
9	Buddy Baker	20,672
10	Cale Yarborough	20,192

RACE WINNERS

Race	Location	Date	Winning Driver
1	Riverside, CA	Jan 17	Dan Gurney
2	Daytona Beach, FL	Feb 12	Darel Dieringer
3	Daytona Beach, FL	Feb 12	Junior Johnson
4	Daytona Beach, FL	Feb 14	Fred Lorenzen
5	Spartanburg, SC	Feb 27	Ned Jarrett
6	Weaverville, NC	Feb 28	Ned Jarrett
7	Richmond, VA	March 7	Junior Johnson
8	Hillsboro, NC	March 14	Ned Jarrett
9	Hampton, GA	April 11	Marvin Panch
10	Greenville, SC	April 17	Dick Hutcherson
11	North Wilkesboro, NC	April 18	Junior Johnson
12	Martinsville, VA	April 25	Fred Lorenzen
13	Columbia, SC	April 28	Tiny Lund
14	Bristol, TN	May 2	Junior Johnson
15	Darlington, SC	May 8	Junior Johnson
16	Hampton, VA	May 14	Ned Jarrett
17	Winston-Salem, NC	May 15	Junior Johnson
18	Hickory, NC	May 16	Junior Johnson
19	Concord, NC	May 23	Fred Lorenzen

RACE WINNERS (CONT.)

Race	Location	Date	Winning Driver
20	Shelby, NC	May 27	Ned Jarrett
21	Asheville, NC	May 29	Junior Johnson
22	Harris, NC	May 30	Ned Jarrett
23	Nashville, TN	June 3	Dick Hutcherson
24	Birmingham, AL	June 6	Ned Jarrett
25	Hampton, GA	June 13	Marvin Panch
26	Greenville, SC	June 19	Dick Hutcherson
27	Myrtle Beach, SC	June 24	Dick Hutcherson
28	Valdosta, GA	June 27	Cale Yarborough
29	Daytona Beach, FL	July 4	A.J. Foyt
30	Manassas, VA	July 8	Junior Johnson
31	Old Bridge, NJ	July 9	Junior Johnson
32	Islip, NY	July 14	Marvin Panch
33	Watkins Glen, NY	July 18	Marvin Panch
34	Bristol, TN	July 25	Ned Jarrett
35	Nashville, TN	July 31	Richard Petty
36	Shelby, NC	Aug 5	Ned Jarrett
37	Weaverville, NC	Aug 8	Richard Petty
38	Maryville, TN	Aug 13	Dick Hutcherson
39	Spartanburg, SC	Aug 14	Ned Jarrett
40	Augusta, GA	Aug 15	Dick Hutcherson
41	Columbus, GA	Aug 19	David Pearson
42	Moyock, NC	Aug 24	Dick Hutcherson
43	Beltsville, MD	Aug 25	Ned Jarrett
44	Winston-Salem, NC	Aug 28	Junior Johnson
45	Darlington, SC	Sept 6	Ned Jarrett
46	Hickory, NC	Sept 10	Richard Petty

RACE WINNERS (CONT.)

Race	Location	Date	Winning Driver
47	New Oxford, PA	Sept 14	Dick Hutcherson
48	Manassas, VA	Sept 17	Richard Petty
49	Richmond, VA	Sept 18	David Pearson
50	Martinsville, VA	Sept 26	Junior Johnson
51	North Wilkesboro, NC	Oct 3	Junior Johnson
52	Concord, NC	Oct 17	Fred Lorenzen
53	Hillsboro, NC	Oct 24	Dick Hutcherson
54	Rockingham, NC	Oct 31	Curtis Turner
55	Moyock, NC	Nov 7	Ned Jarrett

1966

FINAL CHAMPIONSHIP STANDINGS TOP 10

Rank	Driver	Points
1	David Pearson	35,638
2	James Hylton	33,688
3	Richard Petty	22,952
4	Henley Gray	22,468
5	Paul Goldsmith	22,078
6	Wendell Scott	21,702
7	John Sears	21,432
8	J.T. Putney	21,208
9	Neil Castles	20,446
10	Bobby Allison	19,910

RACE WINNERS

Race	Location	Date	Winning Driver
1	Augusta, GA	Nov 14	Richard Petty
2	Riverside, CA	Jan 23	Dan Gurney

Race	Location	Date	Winning Driver
3	Daytona Beach, FL	Feb 25	Paul Goldsmith
4	Daytona Beach, FL	Feb 25	Earl Balmer
5	Daytona Beach, FL	Feb 27	Richard Petty
6	Rockingham, NC	March 13	Paul Goldsmith
7	Bristol, TN	March 20	Dick Hutcherson
8	Hampton, GA	March 27	Jim Hurtubise
9	Hickory, NC	April 3	David Pearson
10	Columbia, SC	April 7	David Pearson
11	Greenville, SC	April 9	David Pearson
12	Winston-Salem, NC	April 11	David Pearson
13	North Wilkesboro, NC	April 17	Jim Paschal
14	Martinsville, VA	April 24	Jim Paschal
15	Darlington, SC	April 30	Richard Petty
16	Hampton, VA	May 7	Richard Petty
17	Macon, GA	May 10	Richard Petty
18	Monroe, NC	May 13	Darel Dieringer
19	Richmond, VA	May 15	David Pearson
20	Concord, NC	May 22	Marvin Panch
21	Moyock, NC	May 29	David Pearson
22	Asheville, NC	June 3	David Pearson
23	Spartanburg, SC	June 4	Elmo Langley
24	Maryville, TN	June 9	David Pearson
25	Weaverville, NC	June 12	Richard Petty
26	Beltsville, MD	June 15	Tiny Lund
27	Greenville, SC	June 25	David Pearson
28	Daytona Beach, FL	July 4	Sam McQuagg
29	Manassas, VA	July 7	Elmo Langley
30	Bridgehampton, NY	July 10	David Pearson
31	Oxford, ME	July 12	Bobby Allison

RACE WINNERS (CONT.)

Race	Location	Date	Winning Driver
32	Fonda, NY	July 14	David Pearson
33	Islip, NY	July 16	Bobby Allison
34	Bristol, TN	July 24	Paul Goldsmith
35	Maryville, TN	July 28	Paul Lewis
36	Nashville, TN	July 30	Richard Petty
37	Hampton, GA	Aug 7	Richard Petty
38	Columbia, SC	Aug 18	David Pearson
39	Weaverville, NC	Aug 21	Darel Dieringer
40	Beltsville, MD	Aug 24	Bobby Allison
41	Winston-Salem, NC	Aug 27	David Pearson
42	Darlington, SC	Sept 5	Darel Dieringer
43	Hickory, NC	Sept 9	David Pearson
44	Richmond, VA	Sept 11	David Pearson
45	Hillsboro, NC	Sept 18	Dick Hutcherson
46	Martinsville, VA	Sept 25	Fred Lorenzen
47	North Wilkesboro, NC	Oct 2	Dick Hutcherson
48	Concord, NC	Oct 16	LeeRoy Yarbrough
49	Rockingham, NC	Oct 30	Fred Lorenzen

1967

FINAL CHAMPIONSHIP STANDINGS TOP 10

Rank	Driver	Points
1	Richard Petty	42,472
2	James Hylton	36,444
3	Dick Hutcherson	33,658
4	Bobby Allison	30,812

Rank	Driver	Points
5	John Sears	29,078
6	Jim Paschal	27,624
7	David Pearson	26,302
8	Neil Castles	23,218
9	Elmo Langley	22,286
10	Wendell Scott	20,700

RACE WINNERS

Race	Location	Date	Winning Driver
1	Augusta, GA	Nov 13	Richard Petty
2	Riverside, CA	Jan 29	Parnelli Jones
3	Daytona Beach, FL	Feb 24	LeeRoy Yarbrough
4	Daytona Beach, FL	Feb 24	Fred Lorenzen
5	Daytona Beach, FL	Feb 26	Mario Andretti
6	Weaverville, NC	March 5	Richard Petty
7	Bristol, TN	March 19	David Pearson
8	Greenville, SC	March 25	David Pearson
9	Winston-Salem, NC	March 27	Bobby Allison
10	Hampton, GA	April 2	Cale Yarborough
11	Columbia, SC	April 6	Richard Petty
12	Hickory, NC	April 9	Richard Petty
13	North Wilkesboro, NC	April 16	Darel Dieringer
14	Martinsville, VA	April 23	Richard Petty
15	Savannah, GA	April 28	Bobby Allison
16	Richmond, VA	April 30	Richard Petty
17	Darlington, SC	May 13	Richard Petty
18	Beltsville, MD	May 19	Jim Paschal
19	Hampton, VA	May 20	Richard Petty
20	Concord, NC	May 28	Jim Paschal
21	Asheville, NC	June 2	Jim Paschal

RACE WINNERS (CONT.)

Race	Location	Date	Winning Driver
22	Macon, GA	June 6	Richard Petty
23	Maryville, TN	June 8	Richard Petty
24	Birmingham, AL	June 10	Bobby Allison
25	Rockingham, NC	June 18	Richard Petty
26	Greenville, SC	June 24	Richard Petty
27	Montgomery, AL	June 27	Jim Paschal
28	Daytona Beach, FL	July 4	Cale Yarborough
29	Trenton, NJ	July 9	Richard Petty
30	Oxford, ME	July 11	Bobby Allison
31	Fonda, NY	July 13	Richard Petty
32	Islip, NY	July 15	Richard Petty
33	Bristol, TN	July 23	Richard Petty
34	Maryville, TN	July 27	Dick Hutcherson
35	Nashville, TN	July 29	Richard Petty
36	Hampton, GA	Aug 6	Dick Hutcherson
37	Winston-Salem, NC	Aug 12	Richard Petty
38	Columbia, SC	Aug 17	Richard Petty
39	Savannah, GA	Aug 25	Richard Petty
40	Darlington, SC	Sept 4	Richard Petty
41	Hickory, NC	Sept 8	Richard Petty
42	Richmond, VA	Sept 10	Richard Petty
43	Beltsville, MD	Sept 15	Richard Petty
44	Hillsboro, NC	Sept 17	Richard Petty
45	Martinsville, VA	Sept 24	Richard Petty
46	North Wilkesboro, NC	Oct 1	Richard Petty
47	Concord, NC	Oct 15	Buddy Baker
48	Rockingham, NC	Oct 29	Bobby Allison
49	Weaverville, NC	Nov 5	Bobby Allison

1968

FINAL CHAMPIONSHIP STANDINGS TOP 10

Rank	Driver	Points
1	David Pearson	3,499
2	Bobby Isaac	3,373
3	Richard Petty	3,123
4	Clyde Lynn	3,041
5	John Sears	3,017
6	Elmo Langley	2,823
7	James Hylton	2,719
8	Jabe Thomas	2,687
9	Wendell Scott	2,685
10	Roy Tyner	2,504

RACE WINNERS

Race	Location	Date	Winning Driver
1	Macon, GA	Nov 12	Bobby Allison
2	Montgomery, AL	Nov 26	Richard Petty
3	Riverside, CA	Jan 21	Dan Gurney
4	Daytona Beach, FL	Feb 25	Cale Yarborough
5	Bristol, TN	March 17	David Pearson
6	Richmond, VA	March 24	David Pearson
7	Hampton, GA	March 31	Cale Yarborough
8	Hickory, NC	April 7	Richard Petty
9	Greenville, SC	April 13	Richard Petty
10	Columbia, SC	April 18	Bobby Isaac
11	North Wilkesboro, NC	April 21	David Pearson
12	Martinsville, VA	April 28	Cale Yarborough
13	Augusta, GA	May 3	Bobby Isaac
14	Weaverville, NC	May 5	David Pearson

RACE WINNERS (CONT.)

Race	Location	Date	Winning Driver
15	Darlington, SC	May 11	David Pearson
16	Beltsville, MD	May 17	David Pearson
17	Hampton, VA	May 18	David Pearson
18	Concord, NC	May 26	Buddy Baker
19	Asheville, NC	May 31	Richard Petty
20	Macon, GA	June 2	David Pearson
21	Maryville, TN	June 6	Richard Petty
22	Birmingham, AL	June 8	Richard Petty
23	Rockingham, NC	June 16	Donnie Allison
24	Greenville, SC	June 22	Richard Petty
25	Daytona Beach, FL	July 4	Cale Yarborough
26	Islip, NY	July 7	Bobby Allison
27	Oxford, ME	July 9	Richard Petty
28	Fonda, NY	July 11	Richard Petty
29	Trenton, NJ	July 14	LeeRoy Yarbrough
30	Bristol, TN	July 21	David Pearson
31	Maryville, TN	July 25	Richard Petty
32	Nashville, TN	July 27	David Pearson
33	Hampton, GA	Aug 4	LeeRoy Yarbrough
34	Columbia, SC	Aug 8	David Pearson
35	Winston-Salem, NC	Aug 10	David Pearson
36	Weaverville, NC	Aug 18	David Pearson
37	South Boston, VA	Aug 23	Richard Petty
38	Hampton, VA	Aug 24	David Pearson
39	Darlington, SC	Sept 2	Cale Yarborough
40	Hickory, NC	Sept 6	David Pearson
41	Richmond, VA	Sept 8	Richard Petty

Race	Location	Date	Winning Driver
42	Beltsville, MD	Sept 13	Bobby Isaac
43	Hillsboro, NC	Sept 15	Richard Petty
44	Martinsville, VA	Sept 22	Richard Petty
45	North Wilkesboro, NC	Sept 29	Richard Petty
46	Augusta, GA	Oct 5	David Pearson
47	Concord, NC	Oct 20	Charlie Glotzbach
48	Rockingham, NC	Oct 27	Richard Petty
49	Jefferson, GA	Nov 3	Cale Yarborough

1969

FINAL CHAMPIONSHIP STANDINGS TOP 10

Rank	Driver	Points
1	David Pearson	4,170
2	Richard Petty	3,813
3	James Hylton	3,750
4	Neil Castles	3,530
5	Elmo Langley	3,383
6	Bobby Isaac	3,301
7	John Sears	3,166
8	Jabe Thomas	3,103
9	Wendell Scott	3,015
10	Cecil Gordon	3,002

RACE WINNERS

Race	Location	Date	Winning Driver
1	Macon, GA	Nov 17	Richard Petty
2	Montgomery, AL	Dec 8	Bobby Allison
3	Riverside, CA	Feb 1	Richard Petty

RACE WINNERS (CONT.)

Race	Location	Date	Winning Driver
4	Daytona Beach, FL	Feb 20	David Pearson
5	Daytona Beach, FL	Feb 20	Bobby Isaac
6	Daytona Beach, FL	Feb 23	LeeRoy Yarbrough
7	Rockingham, NC	March 9	David Pearson
8	Augusta, GA	March 16	David Pearson
9	Bristol, TN	March 23	Bobby Allison
10	Hampton, GA	March 30	Cale Yarborough
11	Columbia, SC	April 3	Bobby Isaac
12	Hickory, NC	April 6	Bobby Isaac
13	Greenville, SC	April 8	Bobby Isaac
14	Richmond, VA	April 13	David Pearson
15	North Wilkesboro, NC	April 20	Bobby Allison
16	Martinsville, VA	April 27	Richard Petty
17	Weaverville, NC	May 4	Bobby Isaac
18	Darlington, SC	May 10	LeeRoy Yarbrough
19	Beltsville, MD	May 16	Bobby Isaac
20	Hampton, VA	May 17	David Pearson
21	Concord, NC	May 25	LeeRoy Yarbrough
22	Macon, GA	June 1	Bobby Isaac
23	Maryville, TN	June 5	Bobby Isaac
24	Brooklyn, MI	June 15	Cale Yarborough
25	Kingsport, TN	June 19	Richard Petty
26	Greenville, SC	June 21	Bobby Isaac
27	Raleigh, NC	June 26	David Pearson
28	Daytona Beach, FL	July 4	LeeRoy Yarbrough
29	Dover, DE	July 6	Richard Petty
30	Thompson, CT	July 10	David Pearson

Race	Location	Date	Winning Driver
31	Trenton, NJ	July 13	David Pearson
32	Beltsville, MD	July 15	Richard Petty
33	Bristol, TN	July 20	David Pearson
34	Nashville, TN	July 26	Richard Petty
35	Maryville, TN	July 27	Richard Petty
36	Hampton, GA	Aug 10	LeeRoy Yarbrough
37	Brooklyn, MI	Aug 17	David Pearson
38	South Boston, VA	Aug 21	Bobby Isaac
39	Winston-Salem, NC	Aug 22	Richard Petty
40	Weaverville, NC	Aug 24	Bobby Isaac
41	Darlington, SC	Sept 1	LeeRoy Yarbrough
42	Hickory, NC	Sept 5	Bobby Isaac
43	Richmond, VA	Sept 7	Bobby Allison
44	Talladega, AL	Sept 14	Richard Brickhouse
45	Columbia, SC	Sept 18	Bobby Isaac
46	Martinsville, VA	Sept 28	Richard Petty
47	North Wilkesboro, NC	Oct 5	David Pearson
48	Concord, NC	Oct 12	Donnie Allison
49	Savannah, GA	Oct 17	Bobby Isaac
50	Augusta, GA	Oct 19	Bobby Isaac
51	Rockingham, NC	Oct 26	LeeRoy Yarbrough
52	Jefferson, GA	Nov 2	Bobby Isaac
53	Macon, GA	Nov 9	Bobby Allison
54	College Station, TX	Dec 7	Bobby Isaac

1970

FINAL CHAMPIONSHIP STANDINGS TOP 10

Rank	Driver	Points
1	Bobby Isaac	3,911
2	Bobby Allison	3,860
3	James Hylton	3,788
4	Richard Petty	3,447
5	Neil Castles	3,158
6	Elmo Langley	3,154
7	Jabe Thomas	3,120
8	Benny Parsons	2,993
9	Dave Marcis	2,820
10	Frank Warren	2,697

RACE WINNERS

Race	Location	Date	Winning Driver
1	Riverside, CA	Jan 18	A.J. Foyt
2	Daytona Beach, FL	Feb 19	Cale Yarborough
3	Daytona Beach, FL	Feb 19	Charlie Glotzbach
4	Daytona Beach, FL	Feb 22	Pete Hamilton
5	Richmond, VA	March 1	James Hylton
6	Rockingham, NC	March 8	Richard Petty
7	Savannah, GA	March 15	Richard Petty
8	Hampton, GA	March 29	Bobby Allison
9	Bristol, TN	April 5	Donnie Allison
10	Talladega, AL	April 12	Pete Hamilton
11	North Wilkesboro, NC	April 18	Richard Petty
12	Columbia, SC	April 30	Richard Petty
13	Darlington, SC	May 9	David Pearson
14	Beltsville, MD	May 15	Bobby Isaac

Race	Location	Date	Winning Driver
15	Hampton, VA	May 18	Bobby Isaac
16	Concord, NC	May 24	Donnie Allison
17	Maryville, TN	May 28	Bobby Isaac
18	Martinsville, VA	May 31	Bobby Isaac
19	Brooklyn, MI	June 7	Cale Yarborough
20	Riverside, CA	June 14	Richard Petty
21	Hickory, NC	June 20	Bobby Isaac
22	Kingsport, TN	June 26	Richard Petty
23	Greenville, SC	June 27	Bobby Isaac
24	Daytona Beach, FL	July 4	Donnie Allison
25	Malta, NY	July 7	Richard Petty
26	Thompson, CT	July 9	Bobby Isaac
27	Trenton, NJ	July 12	Richard Petty
28	Bristol, TN	July 19	Bobby Allison
29	Maryville, TN	July 24	Richard Petty
30	Nashville, TN	July 25	Bobby Isaac
31	Hampton, GA	Aug 2	Richard Petty
32	Columbia, SC	Aug 6	Bobby Isaac
33	Ona, West VA	Aug 11	Richard Petty
34	Brooklyn, MI	Aug 16	Charlie Glotzbach
35	Talladega, AL	Aug 23	Pete Hamilton
36	Winston-Salem, NC	Aug 28	Richard Petty
37	South Boston, VA	Aug 29	Richard Petty
38	Darlington, SC	Sept 7	Buddy Baker
39	Hickory, NC	Sept 11	Bobby Isaac
40	Richmond, VA	Sept 13	Richard Petty
41	Dover, DE	Sept 20	Richard Petty
42	Raleigh, NC	Sept 30	Richard Petty
43	North Wilkesboro, NC	Oct 4	Bobby Isaac

RACE WINNERS (CONT.)

Race	Location	Date	Winning Driver
44	Concord, NC	Oct 11	LeeRoy Yarbrough
45	Martinsville, VA	Oct 18	Richard Petty
46	Macon, GA	Nov 8	Richard Petty
47	Rockingham, NC	Nov 15	Cale Yarborough
48	Hampton, VA	Nov 22	Bobby Allison

1971

FINAL CHAMPIONSHIP STANDINGS TOP 10

Rank	Driver	Points
1	Richard Petty	4,435
2	James Hylton	4,071
3	Cecil Gordon	3,677
4	Bobby Allison	3,636
5	Elmo Langley	3,356
6	Jabe Thomas	3,200
7	Bill Champion	3,058
8	Frank Warren	2,886
9	J.D. McDuffie	2,862
10	Walter Ballard	2,633

RACE WINNERS

Rank	Location	Date	Winning Driver
1	Riverside, CA	Jan 10	Ray Elder
2	Daytona Beach, FL	Feb 11	Pete Hamilton
3	Daytona Beach, FL	Feb 11	David Pearson
4	Daytona Beach, FL	Feb 14	Richard Petty

Rank	Location	Date	Winning Driver
5	Ontario, CA	Feb 28	A.J. Foyt
6	Richmond, VA	March 7	Richard Petty
7	Rockingham, NC	March 14	Richard Petty
8	Hickory, NC	March 21	Richard Petty
9	Bristol, TN	March 28	David Pearson
10	Hampton, GA	April 4	A.J. Foyt
11	Columbia, SC	April 8	Richard Petty
12	Greenville, SC	April 10	Bobby Isaac
13	Maryville, TN	April 15	Richard Petty
14	North Wilkesboro, NC	April 18	Richard Petty
15	Martinsville, VA	April 25	Richard Petty
16	Darlington, SC	May 2	Buddy Baker
17	South Boston, VA	May 9	Benny Parsons
18	Talladega, AL	May 16	Donnie Allison
19	Asheville, NC	May 21	Richard Petty
20	Kingsport, TN	May 23	Bobby Isaac
21	Concord, NC	May 30	Bobby Allison
22	Dover, DE	June 6	Bobby Allison
23	Brooklyn, MI	June 13	Bobby Allison
24	Riverside, CA	June 20	Bobby Allison
25	Houston, TX	June 23	Bobby Allison
26	Greenville, SC	June 26	Richard Petty
27	Daytona Beach, FL	July 4	Bobby Isaac
28	Bristol, TN	July 11	Charlie Glotzbach
29	Malta, NY	July 14	Richard Petty
30	Islip, NY	July 15	Richard Petty
31	Trenton, NJ	July 18	Richard Petty
32	Nashville, TN	July 24	Richard Petty
33	Hampton, GA	Aug 1	Richard Petty
34	Winston-Salem, NC	Aug 6	Bobby Allison

Rank	Location	Date	Winning Driver
35	Ona, West VA	Aug 8	Richard Petty
36	Brooklyn, MI	Aug 15	Bobby Allison
37	Talladega, AL	Aug 22	Bobby Allison
38	Columbia, SC	Aug 27	Richard Petty
39	Hickory, NC	Aug 28	Tiny Lund
40	Darlington, SC	Sept 6	Bobby Allison
41	Martinsville, VA	Sept 26	Bobby Isaac
42	Concord, NC	Oct 10	Bobby Allison
43	Dover, DE	Oct 17	Richard Petty
44	Rockingham, NC	Oct 24	Richard Petty
45	Macon, GA	Nov 7	Bobby Allison
46	Richmond, VA	Nov 14	Richard Petty
47	North Wilkesboro, NC	Nov 22	Tiny Lund
48	College Station, TX	Dec 12	Richard Petty

1972

FINAL CHAMPIONSHIP STANDINGS TOP 10

Rank	Driver	Points
1	Richard Petty	8,701.40
2	Bobby Allison	8,573.50
3	James Hylton	8,158.70
4	Cecil Gordon	7,326.05
5	Benny Parsons	6,844.15
6	Walter Ballard	6,781.45
7	Elmo Langley	6,656.25
8	John Sears	6,298.50
9	Dean Dalton	6,295.05
10	Ben Arnold	6,179.00

RACE WINNERS

Race	Location	Date	Winning Driver
1	Riverside, CA	Jan 23	Richard Petty
2	Daytona Beach, FL	Feb 20	A.J. Foyt
3	Richmond, VA	Feb 27	Richard Petty
4	Ontario, CA	March 5	A.J. Foyt
5	Rockingham, NC	March 12	Bobby Isaac
6	Hampton, GA	March 26	Bobby Allison
7	Bristol, TN	April 9	Bobby Allison
8	Darlington, SC	April 16	David Pearson
9	North Wilkesboro, NC	April 23	Richard Petty
10	Martinsville, VA	April 30	Richard Petty
11	Talladega, AL	May 7	David Pearson
12	Concord, NC	May 28	Buddy Baker
13	Dover, DE	June 4	Bobby Allison
14	Brooklyn, MI	June 11	David Pearson
15	Riverside, CA	June 18	Ray Elder
16	College Station, TX	June 25	Richard Petty
17	Daytona Beach, FL	July 4	David Pearson
18	Bristol, TN	July 9	Bobby Allison
19	Trenton, NJ	July 16	Bobby Allison
20	Hampton, GA	July 23	Bobby Allison
21	Talladega, AL	Aug 6	James Hylton
22	Brooklyn, MI	Aug 20	David Pearson
23	Nashville, TN	Aug 27	Bobby Allison
24	Darlington, SC	Sept 4	Bobby Allison
25	Richmond, VA	Sept 10	Richard Petty
26	Dover, DE	Sept 17	David Pearson
27	Martinsville, VA	Sept 24	Richard Petty

RACE WINNERS (CONT.)

Race	Location	Date	Winning Driver
28	North Wilkesboro, NC	Oct 1	Richard Petty
29	Concord, NC	Oct 8	Bobby Allison
30	Rockingham, NC	Oct 22	Bobby Allison
31	College Station, TX	Nov 12	Buddy Baker

1973

FINAL CHAMPIONSHIP STANDINGS TOP 10

Rank	Driver	Points
1	Benny Parsons	7,173.80
2	Cale Yarborough	7,106.65
3	Cecil Gordon	7,046.80
4	James Hylton	6,972.75
5	Richard Petty	6,877.95
6	Buddy Baker	6,327.60
7	Bobby Allison	6,272.30
8	Walter Ballard	5,955.70
9	Elmo Langley	5,826.85
10	J.D. McDuffie	5,743.90

RACE WINNERS

Race	Location	Date	Winning Driver
1	Riverside, CA	Jan 21	Mark Donohue
2	Daytona Beach, FL	Feb 18	Richard Petty
3	Richmond, VA	Feb 25	Richard Petty
4	Rockingham, NC	March 18	David Pearson
5	Bristol, TN	March 25	Cale Yarborough
6	Hampton, GA	April 1	David Pearson

Race	Location	Date	Winning Driver
7	North Wilkesboro, NC	April 8	Richard Petty
8	Darlington, SC	April 15	David Pearson
9	Martinsville, VA	April 29	David Pearson
10	Talladega, AL	May 6	David Pearson
11	Nashville, TN	May 12	Cale Yarborough
12	Concord, NC	May 27	Buddy Baker
13	Dover, DE	June 3	David Pearson
14	College Station, TX	June 10	Richard Petty
15	Riverside, CA	June 17	Bobby Allison
16	Brooklyn, MI	June 24	David Pearson
17	Daytona Beach, FL	July 4	David Pearson
18	Bristol, TN	July 8	Benny Parsons
19	Hampton, GA	July 22	David Pearson
20	Talladega, AL	Aug 12	Dick Brooks
21	Nashville, TN	Aug 25	Buddy Baker
22	Darlington, SC	Sept 3	Cale Yarborough
23	Richmond, VA	Sept 9	Richard Petty
24	Dover, DE	Sept 16	David Pearson
25	North Wilkesboro, NC	Sept 23	Bobby Allison
26	Martinsville, VA	Sept 30	Richard Petty
27	Concord, NC	Oct 7	Cale Yarborough
28	Rockingham, NC	Oct 21	David Pearson

1974

FINAL CHAMPIONSHIP STANDINGS TOP 10

Rank	Driver	Points
1	Richard Petty	5,037.75
2	Cale Yarborough	4,470.30
3	David Pearson	2,389.25

FINAL CHAMPIONSHIP STANDINGS TOP 10

Rank	Driver	Points
4	Bobby Allison	2,019.19
5	Benny Parsons	1,591.50
6	Dave Marcis	1,378.20
7	Buddy Baker	1,016.88
8	Earl Ross	1,009.47
9	Cecil Gordon	1,000.65
10	Dave Sisco	956.20

RACE WINNERS

Race	Location	Date	Winning Driver
1	Riverside, CA	Jan 26	Cale Yarborough
2	Daytona Beach, FL	Feb 17	Richard Petty
3	Richmond, VA	Feb 24	Bobby Allison
4	Rockingham, NC	March 3	Richard Petty
5	Bristol, TN	March 17	Cale Yarborough
6	Hampton, GA	March 24	Cale Yarborough
7	Darlington, SC	April 7	David Pearson
8	North Wilkesboro, NC	April 21	Richard Petty
9	Martinsville, VA	April 28	Cale Yarborough
10	Talladega, AL	May 5	David Pearson
11	Nashville, TN	May 12	Richard Petty
12	Dover, DE	May 19	Cale Yarborough
13	Concord, NC	May 26	David Pearson
14	Riverside, CA	June 9	Cale Yarborough
15	Brooklyn, MI	June 16	Richard Petty
16	Daytona Beach, FL	July 4	David Pearson
17	Bristol, TN	July 14	Cale Yarborough
18	Nashville, TN	July 20	Cale Yarborough

Race	Location	Date	Winning Driver
19	Hampton, GA	July 28	Richard Petty
20	Long Pond, PA	Aug 4	Richard Petty
21	Talladega, AL	Aug 11	Richard Petty
22	Brooklyn, MI	Aug 25	David Pearson
23	Darlington, SC	Sept 2	Cale Yarborough
24	Richmond, VA	Sept 8	Richard Petty
25	Dover, DE	Sept 15	Richard Petty
26	North Wilkesboro, NC	Sept 22	Cale Yarborough
27	Martinsville, VA	Sept 29	Earl Ross
28	Concord, NC	Oct 6	David Pearson
29	Rockingham, NC	Oct 20	David Pearson
30	Ontario, CA	Nov 24	Bobby Allison

1975

FINAL CHAMPIONSHIP STANDINGS TOP 10

Rank	Driver	Points
1	Richard Petty	4,783
2	Dave Marcis	4,061
3	James Hylton	3,914
4	Benny Parsons	3,820
5	Richard Childress	3,818
6	Cecil Gordon	3,702
7	Darrell Waltrip	3,462
8	Elmo Langley	3,399
9	Cale Yarborough	3,295
10	Dick Brooks	3,182

RACE WINNERS

Race	Location	Date	Winning Driver
1	Riverside, CA	Jan 19	Bobby Allison
2	Daytona Beach, FL	Feb 16	Benny Parsons
3	Richmond, VA	Feb 23	Richard Petty
4	Rockingham, NC	March 2	Cale Yarborough
5	Bristol, TN	March 16	Richard Petty
6	Hampton, GA	March 23	Richard Petty
7	North Wilkesboro, NC	April 6	Richard Petty
8	Darlington, SC	April 13	Bobby Allison
9	Martinsville, VA	April 27	Richard Petty
10	Talladega, AL	May 4	Buddy Baker
11	Nashville, TN	May 10	Darrell Waltrip
12	Dover, DE	May 19	David Pearson
13	Concord, NC	May 25	Richard Petty
14	Riverside, CA	June 8	Richard Petty
15	Brooklyn, MI	June 15	David Pearson
16	Daytona Beach, FL	July 4	Richard Petty
17	Nashville, TN	July 20	Cale Yarborough
18	Long Pond, PA	Aug 3	David Pearson
19	Talladega, AL	Aug 17	Buddy Baker
20	Brooklyn, MI	Aug 24	Richard Petty
21	Darlington, SC	Sept 1	Bobby Allison
22	Dover, DE	Sept 14	Richard Petty
23	North Wilkesboro, NC	Sept 21	Richard Petty
24	Martinsville, VA	Sept 28	Dave Marcis
25	Concord, NC	Oct 5	Richard Petty
26	Richmond, VA	Oct 12	Darrell Waltrip
27	Rockingham, NC	Oct 19	Cale Yarborough
28	Bristol, TN	Nov 2	Richard Petty

Race	Location	Date	Winning Driver
29	Hampton, GA	Nov 9	Buddy Baker
30	Ontario, CA	Nov 23	Buddy Baker

1976

FINAL CHAMPIONSHIP STANDINGS TOP 10

Rank	Driver	Points
1	Cale Yarborough	4,644
2	Richard Petty	4,449
3	Benny Parsons	4,304
4	Bobby Allison	4,097
5	Lennie Pond	3,930
6	Dave Marcis	3,875
7	Buddy Baker	3,745
8	Darrell Waltrip	3,505
9	David Pearson	3,483
10	Dick Brooks	3,447

RACE WINNERS

Race	Location	Date	Winning Driver
1	Riverside, CA	Jan 18	David Pearson
2	Daytona Beach, FL	Feb 15	David Pearson
3	Rockingham, NC	Feb 29	Richard Petty
4	Richmond, VA	March 7	Dave Marcis
5	Bristol, TN	March 14	Cale Yarborough
6	Hampton, GA	March 21	David Pearson
7	North Wilkesboro, NC	April 4	Cale Yarborough
8	Darlington, SC	April 11	David Pearson
9	Martinsville, VA	April 25	Darrell Waltrip
10	Talladega, AL	May 2	Buddy Baker

RACE WINNERS (CONT.)

Race	Location	Date	Winning Driver
11	Nashville, TN	May 8	Cale Yarborough
12	Dover, DE	May 16	Benny Parsons
13	Concord, NC	May 30	David Pearson
14	Riverside, CA	June 13	David Pearson
15	Brooklyn, MI	June 20	David Pearson
16	Daytona Beach, FL	July 4	Cale Yarborough
17	Nashville, TN	July 17	Benny Parsons
18	Long Pond, PA	Aug 1	Richard Petty
19	Talladega, AL	Aug 8	Dave Marcis
20	Brooklyn, MI	Aug 22	David Pearson
21	Bristol, TN	Aug 29	Cale Yarborough
22	Darlington, SC	Sept 6	David Pearson
23	Richmond, VA	Sept 12	Cale Yarborough
24	Dover, DE	Sept 19	Cale Yarborough
25	Martinsville, VA	Sept 26	Cale Yarborough
26	North Wilkesboro, NC	Oct 3	Cale Yarborough
27	Concord, NC	Oct 10	Donnie Allison
28	Rockingham, NC	Oct 24	Richard Petty
29	Hampton, GA	Nov 7	Dave Marcis
30	Ontario, CA	Nov 21	David Pearson

1977

FINAL CHAMPIONSHIP STANDINGS TOP 10

Rank	Driver	Points
1	Cale Yarborough	5,000
2	Richard Petty	4,614

Rank	Driver	Points
3	Benny Parsons	4,570
4	Darrell Waltrip	4,498
5	Buddy Baker	3,961
6	Dick Brooks	3,742
7	James Hylton	3,476
8	Bobby Allison	3,467
9	Richard Childress	3,463
10	Cecil Gordon	3,294

RACE WINNERS

Race	Location	Date	Winning Driver
1	Riverside, CA	Jan 16	David Pearson
2	Daytona Beach, FL	Feb 20	Cale Yarborough
3	Richmond, VA	Feb 27	Cale Yarborough
4	Rockingham, NC	March 13	Richard Petty
5	Hampton, GA	March 20	Richard Petty
6	North Wilkesboro, NC	March 27	Cale Yarborough
7	Darlington, SC	April 3	Darrell Waltrip
8	Bristol, TN	April 17	Cale Yarborough
9	Martinsville, VA	April 24	Cale Yarborough
10	Talladega, AL	May 1	Darrell Waltrip
11	Nashville, TN	May 7	Benny Parsons
12	Dover, DE	May 15	Cale Yarborough
13	Concord, NC	May 29	Richard Petty
14	Riverside, CA	June 12	Richard Petty
15	Brooklyn, MI	June 19	Cale Yarborough
16	Daytona Beach, FL	July 4	Richard Petty
17	Nashville, TN	July 16	Darrell Waltrip
18	Long Pond, PA	July 31	Benny Parsons
19	Talladega, AL	Aug 7	Donnie Allison

RACE WINNERS (CONT.)

Race	Location	Date	Winning Driver
20	Brooklyn, MI	Aug 22	Darrell Waltrip
21	Bristol, TN	Aug 28	Cale Yarborough
22	Darlington, SC	Sept 5	David Pearson
23	Richmond, VA	Sept 11	Neil Bonnett
24	Dover, DE	Sept 18	Benny Parsons
25	Martinsville, VA	Sept 25	Cale Yarborough
26	North Wilkesboro, NC	Oct 2	Darrell Waltrip
27	Concord, NC	Oct 9	Benny Parsons
28	Rockingham, NC	Oct 23	Donnie Allison
29	Hampton, GA	Nov 6	Darrell Waltrip
30	Ontario, CA	Nov 20	Neil Bonnett

1978

FINAL CHAMPIONSHIP STANDINGS TOP 10

Rank	Driver	Points
1	Cale Yarborough	4,841
2	Bobby Allison	4,367
3	Darrell Waltrip	4,362
4	Benny Parsons	4,350
5	Dave Marcis	4,335
6	Richard Petty	3,949
7	Lennie Pond	3,794
8	Dick Brooks	3,769
9	Buddy Arrington	3,626
10	Richard Childress	3,566

RACE WINNERS

Race	Location	Date	Winning Driver
1	Riverside, CA	Jan 22	Cale Yarborough
2	Daytona Beach, FL	Feb 19	Bobby Allison
3	Richmond, VA	Feb 26	Benny Parsons
4	Rockingham, NC	March 5	David Pearson
5	Hampton, GA	March 19	Bobby Allison
6	Bristol, TN	April 2	Darrell Waltrip
7	Darlington, SC	April 9	Benny Parsons
8	North Wilkesboro, NC	April 16	Darrell Waltrip
9	Martinsville, VA	April 23	Darrell Waltrip
10	Talladega, AL	May 14	Cale Yarborough
11	Dover, DE	May 21	David Pearson
12	Concord, NC	May 28	Darrell Waltrip
13	Nashville, TN	June 3	Cale Yarborough
14	Riverside, CA	June 11	Benny Parsons
15	Brooklyn, MI	June 18	Cale Yarborough
16	Daytona Beach, FL	July 4	David Pearson
17	Nashville, TN	July 15	Cale Yarborough
18	Long Pond, PA	July 30	Darrell Waltrip
19	Talladega, AL	Aug 6	Lennie Pond
20	Brooklyn, MI	Aug 20	David Pearson
21	Bristol, TN	Aug 26	Cale Yarborough
22	Darlington, SC	Sept 4	Cale Yarborough
23	Richmond, VA	Sept 10	Darrell Waltrip
24	Dover, DE	Sept 17	Bobby Allison
25	Martinsville, VA	Sept 24	Cale Yarborough
26	North Wilkesboro, NC	Oct 1	Cale Yarborough
27	Concord, NC	Oct 8	Bobby Allison

RACE WINNERS (CONT.)

Race	Location	Date	Winning Driver
28	Rockingham, NC	Oct 22	Cale Yarborough
29	Hampton, GA	Nov 5	Donnie Allison
30	Ontario, CA	Nov 19	Bobby Allison

1979

FINAL CHAMPIONSHIP STANDINGS TOP 10

Rank	Driver	Points
1	Richard Petty	4,830
2	Darrell Waltrip	4,819
3	Bobby Allison	4,633
4	Cale Yarborough	4,604
5	Benny Parsons	4,256
6	Joe Millikan	4,014
7	Dale Earnhardt	3,749
8	Richard Childress	3,735
9	Ricky Rudd	3,642
10	Terry Labonte	3,615

RACE WINNERS

Race	Location	Date	Winning Driver
1	Riverside, CA	Jan 14	Darrell Waltrip
2	Daytona Beach, FL	Feb 18	Richard Petty
3	Rockingham, NC	March 4	Bobby Allison
4	Richmond, VA	March 11	Cale Yarborough
5	Hampton, GA	March 18	Buddy Baker
6	North Wilkesboro, NC	March 25	Bobby Allison

Race	Location	Date	Winning Driver
7	Bristol, TN	April 1	Dale Earnhardt
8	Darlington, SC	April 8	Darrell Waltrip
9	Martinsville, VA	April 22	Richard Petty
10	Talladega, AL	May 6	Bobby Allison
11	Nashville, TN	May 12	Cale Yarborough
12	Dover, DE	May 20	Neil Bonnett
13	Concord, NC	May 27	Darrell Waltrip
14	College Station, TX	June 3	Darrell Waltrip
15	Riverside, CA	June 10	Bobby Allison
16	Brooklyn, MI	June 17	Buddy Baker
17	Daytona Beach, FL	July 4	Neil Bonnett
18	Nashville, TN	July 14	Darrell Waltrip
19	Long Pond, PA	July 30	Cale Yarborough
20	Talladega, AL	Aug 5	Darrell Waltrip
21	Brooklyn, MI	Aug 19	Richard Petty
22	Bristol, TN	Aug 25	Darrell Waltrip
23	Darlington, SC	Sept 3	David Pearson
24	Richmond, VA	Sept 9	Bobby Allison
25	Dover, DE	Sept 16	Richard Petty
26	Martinsville, VA	Sept 23	Buddy Baker
27	Concord, NC	Oct 7	Cale Yarborough
28	North Wilkesboro, NC	Oct 14	Benny Parsons
29	Rockingham, NC	Oct 21	Richard Petty
30	Hampton, GA	Nov 4	Neil Bonnett
31	Ontario, CA	Nov 18	Benny Parsons

1980

FINAL CHAMPIONSHIP STANDINGS TOP 10

Rank	Driver	Points
1	Dale Earnhardt	4,661
2	Cale Yarborough	4,642
3	Benny Parsons	4,278
4	Richard Petty	4,255
5	Darrell Waltrip	4,239
6	Bobby Allison	4,020
7	Jody Ridley	3,972
8	Terry Labonte	3,766
9	Dave Marcis	3,745
10	Richard Childress	3,742

RACE WINNERS

Race	Location	Date	Winning Driver
1	Riverside, CA	Jan 19	Darrell Waltrip
2	Daytona Beach, FL	Feb 17	Buddy Baker
3	Richmond, VA	Feb 24	Darrell Waltrip
4	Rockingham, NC	March 9	Cale Yarborough
5	Hampton, GA	March 16	Dale Earnhardt
6	Bristol, TN	March 30	Dale Earnhardt
7	Darlington, SC	April 13	David Pearson
8	North Wilkesboro, NC	April 20	Richard Petty
9	Martinsville, VA	April 27	Darrell Waltrip
10	Talladega, AL	May 4	Buddy Baker
11	Nashville, TN	May 10	Richard Petty
12	Dover, DE	May 18	Bobby Allison
13	Concord, NC	May 25	Benny Parsons
14	College Station, TX	June 1	Cale Yarborough

RACE WINNERS (CONT.)

Race	Location	Date	Winning Driver
15	Riverside, CA	June 8	Darrell Waltrip
16	Brooklyn, MI	June 15	Benny Parsons
17	Daytona Beach, FL	July 4	Bobby Allison
18	Nashville, TN	July 12	Dale Earnhardt
19	Long Pond, PA	July 27	Neil Bonnett
20	Talladega, AL	Aug 3	Neil Bonnett
21	Brooklyn, MI	Aug 17	Cale Yarborough
22	Bristol, TN	Aug 23	Cale Yarborough
23	Darlington, SC	Sept 1	Terry Labonte
24	Richmond, VA	Sept 7	Bobby Allison
25	Dover, DE	Sept 14	Darrell Waltrip
26	North Wilkesboro, NC	Sept 21	Bobby Allison
27	Martinsville, VA	Sept 28	Dale Earnhardt
28	Concord, NC	Oct 5	Dale Earnhardt
29	Rockingham, NC	Oct 19	Cale Yarborough
30	Hampton, GA	Nov 2	Cale Yarborough
31	Ontario, CA	Nov 15	Benny Parsons

1981

FINAL CHAMPIONSHIP STANDINGS TOP 10

Rank	Driver	Points
1	Darrell Waltrip	4,880
2	Bobby Allison	4,827
3	Harry Gant	4,213
4	Terry Labonte	4,052
5	Jody Ridley	4,002
6	Ricky Rudd	3,991

FINAL CHAMPIONSHIP STANDINGS TOP 10 (CONT.)

Rank	Driver	Points
7	Dale Earnhardt	3,978
8	Richard Petty	3,882
9	Dave Marcis	3,510
10	Benny Parsons	3,452

RACE WINNERS

Race	Location	Date	Winning Driver
1	Riverside, CA	Jan 11	Bobby Allison
2	Daytona Beach, FL	Feb 15	Richard Petty
3	Richmond, VA	Feb 22	Darrell Waltrip
4	Rockingham, NC	March 1	Darrell Waltrip
5	Hampton, GA	March 15	Cale Yarborough
6	Bristol, TN	March 29	Darrell Waltrip
7	North Wilkesboro, NC	April 5	Richard Petty
8	Darlington, SC	April 12	Darrell Waltrip
9	Martinsville, VA	April 26	Morgan Shepherd
10	Talladega, AL	May 3	Bobby Allison
11	Nashville, TN	May 9	Benny Parsons
12	Dover, DE	May 17	Jody Ridley
13	Concord, NC	May 24	Bobby Allison
14	College Station, TX	June 7	Benny Parsons
15	Riverside, CA	June 14	Darrell Waltrip
16	Brooklyn, MI	June 21	Bobby Allison
17	Daytona Beach, FL	July 4	Cale Yarborough
18	Nashville, TN	July 11	Darrell Waltrip
19	Long Pond, PA	July 26	Darrell Waltrip
20	Talladega, AL	Aug 2	Ron Bouchard

RACE WINNERS (CONT.)

Race	Location	Date	Winning Driver
21	Brooklyn, MI	Aug 16	Richard Petty
22	Bristol, TN	Aug 22	Darrell Waltrip
23	Darlington, SC	Sept 7	Neil Bonnett
24	Richmond, VA	Sept 13	Benny Parsons
25	Dover, DE	Sept 20	Neil Bonnett
26	Martinsville, VA	Sept 27	Darrell Waltrip
27	North Wilkesboro, NC	Oct 4	Darrell Waltrip
28	Concord, NC	Oct 11	Darrell Waltrip
29	Rockingham, NC	Nov 1	Darrell Waltrip
30	Hampton, GA	Nov 8	Neil Bonnett
31	Riverside, CA	Nov 22	Bobby Allison

1982

FINAL CHAMPIONSHIP STANDINGS TOP 10

Rank	Driver	Points
1	Darrell Waltrip	4,489
2	Bobby Allison	4,417
3	Terry Labonte	4,211
4	Harry Gant	3,877
5	Richard Petty	3,814
6	Dave Marcis	3,666
7	Buddy Arrington	3,642
8	Ron Bouchard	3,545
9	Ricky Rudd	3,537
10	Morgan Shepherd	3,451

RACE WINNERS

Race	Location	Date	Winning Driver
1	Daytona Beach, FL	Feb 14	Bobby Allison
2	Richmond, VA	Feb 21	Dave Marcis
3	Bristol, TN	March 14	Darrell Waltrip
4	Hampton, GA	March 21	Darrell Waltrip
5	Rockingham, NC	March 28	Cale Yarborough
6	Darlington, SC	April 4	Dale Earnhardt
7	North Wilkesboro, NC	April 18	Darrell Waltrip
8	Martinsville, VA	April 25	Harry Gant
9	Talladega, AL	May 2	Darrell Waltrip
10	Nashville, TN	May 8	Darrell Waltrip
11	Dover, DE	May 16	Bobby Allison
12	Concord, NC	May 30	Neil Bonnett
13	Long Pond, PA	June 6	Bobby Allison
14	Riverside, CA	June 13	Tim Richmond
15	Brooklyn, MI	June 20	Cale Yarborough
16	Daytona Beach, FL	July 4	Bobby Allison
17	Nashville, TN	July 10	Darrell Waltrip
18	Long Pond, PA	July 25	Bobby Allison
19	Talladega, AL	Aug 1	Darrell Waltrip
20	Brooklyn, MI	Aug 22	Bobby Allison
21	Bristol, TN	Aug 28	Darrell Waltrip
22	Darlington, SC	Sept 6	Cale Yarborough
23	Richmond, VA	Sept 12	Bobby Allison
24	Dover, DE	Sept 19	Darrell Waltrip
25	North Wilkesboro, NC	Oct 3	Darrell Waltrip
26	Concord, NC	Oct 10	Harry Gant
27	Martinsville, VA	Oct 17	Darrell Waltrip

Race	Location	Date	Winning Driver
28	Rockingham, NC	Oct 31	Darrell Waltrip
29	Hampton, GA	Nov 7	Bobby Allison
30	Riverside, CA	Nov 21	Tim Richmond

1983

FINAL CHAMPIONSHIP STANDINGS TOP 10

Rank	Driver	Points
1	Bobby Allison	4,667
2	Darrell Waltrip	4,620
3	Bill Elliott	4,279
4	Richard Petty	4,042
5	Terry Labonte	4,009
6	Neil Bonnett	3,837
7	Harry Gant	3,790
8	Dale Earnhardt	3,732
9	Ricky Rudd	3,693
10	Tim Richmond	3,592

RACE WINNERS

Race	Location	Date	Winning Driver
1	Daytona Beach, FL	Feb 20	Cale Yarborough
2	Richmond, VA	Feb 27	Bobby Allison
3	Rockingham, NC	March 13	Richard Petty
4	Hampton, GA	March 27	Cale Yarborough
5	Darlington, SC	April 10	Harry Gant
6	North Wilkesboro, NC	April 17	Darrell Waltrip
7	Martinsville, VA	April 24	Darrell Waltrip
8	Talladega, AL	May 1	Richard Petty
9	Nashville, TN	May 7	Darrell Waltrip
10	Dover, DE	May 15	Bobby Allison

RACE WINNERS (CONT.)

Race	Location	Date	Winning Driver
11	Bristol, TN	May 21	Darrell Waltrip
12	Concord, NC	May 29	Neil Bonnett
13	Riverside, CA	June 5	Ricky Rudd
14	Long Pond, PA	June 12	Bobby Allison
15	Brooklyn, MI	June 19	Cale Yarborough
16	Daytona Beach, FL	July 4	Buddy Baker
17	Nashville, TN	July 16	Dale Earnhardt
18	Long Pond, PA	July 24	Tim Richmond
19	Talladega, AL	July 31	Dale Earnhardt
20	Brooklyn, MI	Aug 21	Cale Yarborough
21	Bristol, TN	Aug 27	Darrell Waltrip
22	Darlington, SC	Sept 5	Bobby Allison
23	Richmond, VA	Sept 11	Bobby Allison
24	Dover, DE	Sept 18	Bobby Allison
25	Martinsville, VA	Sept 25	Ricky Rudd
26	North Wilkesboro, NC	Oct 2	Darrell Waltrip
27	Concord, NC	Oct 9	Richard Petty
28	Rockingham, NC	Oct 30	Terry Labonte
29	Hampton, GA	Nov 6	Neil Bonnett
30	Riverside, CA	Nov 20	Bill Elliott

1984

FINAL CHAMPIONSHIP STANDINGS TOP 10

Rank	Driver	Points
1	Terry Labonte	4,508
2	Harry Gant	4,443
3	Bill Elliott	4,377
4	Dale Earnhardt	4,265

Rank	Driver	Points
5	Darrell Waltrip	4,235
6	Bobby Allison	4,094
7	Ricky Rudd	3,918
8	Neil Bonnett	3,797
9	Geoffrey Bodine	3,734
10	Richard Petty	3,643

RACE WINNERS

Race	Location	Date	Winning Driver
1	Daytona Beach, FL	Feb 19	Cale Yarborough
2	Richmond, VA	Feb 26	Ricky Rudd
3	Rockingham, NC	March 4	Bobby Allison
4	Hampton, GA	March 18	Benny Parsons
5	Bristol, TN	April 1	Darrell Waltrip
6	North Wilkesboro, NC	April 8	Tim Richmond
7	Darlington, SC	April 15	Darrell Waltrip
8	Martinsville, VA	April 29	Geoffrey Bodine
9	Talladega, AL	May 6	Cale Yarborough
10	Nashville, TN	May 12	Darrell Waltrip
11	Dover, DE	May 20	Richard Petty
12	Concord, NC	May 27	Bobby Allison
13	Riverside, CA	June 3	Terry Labonte
14	Long Pond, PA	June 10	Cale Yarborough
15	Brooklyn, MI	June 17	Bill Elliott
16	Daytona Beach, FL	July 4	Richard Petty
17	Nashville, TN	July 14	Geoffrey Bodine
18	Long Pond, PA	July 22	Harry Gant
19	Talladega, AL	July 29	Dale Earnhardt
20	Brooklyn, MI	Aug 12	Darrell Waltrip

RACE WINNERS (CONT.)

Race	Location	Date	Winning Driver
21	Bristol, TN	Aug 25	Terry Labonte
22	Darlington, SC	Sept 2	Harry Gant
23	Richmond, VA	Sept 9	Darrell Waltrip
24	Dover, DE	Sept 16	Harry Gant
25	Martinsville, VA	Sept 23	Darrell Waltrip
26	Concord, NC	Oct 7	Bill Elliott
27	North Wilkesboro, NC	Oct 14	Darrell Waltrip
28	Rockingham, NC	Oct 21	Bill Elliott
29	Hampton, GA	Nov 11	Dale Earnhardt
30	Riverside, CA	Nov 18	Geoffrey Bodine

1985

FINAL CHAMPIONSHIP STANDINGS TOP 10

Rank	Driver	Points
1	Darrell Waltrip	4,292
2	Bill Elliott	4,191
3	Harry Gant	4,028
4	Neil Bonnett	3,897
5	Geoffrey Bodine	3,862
6	Ricky Rudd	3,857
7	Terry Labonte	3,683
8	Dale Earnhardt	3,561
9	Kyle Petty	3,523
10	Lake Speed	3,507

RACE WINNERS

Race	Location	Date	Winning Driver
1	Daytona Beach, FL	Feb 17	Bill Elliott
2	Richmond, VA	Feb 24	Dale Earnhardt
3	Rockingham, NC	March 3	Neil Bonnett
4	Hampton, GA	March 17	Bill Elliott
5	Bristol, TN	April 6	Dale Earnhardt
6	Darlington, SC	April 14	Bill Elliott
7	North Wilkesboro, NC	April 21	Neil Bonnett
8	Martinsville, VA	April 28	Harry Gant
9	Talladega, AL	May 5	Bill Elliott
10	Dover, DE	May 19	Bill Elliott
11	Concord, NC	May 26	Darrell Waltrip
12	Riverside, CA	June 2	Terry Labonte
13	Long Pond, PA	June 9	Bill Elliott
14	Brooklyn, MI	June 16	Bill Elliott
15	Daytona Beach, FL	July 4	Greg Sacks
16	Long Pond, PA	July 21	Bill Elliott
17	Talladega, AL	July 28	Cale Yarborough
18	Brooklyn, MI	Aug 11	Bill Elliott
19	Bristol, TN	Aug 24	Dale Earnhardt
20	Darlington, SC	Sept 1	Bill Elliott
21	Richmond, VA	Sept 8	Darrell Waltrip
22	Dover, DE	Sept 15	Harry Gant
23	Martinsville, VA	Sept 22	Dale Earnhardt
24	North Wilkesboro, NC	Sept 29	Harry Gant
25	Concord, NC	Oct 6	Cale Yarborough
26	Rockingham, NC	Oct 20	Darrell Waltrip
27	Hampton, GA	Nov 3	Bill Elliott
28	Riverside, CA	Nov 17	Ricky Rudd

1986

FINAL CHAMPIONSHIP STANDINGS TOP 10

Rank	Driver	Points
1	Dale Earnhardt	4,468
2	Darrell Waltrip	4,180
3	Tim Richmond	4,174
4	Bill Elliott	3,844
5	Ricky Rudd	3,823
6	Rusty Wallace	3,757
7	Bobby Allison	3,698
8	Geoffrey Bodine	3,678
9	Bobby Hillin Jr.	3,541
10	Kyle Petty	3,537

RACE WINNERS

Race	Location	Date	Winning Driver
1	Daytona Beach, FL	Feb 16	Geoffrey Bodine
2	Richmond, VA	Feb 23	Kyle Petty
3	Rockingham, NC	March 2	Terry Labonte
4	Hampton, GA	March 16	Morgan Shepherd
5	Bristol, TN	April 6	Rusty Wallace
6	Darlington, SC	April 13	Dale Earnhardt
7	North Wilkesboro, NC	April 20	Dale Earnhardt
8	Martinsville, VA	April 27	Ricky Rudd
9	Talladega, AL	May 4	Bobby Allison
10	Dover, DE	May 18	Geoffrey Bodine
11	Concord, NC	May 25	Dale Earnhardt
12	Riverside, CA	June 1	Darrell Waltrip
13	Long Pond, PA	June 8	Tim Richmond
14	Brooklyn, MI	June 15	Bill Elliott

Race	Location	Date	Winning Driver
15	Daytona Beach, FA	July 4	Tim Richmond
16	Long Pond, PA	July 20	Tim Richmond
17	Talladega, AL	July 27	Bobby Hillin Jr.
18	Watkins Glen, NY	Aug 10	Tim Richmond
19	Brooklyn, MI	Aug 17	Bill Elliott
20	Bristol, TN	Aug 23	Darrell Waltrip
21	Darlington, SC	Aug 31	Tim Richmond
22	Richmond, VA	Sept 7	Tim Richmond
23	Dover, DE	Sept 14	Ricky Rudd
24	Martinsville, VA	Sept 21	Rusty Wallace
25	North Wilkesboro, NC	Sept 28	Darrell Waltrip
26	Concord, NC	Oct 5	Dale Earnhardt
27	Rockingham, NC	Oct 19	Neil Bonnett
28	Hampton, GA	Nov 2	Dale Earnhardt
29	Riverside, CA	Nov 16	Tim Richmond

1987

FINAL CHAMPIONSHIP STANDINGS TOP 10

Rank	Driver	Points
1	Dale Earnhardt	4,696
2	Bill Elliott	4,207
3	Terry Labonte	4,007
4	Darrell Waltrip	3,911
5	Rusty Wallace	3,818
6	Ricky Rudd	3,742
7	Kyle Petty	3,737
8	Richard Petty	3,708
9	Bobby Allison	3,525
10	Ken Schrader	3,405

RACE WINNERS

Race	Location	Date	Winning Driver
1	Daytona Beach, FL	Feb 15	Bill Elliott
2	Rockingham, NC	March 1	Dale Earnhardt
3	Richmond, VA	March 8	Dale Earnhardt
4	Hampton, GA	March 15	Ricky Rudd
5	Darlington, SC	March 29	Dale Earnhardt
6	North Wilkesboro, NC	April 5	Dale Earnhardt
7	Bristol, TN	April 12	Dale Earnhardt
8	Martinsville, VA	April 26	Dale Earnhardt
9	Talladega, AL	May 3	Davey Allison
10	Concord, NC	May 24	Kyle Petty
11	Dover, DE	May 31	Davey Allison
12	Long Pond, PA	June 14	Tim Richmond
13	Riverside, CA	June 21	Tim Richmond
14	Brooklyn, MI	June 28	Dale Earnhardt
15	Daytona Beach, FL	July 4	Bobby Allison
16	Long Pond, PA	July 19	Dale Earnhardt
17	Talladega, AL	July 26	Bill Elliott
18	Watkins Glen, NY	Aug 10	Rusty Wallace
19	Brooklyn, MI	Aug 16	Bill Elliott
20	Bristol, TN	Aug 22	Dale Earnhardt
21	Darlington, SC	Sept 6	Dale Earnhardt
22	Richmond, VA	Sept 13	Dale Earnhardt
23	Dover, DE	Sept 20	Ricky Rudd
24	Martinsville, VA	Sept 27	Darrell Waltrip
25	North Wilkesboro, NC	Oct 4	Terry Labonte
26	Concord, NC	Oct 11	Bill Elliott
27	Rockingham, NC	Oct 25	Bill Elliott

Race	Location	Date	Winning Driver
28	Riverside, CA	Nov 8	Rusty Wallace
29	Hampton, GA	Nov 22	Bill Elliott

1988

FINAL CHAMPIONSHIP STANDINGS TOP 10

Rank	Driver	Points
1	Bill Elliott	4,488
2	Rusty Wallace	4,464
3	Dale Earnhardt	4,256
4	Terry Labonte	4,007
5	Ken Schrader	3,858
6	Geoffrey Bodine	3,799
7	Darrell Waltrip	3,764
8	Davey Allison	3,631
9	Phil Parsons	3,630
10	Sterling Marlin	3,621

RACE WINNERS

Race	Location	Date	Winning Driver
1	Daytona Beach, FL	Feb 14	Bobby Allison
2	Richmond, VA	Feb 21	Neil Bonnett
3	Rockingham, NC	March 6	Neil Bonnett
4	Hampton, GA	March 20	Dale Earnhardt
5	Darlington, SC	March 27	Lake Speed
6	Bristol, TN	April 10	Bill Elliott
7	North Wilkesboro, NC	April 17	Terry Labonte
8	Martinsville, VA	April 24	Dale Earnhardt
9	Talladega, AL	May 1	Phil Parsons
10	Concord, NC	May 29	Darrell Waltrip

RACE WINNERS (CONT.)

Race	Location	Date	Winning Driver
11	Dover, DE	June 5	Bill Elliott
12	Riverside, CA	June 12	Rusty Wallace
13	Long Pond, PA	June 19	Geoffrey Bodine
14	Brooklyn, MI	June 26	Rusty Wallace
15	Daytona Beach, FL	July 2	Bill Elliott
16	Long Pond, PA	July 24	Bill Elliott
17	Talladega, AL	July 31	Ken Schrader
18	Watkins Glen, NY	Aug 14	Ricky Rudd
19	Brooklyn, MI	Aug 21	Davey Allison
20	Bristol, TN	Aug 27	Dale Earnhardt
21	Darlington, SC	Sept 4	Bill Elliott
22	Richmond, VA	Sept 11	Davey Allison
23	Dover, DE	Sept 18	Bill Elliott
24	Martinsville, VA	Sept 25	Darrell Waltrip
25	Concord, NC	Oct 9	Rusty Wallace
26	North Wilkesboro, NC	Oct 16	Rusty Wallace
27	Rockingham, NC	Oct 23	Rusty Wallace
28	Phoenix, AZ	Nov 6	Alan Kulwicki
29	Hampton, GA	Nov 20	Rusty Wallace

1989

FINAL CHAMPIONSHIP STANDINGS TOP 10

Rank	Driver	Points
1	Rusty Wallace	4,176
2	Dale Earnhardt	4,164
3	Mark Martin	4,053
4	Darrell Waltrip	3,971
5	Ken Schrader	3,786
6	Bill Elliott	3,774
7	Harry Gant	3,610
8	Ricky Rudd	3,608
9	Geoffrey Bodine	3,600
10	Terry Labonte	3,569

RACE WINNERS

Race	Location	Date	Winning Driver
1	Daytona Beach, FL	Feb 19	Darrell Waltrip
2	Rockingham, NC	March 5	Rusty Wallace
3	Hampton, GA	March 19	Darrell Waltrip
4	Richmond, VA	March 26	Rusty Wallace
5	Darlington, SC	April 2	Harry Gant
6	Bristol, TN	April 9	Rusty Wallace
7	North Wilkesboro, NC	April 16	Dale Earnhardt
8	Martinsville, VA	April 23	Darrell Waltrip
9	Talladega, AL	May 7	Davey Allison
10	Concord, NC	May 28	Darrell Waltrip
11	Dover, DE	June 4	Dale Earnhardt
12	Sonoma, CA	June 11	Ricky Rudd
13	Long Pond, PA	June 18	Terry Labonte
14	Brooklyn, MI	June 25	Bill Elliott

Race	Location	Date	Winning Driver
15	Daytona Beach, FL	July 1	Davey Allison
16	Long Pond, PA	July 23	Bill Elliott
17	Talladega, AL	July 30	Terry Labonte
18	Watkins Glen, NY	Aug 13	Rusty Wallace
19	Brooklyn, MI	Aug 20	Rusty Wallace
20	Bristol, TN	Aug 26	Darrell Waltrip
21	Darlington, SC	Sept 3	Dale Earnhardt
22	Richmond, VA	Sept 10	Rusty Wallace
23	Dover, DE	Sept 17	Dale Earnhardt
24	Martinsville, VA	Sept 24	Darrell Waltrip
25	Concord, NC	Oct 8	Ken Schrader
26	North Wilkesboro, NC	Oct 15	Geoffrey Bodine
27	Rockingham, NC	Oct 22	Mark Martin
28	Phoenix, AZ	Nov 5	Bill Elliott
29	Hampton, GA	Nov 19	Dale Earnhardt

1990

FINAL CHAMPIONSHIP STANDINGS TOP 10

Rank	Driver	Points
1	Dale Earnhardt	4,430
2	Mark Martin	4,404
3	Geoffrey Bodine	4,017
4	Bill Elliott	3,999
5	Morgan Shepherd	3,689
6	Rusty Wallace	3,676
7	Ricky Rudd	3,601
8	Alan Kulwicki	3,599
9	Ernie Irvan	3,593
10	Ken Schrader	3,572

RACE WINNERS

Race	Location	Date	Winning Driver
1	Daytona Beach, FL	Feb 18	Derrike Cope
2	Richmond, VA	Feb 25	Mark Martin
3	Rockingham, NC	March 4	Kyle Petty
4	Hampton, GA	March 18	Dale Earnhardt
5	Darlington, SC	April 1	Dale Earnhardt
6	Bristol, TN	April 8	Davey Allison
7	North Wilkesboro, NC	April 22	Brett Bodine
8	Martinsville, VA	April 29	Geoffrey Bodine
9	Talladega, AL	May 6	Dale Earnhardt
10	Concord, NC	May 27	Rusty Wallace
11	Dover, DE	June 3	Derrike Cope
12	Sonoma, CA	June 10	Rusty Wallace
13	Long Pond, PA	June 17	Harry Gant
14	Brooklyn, MI	June 24	Dale Earnhardt
15	Daytona Beach, FL	July 7	Dale Earnhardt
16	Long Pond, PA	July 22	Geoffrey Bodine
17	Talladega, AL	July 29	Dale Earnhardt
18	Watkins Glen, NY	Aug 12	Ricky Rudd
19	Brooklyn, MI	Aug 19	Mark Martin
20	Bristol, TN	Aug 25	Ernie Irvan
21	Darlington, SC	Sept 2	Dale Earnhardt
22	Richmond, VA	Sept 9	Dale Earnhardt
23	Dover, DE	Sept 16	Bill Elliott
24	Martinsville, VA	Sept 23	Geoffrey Bodine
25	North Wilkesboro, NC	Sept 30	Mark Martin
26	Concord, NC	Oct 7	Davey Allison
27	Rockingham, NC	Oct 21	Alan Kulwicki

RACE WINNERS (CONT.)

Race	Location	Date	Winning Driver
28	Phoenix, AZ	Nov 4	Dale Earnhardt
29	Hampton, GA	Nov 18	Morgan Shepherd

1991

FINAL CHAMPIONSHIP STANDINGS TOP 10

Rank	Driver	Points
1	Dale Earnhardt	4,287
2	Ricky Rudd	4,092
3	Davey Allison	4,088
4	Harry Gant	3,985
5	Ernie Irvan	3,925
6	Mark Martin	3,914
7	Sterling Marlin	3,839
8	Darrell Waltrip	3,711
9	Ken Schrader	3,690
10	Rusty Wallace	3,582

RACE WINNERS

Race	Location	Date	Winning Driver
1	Daytona Beach, FL	Feb 17	Ernie Irvan
2	Richmond, VA	Feb 24	Dale Earnhardt
3	Rockingham, NC	March 3	Kyle Petty
4	Hampton, GA	March 18	Ken Schrader
5	Darlington, SC	April 7	Ricky Rudd
6	Bristol, TN	April 14	Rusty Wallace
7	North Wilkesboro, NC	April 21	Darrell Waltrip
8	Martinsville, VA	April 28	Dale Earnhardt

Race	Location	Date	Winning Driver
9	Talladega, AL	May 6	Harry Gant
10	Concord, NC	May 26	Davey Allison
11	Dover, DE	June 2	Ken Schrader
12	Sonoma, CA	June 9	Davey Allison
13	Long Pond, PA	June 16	Darrell Waltrip
14	Brooklyn, MI	June 23	Davey Allison
15	Daytona Beach, FL	July 6	Bill Elliott
16	Long Pond, PA	July 21	Rusty Wallace
17	Talladega, AL	July 28	Dale Earnhardt
18	Watkins Glen, NY	Aug 11	Ernie Irvan
19	Brooklyn, MI	Aug 18	Dale Jarrett
20	Bristol, TN	Aug 24	Alan Kulwicki
21	Darlington, SC	Sept 1	Harry Gant
22	Richmond, VA	Sept 7	Harry Gant
23	Dover, DE	Sept 15	Harry Gant
24	Martinsville, VA	Sept 22	Harry Gant
25	North Wilkesboro, NC	Sept 29	Dale Earnhardt
26	Concord, NC	Oct 6	Geoffrey Bodine
27	Rockingham, NC	Oct 20	Davey Allison
28	Phoenix, AZ	Nov 3	Davey Allison
29	Hampton, GA	Nov 17	Mark Martin

1992

FINAL CHAMPIONSHIP STANDINGS TOP 10

Rank	Driver	Points
1	Alan Kulwicki	4,078
2	Bill Elliott	4,068
3	Davey Allison	4,015
4	Harry Gant	3,955

FINAL CHAMPIONSHIP STANDINGS TOP 10 (CONT.)

Rank	Driver	Points
5	Kyle Petty	3,945
6	Mark Martin	3,887
7	Ricky Rudd	3,735
8	Terry Labonte	3,674
9	Darrell Waltrip	3,659
10	Sterling Marlin	3,603

RACE WINNERS

Race	Location	Date	Winning Driver
1	Daytona Beach, FL	Feb 16	Davey Allison
2	Rockingham, NC	March 1	Bill Elliott
3	Richmond, VA	March 8	Bill Elliott
4	Hampton, GA	March 15	Bill Elliott
5	Darlington, SC	March 29	Bill Elliott
6	Bristol, TN	April 5	Alan Kulwicki
7	North Wilkesboro, NC	April 12	Davey Allison
8	Martinsville, VA	April 26	Mark Martin
9	Talladega, AL	May 3	Davey Allison
10	Concord, NC	May 24	Dale Earnhardt
11	Dover, DE	May 31	Harry Gant
12	Sonoma, CA	June 7	Ernie Irvan
13	Long Pond, PA	June 14	Alan Kulwicki
14	Brooklyn, MI	June 21	Davey Allison
15	Daytona Beach, FL	July 4	Ernie Irvan
16	Long Pond, PA	July 19	Darrell Waltrip
17	Talladega, AL	July 26	Ernie Irvan
18	Watkins Glen, NY	Aug 9	Kyle Petty
19	Brooklyn, MI	Aug 16	Harry Gant
20	Bristol, TN	Aug 29	Darrell Waltrip

Race	Location	Date	Winning Driver
21	Darlington, SC	Sept 6	Darrell Waltrip
22	Richmond, VA	Sept 12	Rusty Wallace
23	Dover, DE	Sept 20	Ricky Rudd
24	Martinsville, VA	Sept 28	Geoffrey Bodine
25	North Wilkesboro, NC	Oct 5	Geoffrey Bodine
26	Concord, NC	Oct 11	Mark Martin
27	Rockingham, NC	Oct 25	Kyle Petty
28	Phoenix, AZ	Nov 1	Davey Allison
29	Hampton, GA	Nov 15	Bill Elliott

ACKNOWLEDGMENTS

The list of benefactors on this project is of course lengthy.

But on the other hand, it is one helluva list. Accordingly, we must start at the top, thanking Bill France Sr.'s two sons.

Sadly, one debt of gratitude must be posthumously offered.

Big Bill's eldest son, William Clifton France, known simply as Bill Jr. to so many . . . it's hard to describe what he has meant to me career-wise. More than a decade ago he saw something he liked in a new hire – no, let's be accurate here; he *read* something he liked that I had written – and we were off and running, the old man having recruited me for his speeches. The result was an impromptu five-year course in NASCAR history memorable for salty language and sage insight. The experiences with

Bill Jr., who died on June 4, 2007, laid the groundwork for the book I would write on his life two years later – and for this book on his father. The two books – it is hard for me to imagine one without the other.

More importantly, he took me under his wing, which, as those who knew him might imagine, was sort of a double-edged sword. Bill France Jr. became highly interested in what I was doing on a daily basis, which was, of course, the good news *and* the bad news. But it was always enlightening, certainly entertaining, and, in the last year of his life, incredibly poignant. Like so many others involved in the auto racing industry, I miss him daily.

James Carl France – Jim – is a different cat, to borrow from old-school NASCAR vernacular. Close to the vest . . . that's him. Thing is, you seldom catch him wearing one. Typically casual in dress and low-key in demeanor, Jim is known as the quiet France, the behind-the-scenes leader. But make no mistake, he leads, as NASCAR's vice chairman and the chairman of both the International Speedway Corporation and the International Motor Sports Association.

He led the way on this project, championing the idea of approaching our publisher, Random House, about a project he knew in his heart was long overdue. Once the deal was struck, he went from champion to facilitator in terms of family history and photographs. Having me write this book was his idea. It has been an honor bringing that idea to fruition.

Jim France was invaluable, but so, too, was Jim Foster, the former NASCAR and ISC executive who actually started a book on Bill Sr. years ago but never got around to finishing, as he was too busy helping run a sport. At Jim France's behest, Foster graciously offered that incomplete manuscript as a research resource for this project along with his own priceless stories, which is evident throughout these pages.

Let's just say that deep appreciation goes out to Jim Foster.

As it does to Jim France's children – Amy, J.C., and Jennifer – for their help in choosing photography for this book from their family's private collection, and to the other family members interviewed – Bill Jr.'s widow, Betty Jane France, and their children: ISC CEO Lesa France Kennedy and NASCAR chairman and CEO Brian France. And let's include a de facto member of the France Family, the esteemed Washington, D.C., attorney John Cassidy, who for years Bill Sr.'s key legal counsel but more importantly his confidant and friend. Cassidy's reminiscences were pure gold.

How about Richard Petty? "The King" readily agreed to supply a foreword, even though he and his father, Lee, didn't always agree with Big Bill France.

The late Jim Hunter, former NASCAR vice president, was also involved in this book's foundation, although neither of us knew that was happening when Hunter would weave magical, colorful stories of Bill Sr.'s days as NASCAR's leader.

Words of gratitude and remembrance are mandatory for the late John Bishop and his family. John and his wife, Peggy, co-founded the International Motor Sports Association with Bill Sr. in 1969, and in the spring of 2014 he detailed those grand times for this book, via an animated 90-minute phone conversation from his home in San Rafael, California. Several months later he died at the age of 87. For years, John Bishop *was* sports car racing in North America, as Big Bill's partner. He was a gem.

Editors – God love 'em – were crucial, starting with NASCAR Senior Communications Manager (and fine wordsmith) Mike Forde and moving on to the team at Random House. Collectively, they reined in this copy and added to it when needed.

Support and encouragement from the NASCAR licensing team in Charlotte, North Carolina – Blake Davidson, Nick Rend, Kristi Joyal, et al., was likewise a key. And I can't forget NASCAR Marketing Counsel Jason Weaver, who explained contractual language on a near-daily basis for several months.

Thanks to all.

Cheers,

H.A. Branham

BIBLIOGRAPHY AND OTHER SOURCES

Chapter 1 – Validation of the Vision

Interviews with John Cassidy, Brian France, Jim France, Tom Higgins, Jim Hunter, Winston Kelley, Ramsey Poston.

Chapter 2 – An Early Racing Sensibility

Interviews with John Cassidy, Betty Faulk, Larry Jendras, Jim Foster, Judy Jones. . . . Jim Foster interview with Bill France Sr. . . . Jendras provided special insight into the racing history of the Washington D.C./Beltway area. . . . Stories from Washington Post on 1920 death of James France. . . . Wikipedia and Ancestry.com proved invaluable to France family research.

Chapter 3 – Coming to Daytona

Interviews with Seth Bramson, Bill France Jr., Jim France, Betty Faulk, Godwin Kelly, Humpy Wheeler. Bramson was particularly helpful in drawing historical parallels between Florida railroad pioneer Henry Flagler and Bill France. . . . Another of Jim Foster's interviews with Bill France Sr. was key as well.

Chapter 4 – The 1940s: The Beach, the War – and NASCAR

Interviews with Bill France Jr., Ed Hinton, Jim Hunter. . . . Jim Foster interview with Bill France Sr. . . . Statistical assistance/ verification from NASCAR Hall of Fame historian Buz McKim.

Chapter 5 – The 1950s: From Sand and Dirt to Darlington and Daytona

Interviews with Joie Chitwood III, Betty Jane France, Bill France Jr., Jim France, Jim Hunter, Jonathan Ingram, Buz McKim, Richard Petty, Ken Squier, Rex White. . . . Darlington, S.C. history at Darlingtonsconline.com. . . . United Press International stories, June 6, 1957. . . . Transcript of Bill France Sr. public announcement regarding Daytona International Speedway, November 9, 1957. . . . White gave a unique insider's remembrance of the first Daytona 500. . . . Transcript of 2007 NASCAR Sprint Cup Awards speech by Tom Brokaw, a tribute to Bill France Jr. that expanded into broad-brush thoughts on the sport of NASCAR and its place in Americana.

Chapter 6 – The 1960s: From the Teamsters to Talladega

Interviews with Bobby Allison, Scott Atherton, John Bishop, John Cassidy, Richard Childress, Brian France, Jim France, A.J. Foyt, Mike Helton, Tom Higgins, David Hobbs, Jim Hunter, Junior

Johnson, Richard Petty, Humpy Wheeler. . . . Jim Foster interview with Bill France Sr. . . . Personal scrapbook of 1969 Talladega winner Richard Brickhouse, with stories from Associated Press, United Press International, *Charlotte Observer*.

Chapter 7 – The 1970s: Talladega Aftermath, RJR, and Bill France Jr.

Interviews with James Bockoven, Richard Childress, Betty Faulk, A.J. Foyt, Mike Helton, Ed Hinton, Jim Hunter, Jonathan Ingram, Junior Johnson, Cliff Pennell.

Chapter 8 – The 1980s: Closing Laps

Interviews with Holly Cain, John Cassidy, Juanita Epton, Betty Faulk, Betty Jane France, Bill France Jr., Jim France, Jim Hunter, Lesa France Kennedy, Jeff Gordon, Ed Hinton, Rex White. . . . Letters from Anne Bledsoe France to her sister Juanita Bledsoe Miller, courtesy of the NASCAR Hall of Fame.

Chapter 9 – Saying Goodbye

Interviews with Joy Burke, John Cassidy, Ken Clapp, Jeff Dowling, Betty Faulk, A.J. Foyt, Betty Jane France, Jim France, Mike Helton, Ed Hinton, Godwin Kelly, Richard Petty, Steve Waid, Humpy Wheeler. . . . Stories on Bill France Sr.'s death from the *Daytona Beach News-Journal*, *USA TODAY*, the *Los Angeles Times*, and *Atlanta Journal-Constitution*.

Chapter 10 – What Would Bill Sr. Think?

Interviews with Bobby Allison, Scott Atherton, John Bishop, Richard Childress, Joie Chitwood III, Ken Clapp, John Cooper, A.J. Foyt, Betty Jane France, Brian France, Jim France, Ed

Hinton, Ned Jarrett, Junior Johnson, Judy Jones, Winston Kelley, Lesa France Kennedy, Ken Squier, Steve Waid, Darrell Waltrip, Humpy Wheeler.

Bechtel, Mark. *He Crashed Me So I Crashed Him Back: The True Story of the Year the King, Jaws, Earnhardt, and the Rest of NASCAR's Feudin', Fightin' Good Ol' Boys Put Stock Car Racing on the Map.* Back Bay Books/Little, Brown and Company, 2010.

Bramson, Seth. *The Greatest Railroad Story Ever Told: Henry Flagler & the Florida East Coast Railway's Key West Extension.* The History Press, 2011.

Branham, H.A. *Bill France Jr. – The Man Who Made NASCAR.* Triumph Books, 2010.

Branham, H.A. *The NASCAR Family Album.* Chronicle Books, 2007.

Branham, H.A. and Buz McKim. *The NASCAR Vault.* becker&-mayer!, 2003.

Edelstein, Robert. *NASCAR Generations: The Legacy of Family in NASCAR Racing.* HarperCollins, 2000.

Fielden, Greg. *Forty Years of Stock Car Racing.* The Galfield Press, 1988.

Foyt, A.J. with William Neely. *A.J. – My Life As America's Greatest Race Car Driver.* Times Books, 1983.

Golenbock, Peter. *Miracle: Bobby Allison and the Saga of the Alabama Gang.* St. Martin's Press, 2006.

Hinton, Edward. *Daytona Dynasty.* ESPN.com, 2013.

Hinton, Edward. *Daytona: From the Birth of Speed to the Death of the Man in Black.* Warner Books, 2001.

Ingram, Jonathan. *Origins of Stock Car Racing.* Racin'Today.com, 2010.

Martin, Sydney. *Florida's Flagler*. University of Georgia Press, 1977.

Neely, William. *Daytona U.S.A.: The Official History of Daytona and Ormond Beach Racing from 1902 to Today's NASCAR Super Speedway*. Aztec, 1979.

Malley, J.J. *Daytona 24 Hours: The Definitive History of America's Great Endurance Race*. David Bull Publishing, 2003.

Poole, David. *Race with Destiny: The Year that Changed NASCAR Forever*. Albion Press, 2002.

Punnett, Dick. *Racing on the Rim: A History of the Annual Automobile Racing Tournaments Held on the Sands of Ormond-Daytona Beach, Florida 1903-1910*. Tomoka Press, 2004.

Thompson, Neal. *Driving with the Devil: Southern Moonshine, Detroit Wheels and the Birth of NASCAR*. Three Rivers Press, 2007.

Yunick, Smokey. *Best Damn Garage in Town: My Life & Adventures*. Carbon Press, 2001.

Wolfe, Thomas. "The Last American Hero Is Junior Johnson. Yes!" *Esquire Magazine*, March 1965.

Zeller, Bob. *Daytona 500: An Official History*. David Bull Publishing, 2002.

INDEX